THE LIBRARY
ST. MARY'S COLLEGE OF MARYLAND
ST. MARY'S CITY, MARYLAND 20686

P9-ASK-597

The Jicarilla Apaches

A Study in Survival

The Jicarilla Apaches

A Study in Survival

DOLORES A. GUNNERSON

Northern Illinois University Press
DeKalb, Illinois

Acknowledgments—for material reproduced from Page 90 of *Fray Alonso de Benavides' Revised Memorial of 1634,* by F. W. Hodge, G. P. Hammond and A. Rey. Albuquerque: University of New Mexico Press, 1945. *By permission.* Pages 300–303 of "The Report of Fray Alonso de Posada in Relation to Quivira and Teguayo," by S. Lyman Tyler and H. Darrel Taylor, *New Mexico Historical Review* 33 (1958): 285–314. *By permission.* Page 194 of *After Coronado: Spanish Explorations Northeast of New Mexico, 1696–1727,* by Alfred B. Thomas. Norman: University of Oklahoma Press, 1935. Pages 135–37 of *The Plains Indians and New Mexico, 1751–1778,* by Alfred B. Thomas. Albuquerque: University of New Mexico Press, 1940. *By permission.*

Excerpts throughout the text have been reprinted by permission of the publishers for the following: Forbes, Jack D. *Apache, Navaho, and Spaniard.* Norman: University of Oklahoma Press, 1960. Hackett, Charles W., ed. and trans. *Historical Documents Relating to New Mexico, Nueva Vizcaya, and Approaches Thereto, to 1773.* 3 vols. 1923–1937. Carnegie Institution of Washington Publication 330. Hammond, George P., and Agapito Rey. *Obregón's History of 16th Century Explorations in Western America.* Los Angeles: Wetzel Publishing Co., Inc., 1928. Hammond, George P., and Agapito Rey. *Don Juan de Oñate. Colonizer of New Mexico 1595–1628.* 2 vols. Albuquerque: University of New Mexico Press, 1953. Hammond, George P., and Agapito Rey. *The Rediscovery of New Mexico 1580–1594.* Albuquerque: University of New Mexico Press, 1966. Thomas, Alfred B. *After Coronado: Spanish Explorations Northeast of New Mexico, 1696–1727.* Norman: University of Oklahoma Press, 1935.

Library of Congress Cataloging in Publication Data

Gunnerson, Dolores A   1923–
    The Jicarilla Apaches.

    Bibliography: p.
    1. Jicarilla Indians. I. Title.
E99.J5G86   970.3   72–2582
ISBN 0–87580–033–5

Copyright © 1974 by Northern Illinois University Press

Published by the Northern Illinois University Press
DeKalb, Illinois 60115
Manufactured in the United States of America
All Rights Reserved

FOR
Alfred Barnaby Thomas
whose published works
inspired this study

Contents

Preface, xi

List of Figures

Figure 7, following page 240

Section of Lafora's map of 1771
showing "Apaches Carlanes y Xicarillas"
just east of mouth of Gallinas River

Figure 8, page 291

A section of Humboldt's map of
New Spain drawn in 1803, showing the
Llanero Apaches on the Plains east of settled
New Mexico and mountain ranges that
sheltered various Apache tribes ca. 1800

In the late 1940s as a student at the University of Nebraska, I
participated for three summers in an archeological field school
under the direction of Dr. John L. Champe. Each year we
camped at White Cat Village, the Dismal River site where most
of our excavating was done. The archeological complex represented was, in 1949, attributed to Cuartelejo and/or Paloma
Apaches by Champe, who drew on the work of Alfred Barnaby
Thomas, thus introducing his students to the publications of this
important historian and to the discipline of ethnohistory. As the
field seasons passed, I became increasingly interested in the ulti-
mate fate of the Central Plains Apaches. The Cuartelejos and
Palomas had lived briefly in Thomas's *After Coronado* and *The
Plains Indians and New Mexico*, then seemingly disappeared.
Where had they gone? Who were their descendants?

After extensive reading in published materials, done for the most part while a graduate student at the University of Utah, I surmised that the Cuartelejo and Paloma Apaches had become part of the Llanero or Plains Band of the modern tribe known as Jicarilla Apaches, and perusal of Twitchell's calendar of the Spanish Archives of New Mexico convinced me that I should continue my research in Santa Fé. Fortunately, a Wenner–Gren Foundation Grant enabled me to spend the summer of 1959 using archival materials and books in the New Mexico State Historical Society Library in the Palace of the Governors. I will always be grateful to Bruce T. Ellis for permission to use the Society's collections; to Gertrude Hill, then Head Librarian, and her ever-pleasant and helpful staff; and to Robert Feynn, Archivist at that time, who gave me much personal assistance, carrying boxes of documents from vault to library, reproducing selected items, and transcribing one or two that could not be photocopied. Margaret Metcalf Howie generously helped check papers from the Territorial Period.

In coping with archaic Spanish and with terms from various American Indian languages, I was greatly aided by what I learned of linguistics from Dr. Charles E. Dibble, Dr. Gerald K. Gresseth, and Dr. William R. Slager of the University of Utah. In eliciting information from informants I have frequently had reason to be thankful for training in ethnological field techniques received under Dr. Robert Anderson. To Dr. Dibble in particular, who directed my Ph.D. dissertation, I owe immeasurable thanks for patience and understanding.

The Palace of the Governors was locked during the noon hour in 1959, and after the brief time it took to eat a sandwich in the Plaza I often sat for a while by the bed of the late Father Berard Haile in nearby St. Vincent's hospital learning (when there was no baseball game on TV) of the Navajos and their language. That experience will not be forgotten.

For many years I have accompanied James H. Gunnerson on archeological field expeditions that took us into much of the area inhabited by Southern Athabascans—from northwestern

Nebraska to El Paso and from Monument Valley down to Cochise's country in Arizona. This experience has added geographical reality to what might otherwise have been primarily an armchair exercise.

As I have noted in the body of this work, Carol Condie Stout of Albuquerque, New Mexico, at times kindly elicited needed linguistic data from Navajo informants.

I did much of the transliteration and/or translation of the Spanish documents utilized for this work in Sante Fé in 1959. However, this task, often slowed by idiosyncrasies of the handwriting to be deciphered, has continued over the years. For a few of the documents I sought an independent check on my interpretations from Dr. William F. Harrison of the Northern Illinois University Department of Foreign Languages. Where the Spanish can be translated or interpreted in more than one way, I have presented the version consistent with the historical and anthropological context. For anyone interested in consulting the documents, the Spanish Archives of New Mexico are now readily available on microfilm.

I owe much to institutions. The Newberry Library collection of Americana and the helpfulness of the personnel in the library's Rare Book Room has in itself been a stimulus to research. The Bancroft Library made available microfilm of the "New Mexico Originals" so painstakingly listed by Father Angélico Chávez. And the Museum of New Mexico at Santa Fé—all of its branches —has provided inspiration over the years simply by its very existence.

My basic debt, of course, is to the University of Utah Research Committee for granting me fellowships and to the Wenner–Gren Foundation for supporting my work in Santa Fé, funds from both agencies having been obtained through the helpfulness of Dr. Jesse D. Jennings of the University of Utah.

In this work I have traced the Cuartelejo and Paloma Apaches, in archeological terms the Dismal River people of the Central Plains, through nearly a century in which they joined part of the Carlana Apaches of southeastern Colorado for protection against enemy tribes to finally lose their identity among the Carlanas. These three allied bands, intimates of the Jicarillas proper of northeastern New Mexico, were also friends and allies of the Spanish settlers in that province. However, threatened on the one hand by enemy Indians and on the other hand by the desire of their Spanish protectors to restrict them to a mission settlement, the Carlanas, Palomas, and Cuartelejos for the most part hovered cautiously just beyond the vicinity of the New Mexico villages. Then, after drifting gradually southward, they appeared in Texas and Coahuila under new names, first being called Lipiyanes and Llaneros, and finally just Llaneros. Caught in the increasingly efficient dragnet operations of Spanish presidial troops and Indian auxiliaries directed basically against other Apacheans, the Llaneros finally returned to New Mexico. There, in 1798 and 1801, they explicitly claimed to be part of the Jicarillas and, in spite of initial Spanish opposition, remained as the Llanero Band of the present Jicarilla tribe.

In tracing the history of the Llaneros I had to consider also the mountain-dwelling Jicarillas proper, searching back through the earliest relevant Spanish sources for their origins. By re-examining materials bearing on the sixteenth and seventeenth centuries, I have achieved incidentally what I believe to be a few new insights into the course of Spanish exploration and also into the nature of Apache-Pueblo relations. I became fascinated, too, by the fact that the Mountain (Hoyero?) Band of the Jicarillas had survived nearly two centuries of precarious existence as displaced persons with the core of their culture intact, and a second objective of the study became not merely to chronicle the events of Jicarilla history but to deduce therefrom the mechanisms by which this was accomplished.

I have, in fact, called this work a "study in survival." It could also be called a study in human relations, for the Mountain Jicarillas saved themselves, and apparently also their kinsmen from the Plains, by their ability to adapt to changing social and political (i.e., human) situations. Because the multiplicity of peoples and events treated has made this presentation complex, I have deliberately provided generalized, undocumented overviews and recapitulations for the detailed, documented sections. In the documented sections, however, every fact or idea in this work that has been taken from another publication has been appropriately related to its source through citations within the text and in the Bibliography.

Part 1

The Apacheans before 1700

Chapter One

From *Conquistadores*
to *Colonistas*

From Dulce, the Jicarilla Apache agency town in the mountains of north-central New Mexico, it is not far to the Pueblo of Taos, as distance is reckoned today. By truck and by car the Jicarillas come to Taos on important feast days, and during the Jicarilla fiesta at Stone Lake, in turn, Taos Pueblo is nearly deserted. "It is just like the old days," said an aged Taos woman, "except that we don't go in wagons any more."[1] For her the old days stretched even beyond the reservation years of the Jicarillas, back to a time when these Apaches were living in the mountains around her pueblo (figure 1). And where the memories of living informants end, the Jicarilla chronicle can be pieced together

---

1 This information was collected in 1957 from both Taos Indians and Anglo-Americans long resident in the Taos area. The amount of Taos-Jicarilla interaction may have decreased since that date.

Figure 1. *Map of New Mexico showing locations of the Jicarilla Reservation and various places frequented by the Jicarillas.*

from documents—American, Mexican, and Spanish. When the present name of the Jicarillas first appeared in records, in the early 1700s, they were living east of Taos, across the mountains now called the Sangre de Cristos, farming in canyons that open onto the Plains. In those days the Jicarillas "entered at peace in Taos and always kept it," trading and bringing gossip from their Apachean kindred who lived far out in the buffalo country. Some two centuries later, ca. 1900, Jicarilla tradition held that the heart of the world was near Taos. There they had emerged from lower regions at the time of their creation, and in Taos Pueblo their great culture hero, Monster Slayer, left his mother and younger brother for protection when he set out to rid the world of its evils. There, too, according to tradition, trophies of his exploits were preserved.

The Jicarillas were assuredly known in the Southwest before 1700, but by a different name, and their identity, like that of other Apachean groups, was frequently obscured by the tendency of observers to use only the generic name "Apaches." For this reason and because their story, once it begins, is best understood in terms of previous Apache-Pueblo-Spanish relations, this study of Jicarilla history is prefaced with a consideration of earlier events.

All the modern Apachean tribes (which includes the Navajos) speak closely related dialects of Southern Athabascan, a branch of the widespread Athabascan linguistic stock. Because the largest area inhabited by speakers of Athabascan covers much of Alaska and western Canada, and for various other reasons, it is generally believed that the Southern Athabascans, or Apacheans, separated from the northern bloc and reached their historic locations as a result of southward migration. However, the route that they followed and the time of their arrival in the Southwest has long been a matter of controversy.

The bulk of historical and anthropological evidence strongly suggests that the Southern Athabascans first became known to the Pueblo people about 1525 A.D. as Plains nomads who came into the Río Grande area from the north and east. However, this reconstruction of events, first systematically formulated in 1956 by the present author, is the antithesis of opinions advanced by many who have considered the problem.

Faced by the need to explain the abandonment of prehistoric pueblos on both the northern and southern frontiers of the Anasazi area, early researchers invoked as the cause an "enemy people"—fierce outsiders who were supposed to have brought new culture traits into the Pueblo area about 1000 A.D., forced the Anasazi to crowd together in large, defensive communities and build strategic "watchtowers," and finally forced them to withdraw permanently from their northernmost settlements in the late 1200s. Supposedly, these enemy people spread throughout the entire Pueblo area so that in the late 1300s they were in a position to destroy communities in the southern part of the region, which was also abandoned.

Understandably, the Apachean tribes, some of whom were as predatory in fact as they could be represented in fiction, were prime candidates for the role of enemy people, and most students concerned with the matter were content to project the historic behavior of the most hostile Apaches into prehistory. Without analyzing in detail actual patterns of intergroup relations in the Southwest, they generalized that at all times and in all parts of the world the village dweller and the nomad have been bitter enemies, thus contributing to the false impression that in the Southwest there existed a simple dichotomy—all Apacheans were enemies of all Pueblo peoples. In brief, there has been a tripartite idea that Apache harassment of the Pueblos: (1) began in prehistoric times, (2) was unanimous, and (3) resulted in major devastation. Although unsupported and even controverted by direct evidence, this hypothesis is dying hard. The logical considerations that led to its decline led also to the alternative suggestion that evidence of prehistoric conflict in the Southwest was actually the result of Pueblos fighting among themselves. However, again because of the tendency to project historic behavior —this time the recent "docility" of the Pueblo people—into prehistoric times, this latter alternative has been largely ignored, although it is supported by early Spanish accounts as the concept of a prehistoric Apachean menace is not.

Even before 1540, Spaniards in Mexico heard rumors of conflict among the still legendary pueblos to the north, and Coronado, who did not report nomadic tribes living in the country
around the Pueblos, noted marked hostility among Pueblo groups
themselves. The only nomadic people mentioned by the Pueblo
Indians and observed by the Spaniards in 1540–1542 were the
Querechos and Teyas, who followed the buffalo about on the
Plains. Pueblo Indian informants told the Spaniards that these
plainsmen, who can be identified as Southern Athabascans, had
invaded the Pueblo area from the north about 1525. Failing to
conquer the village peoples, they had established friendship with
them instead and by 1540 were carrying on an intensive and
mutually beneficial trade with the eastern Pueblos.

Apparently a sort of political equilibrium existed in New
Mexico in 1540, which the presence of Coronado's soldiers soon
threatened. The army of Spaniards brought economic and social
problems to which the Pueblos concerned (those in the Albuquerque-Bernalillo area) responded with violence. Numerous
Indians were killed before the rebellion was suppressed, and the
bloodshed, some of it brutal by any standards, must have made
a profound impression on the natives. Nevertheless, the Indians of
Pecos, who coveted fields on the Río Grande, were quick to offer
the Spaniards military aid in the hope of getting land there as a
reward.

Coronado refused to become involved in native intrigues and
left New Mexico before his *entrada* could have a really significant
immediate effect on the Indian situation. Yet, it may be of cru-
cial importance for the reconstruction of Apachean history that
explorers who followed him (and gave the Indians additional
cause to fear white men) found "wild tribes" called Querechos
in mountainous areas near both Acoma and the Hopi Pueblos, as
Coronado had not. Both the Acomas and Hopis called upon their
Querecho neighbors to aid them against the Spaniards, and it is
here suggested that these Pueblos (and perhaps others), antici-
pating further Spanish expeditions, deliberately encouraged
Querechos from the Plains to settle near them after Coronado's
departure. In view of the communication known to have existed

between Mexican and New Mexican Indians before Coronado's *entrada*, it is unlikely that the northward advance of the Spanish frontier in Mexico after 1542 had gone unnoticed by the Pueblo Indians.

Possibly, mountain Querechos were serving their Pueblo friends against other Pueblos in the late 1500s, since Spanish accounts of that period show that inter-Pueblo hostilities had not diminished. Documents of ca. 1600 relating to Oñate's rule in New Mexico indicate that nomadic tribes living in the mountain ranges between the Pueblos had begun attacking village dwellers to get farm produce before the Spanish colonists of 1598 arrived, but whether these raids were inspired by Pueblo allies, simple need, or both is not clear. It was Oñate who introduced the term "Apache" into the literature on New Mexico, applying it first to mountain people, and it is virtually certain that the New Mexico mountain people who came to be known as Apaches were those who had been known earlier as mountain Querechos.

Originally, Oñate and his followers seemed to distinguish between "Apaches" of the mountains and "Vaqueros" of the Plains, but, as will be shown, it is possible to trace in the relevant documents a rapidly growing recognition that the plains Vaqueros and mountain Apaches were of a common stock, and soon both groups were called Apaches by the Spaniards.

The advent of permanent Spanish colonists in 1598 heightened the tensions that already existed between Indian groups in New Mexico. By submitting to the Spaniards and becoming nominal Christians, Río Grande villagers incurred or enhanced the enmity of the outlying Pueblos—Taos, Picurís, Pecos, Acoma, and Jémez. The mountain Apache allies of these border Pueblos also seem to have become more hostile to the "Christian" Pueblos, soon even directing their raids against the Spaniards. Thus, to the prehistoric economic reasons for intertribal warfare was added an historic, religious one—the dislike of anti-Christian Indians for "Christian" Indians. Still, the native political situation was never, as early scholars suggested, a simple dichotomy—nomad against villager, Apachean against Pueblo Indian, or, later, non-Christian against Christian. There are first hints and later outright statements in the documents that can only be interpreted to mean that even before 1600, certain *mountain* Apache tribes were at war with some Pueblos while maintaining friendly relations with others. After their original incursion the *Plains* Apaches were, in contrast, friendly to all villagers. Attacks by mountain Apaches on the Spaniards increased as the years went by, but the Plains Apaches were apparently happy to accept the colonists as new trading partners and attempted to maintain their friendship even after the New Mexico Spaniards began to send slave raiders against them about 1620.

Relations between the Spaniards and the Pueblo groups took still another course. Rather than pay tribute and conform to Spanish customs, many individuals and small groups from the Spanish-controlled Río Grande villages sought refuge at hostile border Pueblos or even among the Apaches. These defections probably brought about a marked increase in Pueblo influence on Apache culture beginning just before 1600 and accelerating as the economic and religious demands of the conquerors increased. The Pueblo Indians that remained submissive not only bore the heavy burden of supporting the colonists but were confused and demoralized by internal dissension among the white men and by the conflicting demands of civil and religious authorities. Famine, which increased the Spanish drain on Pueblo food supplies, along with the intensive efforts of the Franciscans to stamp out Pueblo religious customs, finally made the presence of the Spaniards so intolerable that the Pueblos were able to ignore their own differences and unite long enough to carry on the relatively large-scale warfare necessary to drive out the intruders. In this rebellion they received little actual help from their Apache allies, who customarily made only sudden brief raids for loot. Thus, it was largely by their own efforts that the Pueblo Indians, after several abortive attempts, forced the Spaniards out of New Mexico in 1680; however, their constant assertions that Apaches were coming to aid them undoubtedly affected Spanish morale, for by that time the devastating raids of some Apacheans had all but demoralized the Spaniards.

With the retreat of the colonists to the El Paso area, the

Pueblos again began to fight among themselves, and most of the damage inflicted on these towns between the rebellion and the Spanish reoccupation was not done by Apaches, as the Spaniards had anticipated, but by other Pueblos. Selective Apache-Pueblo relations in which the various Apache bands frequented some pueblos and attacked others apparently became well-established while the Spaniards were absent, if they had not been before. Thus, the New Mexico that General Vargas reconquered late in the seventeenth century was characterized by shifting alliances among Pueblos and by Apache-Pueblo relations that were more complex than ever, or possibly only seemed so because more records from this period have survived.

Some of the special Apache-Pueblo friendships were documented before 1700. Navajos in the vicinity of Jémez were friends of that pueblo. "Salinero" Apaches were intimate with the Zuñis, who had, on the other hand, suffered greatly from Navajo raids. Plains Apaches came periodically to the great trading center of Pecos, among them Faraon Apaches from the Canadian River to the east, who were special allies of the Pecos Indians. The Chipaynes, a band of the Faraons, traded regularly at Picurís, and both the Picurís and Taos Indians were friendly with mountain Apaches called Achos, who in the late 1600s lived on the Red River north of Taos. The "Jicarilla" Apaches were not mentioned as such until 1700, but Jicarilla was very probably only a new name for Apaches who had already occupied the mountain-plains borderland east of Taos for more than a century. Linguistic evidence, for example, makes it possible to equate the Jicarillas with the Quinia Apaches who lived in that same area in the early 1600s. Archeological remains attributable to Apacheans and dating from ca. 1600 (and probably even earlier) have been found in the vicinity of Cimarrón and elsewhere in northeastern New Mexico. Both archeological and ethnohistorical research has shown that these mountain or "foothills" Apacheans had adopted many Pueblo and/or Spanish Colonial culture traits by the early 1700s. By this time, also, they had well-established relationships with the Indians of Taos and Picurís Pueblos and seem to have been friendly with at least the conservative faction at Pecos as well.

The obscurity of the Jicarillas in the sixteenth and seventeenth centuries and the relative obscurity of all the mountain Apaches living north and east of Taos can be variously explained. These Apaches lived beyond the area of which the Spaniards had detailed knowledge and beyond the sphere of effective Spanish control. Moreover, their mountains afforded a dependable food supply that could be supplemented from buffalo herds on the adjacent plains. The Jicarillas and other mountain or foothills Apache groups in their locality probably seldom had cause to attack either Pueblos or Spanish communities and hence received little space in official reports. In fact, the Jicarillas, although unspectacular, were unique among the Apaches in their enduring friendship for the settled peoples of New Mexico, as their history reveals.

Chapter Two

The Apaches:
1525–1609

Early Rumors Concerning New Mexico
1530–1540

Spaniards had not had many years to establish themselves in the Valley of Mexico before rumors of fabulous cities to the north made officials of church and state alike eager for new exploration in that direction. As Bandelier has pointed out, little information concerning the origins of the civilized Mexican Indians, with their golden treasures, seems to have been obtained during the initial period of Spanish conquest and administrative organization. Friars, however, may have begun as early as 1529 to collect migration legends which mentioned "Seven Caves" as a place where the Aztecs had remained for many years on their way south. This story may or may not have been blended quickly with

European legends of "Seven Cities," whose location had already been sought in vain by Spanish explorers in the New World (Bandelier 1890: 3–11).

As early as 1530, stories of seven large pueblos in an interior land rich in gold and silver were told to the *conquistador* Guzmán by one of his Mexican Indian servants who claimed to have been to those pueblos as a small boy with trading expeditions (Winship 1896: 472–73; Bandelier 1890: 11–12). Guzmán tried to find the Seven Cities and failed. Then, in 1536, Cabeza de Vaca and three other survivors of the Narváez expedition to "Florida" wandered across southern Texas and Mexico to the Pacific coast (Hallenbeck 1940; Sauer 1932, 1937; Undreiner 1947), were found by Spaniards, taken to Mexico City, and there told stories they had heard in northern Mexico of people who lived in very large houses still farther to the north and who had much turquoise (Bandelier 1890: 42; 1910: 5).

Viceroy Mendoza, himself only recently arrived in New Spain (1535), was much affected by their accounts. He had, according to Obregón, already become interested in the "chronicles, hieroglyphs and pictures" from Montezuma's palace which told of the migrations of the ancient Mexicans, and he associated these with the settlements that Cabeza de Vaca had heard of (Hammond and Rey 1928: 10–11; hereafter referred to as H & R), probably also assuming that the culture and riches of the Aztecs would characterize settlements in the regions from which they had presumably come. If such thinking on the part of Mendoza was indeed responsible for his strong support of northward exploration then it would not be incorrect to say that the migration legends of the Aztecs led to the discovery of the New Mexico Pueblos and lured Coronado on to Quivira across the Buffalo Plains where he and his men were the first Europeans to see Indians representing another major New World stock—the Athabascans.

Whatever his motives, Mendoza attempted to persuade one of the Spaniards of Cabeza de Vaca's party to lead an expedition to the fabled country. Failing in this, he sent out a Franciscan friar, Marcos de Niza, in September 1538, to explore northward (Winship 1896: 354; Bandelier 1892: 2). The friar's formal testimony about what he had seen corroborated the accounts of Cabeza de Vaca's party (H & R 1940: 63–82),[1] and exaggerations of his verbal statements by others (Bandelier 1892: 21–27; Winship 1896: 362–68; H & R 1940: 79) greatly excited the people. Soon after the friar's return to Mexico City in fall 1539, Viceroy Mendoza, who had apparently also long been seeking a reasonable pretext for getting rid of the restless adventurers in New Spain, began to organize Coronado's expedition (Bandelier 1892: 25–27; 1910: 5; H & R 1940: 5).

Some writers have doubted that Fray Marcos ever reached the Zuñi Pueblos on his first trip north, but the fact that he was able to guide Coronado there suggests that he had at least come close (Schroeder 1955–1956: 266–67). More important for the present study, his accounts of relations between various peoples living in the region he traversed agree with information obtained later. He learned, for example, that the Ópatas of Sonora customarily went to "Cíbola" (the name applied by north-Mexican Indians to the Zuñi Pueblos) where they did day-labor in exchange for tanned buffalo hides, turquoise, and other items. Moreover, even the Ópatas knew of other Pueblos located well beyond Cíbola that later proved to be the Hopi villages and Acoma (Bandelier 1890: 133–34; 1892: 3–5). In spite of the information these Mexican Indians had of the Pueblo country that came to be known as New Mexico, nowhere among them did Fray Marcos hear of Indians whose description suggests Apaches (Schroeder 1952; 1955–1956) nor of any human barrier to their contacts with Cíbola. Neither did he hear of nomadic tribes threatening the New Mexico Pueblos. He did hear, however, of conflict between Pueblo peoples themselves.

Among Indians identified as the Sobaipuri of southern Arizona, Fray Marcos gained additional information on Cíbola and even met an old Zuñi man who told him that the "seven towns" (the Zuñi Pueblos) fought with another group of Pueblos to the

---

1 I refer to both Winship's version of the narratives of the Coronado expedition and the version by Hammond and Rey, in part because they differ and in part because over the years I have sometimes had access to only one or the other work. The same is true of other sources for which I have cited more than one version or edition.

southeast of them, the kingdom of Marata (Bandelier 1890: 142, 144–46; 1892: 5–6). Bandelier associated Marata with well-preserved ruins still to be found southeast of Zuñi, and this early advocate of the idea that the Apaches were the enemy people states, "the cause of their ruin would appear to be, not the hostility of the Apaches, but intertribal strife and the final absorption of the people by the more powerful cluster in the Zuñi basin" (Bandelier 1892: 5–6).

These indications that the Zuñis were not particularly peaceful are augmented by the fate of Esteban, a Negro or Moor who had been with Cabeza de Vaca's party on its wanderings and who was later purchased by the viceroy so he could accompany Fray Marcos to the north. Esteban was sent on ahead of the friar as an emissary but behaved so insolently that he was killed by the Zuñis, as were some of the Mexican Indians who accompanied him. Those who escaped not only mourned for their dead but complained to Fray Marcos that they would no longer dare go to Cíbola as they had before (H & R 1940: 75–76). Thus, the first Spanish expedition into New Mexico inadvertently resulted in the disruption of friendly contacts between native groups. It also introduced into the literature the term "Cíbola," which was to be applied to the Zuñi towns, the Pueblo area in general, and the Buffalo Plains east of it. As a synonym for the chimera that Bancroft called the "Northern Mystery," however, the name Cíbola was eventually replaced by "Copalá" and later by "Quivira," as one never-never land after another disappointed its discoverer and was rejected in favor of a newer dream. Since it was the repeated efforts of Iberian adventurers to find a "new" Mexico (in the sense of another kingdom like that of the Aztecs) that led indirectly to what we know of the sixteenth-century Apacheans, various *entradas* must be considered.

The Coronado Expedition
1540–1542

With Fray Marcos as guide, Coronado approached the Zuñi Pueblos in 1540. One of his soldiers, Pedro de Castañeda, who later wrote what is the most detailed account of the journey, mentioned seeing on the way one group of "barbarous" people who cannot be either eliminated or identified as Apaches on the basis of his description. However, in light of a study by Undreiner (1947), Schroeder (1955–1956: 33) identifies Castañeda's barbarous people as Yavapai.

When the *conquistadores* reached the Zuñi Pueblo of Hawikuh, the Indians put up a spirited resistance before they were forced to surrender (H & R 1940: 167–69). Having captured Hawikuh, Coronado lost little time in undertaking one of the principal tasks given him by the viceroy of New Spain—obtaining information about the country and its people. By questioning the Zuñis, he learned of the Hopi Pueblos to the northwest. The Zuñis told him that they were not on good terms with the Hopis, who were warlike (H & R 1940: 213–14). Subsequently, the Spaniards heard that the Indians of Acoma Pueblo were "robbers feared throughout the land" (H & R 1940: 218); the warriors of Pecos Pueblo were also much feared. Casteñeda commented: "The people of this town [Pecos] pride themselves because no one has been able to subjugate them while they dominate the pueblos they wish" (H & R 1940: 256–57).

Coronado established winter quarters at a pueblo in what he called the province of Tiguex, which extended along the Río Grande River in the present Albuquerque-Bernalillo area (H & R 1940: 219), but when the Spaniards made excessive demands for food and clothing and molested a Pueblo woman, the people of Tiguex rebelled. In an attempt to take advantage of this situation, "head men" of Pecos came to visit Coronado and offered to help him against the people of Tiguex, if he would give Pecos a pueblo on the Río Grande. They said that Pecos was short of land, that there was plenty of land at Tiguex, and that the Pecos people were enemies of the Tiguex Indians anyway (H & R 1940: 328). Here, land shortage appears as a specific reason for inter-Pueblo conflict, but it is also apparent that a pattern of generalized inter-Pueblo hostility was already well-established before the Spaniards arrived. One member of Coronado's party even said that the pueblos were settled the way they were in part because of the wars they waged against one another (H & R 1940: 294).

Before Coronado had an opportunity to become embroiled in Pueblo intrigues, his interest was shifted to the Plains. Living in Pecos in 1540 were at least three slaves from villages of sedentary farming Indians beyond the High Plains to the east. Two of these slaves were from Quivira (H & R 1940: 235, 237), an area in what is now central Kansas, inhabited then by the Wichita Indians (Wedel 1942). The other slave, whom the Spaniards nicknamed "the Turk," may have been from even farther east or north (H & R 1940: 219). The Spaniards obtained the Turk from the Pecos Indians and listened eagerly to stories he told about gold and silver at Quivira and settlements beyond (H & R 1940: 221). Coronado decided to go to Quivira, taking the Turk along as guide. As it turned out, the Turk had been asked by the Pecos Indians to lose the Spaniards on the Plains, and this he tried to do by leading them far to the south of the most direct route.

Beyond the Canadian River Coronado found the Plains lush with grass, teeming with buffalo, and populated by nomadic hunters whom Pueblo people called Querechos and Teyas. Although these Indians seem to have been newcomers to the Southern Plains, they had a way of life already closely adapted to this environment. The Spaniards, amazed and impressed by the efficiency with which the Querechos and Teyas exploited the bison to satisfy most of their material needs, commented on possessions that gave the plainsmen almost as much mobility as the herds on which they depended. These were sewn skin tents that could be quickly pitched and struck and well-trained pack dogs that carried tents and household gear on their backs and dragged the tent poles at their sides.

Other explorers observed dog-nomads in the sixteenth century, but it was not until Oñate and his followers reached New Mexico and penetrated the Plains that Spaniards began to refer to such peoples as Apaches. The Apaches whom Oñate called "masters of the plains" at the turn of the seventeenth century (1598–

1609) were living in the same manner as the Teyas and Querechos of 1540–1542, and their sewn skin tents and pack dogs still
excited admiring comments from Spanish observers. This continuity of culture alone is enough to suggest that Coronado's
Querechos and Teyas and Oñate's Plains Apaches were of the
same stock. The fact that no chronicler of either expedition attributes dog-nomadism to other groups that were observed
strengthens this probability. There now seems to be general agreement that the Querechos were Apacheans, but since the ethnic
identity of the Teyas is still occasionally questioned (cf. Schroeder 1962: 8–9), the relevant evidence should be presented more
fully.

Additional support for the identification of both the Querechos and Teyas as Apacheans is furnished by the fact that some
of the Pueblo people apply to Apacheans now the same names
that they applied to the dog-nomads of Coronado's time. Jaramillo, one of Coronado's soldiers, said: "We found Indians among
these first cows [buffaloes], who were, on this account, called
Querechos by those in the flat-roof houses" (Winship 1896:
588). And Castañeda explains the name Teya thus: "They [the
Pueblo people] usually call these people Teyas or brave men,
just as the Mexicans say chichimecas or braves, for the Teyas
whom the army saw were brave" (Winship 1896: 524). Fortunately, working at Jémez in the late 1800s and early 1900s, F. W.
Hodge and J. P. Harrington found equivalents of the names Teya
and Querecho in both the Pecos and Jémez dialects of Towa.

It is probable that the names Querecho and Teya originated at
Pecos, which was not only the largest and most powerful of the
Pueblos in 1540 but was also easily accessible from the Plains and
seems to have been the most important center for trade with the
Plains Apaches even before Coronado's time. Knowledge of the
Pecos dialect is limited, however, because this pueblo, long since
weakened by Comanche attacks and disease, was abandoned in
1838, the seventeen remaining inhabitants going to live with their
closest linguistic relatives, the Jémez.

Because Hodge's linguistic research was done at Jémez while
an aged native of Pecos still survived there, he was able to ascer-

tain that the Pecos generic term for the Apacheans (presumably
including both Eastern and Western Apaches) was *Tágukerésh*
and that the Pecos specific term for the Navajo tribe was *Keretsâ*.
Hodge concluded that the sixteenth-century name Querecho
represented one or the other of these forms (Hodge 1907–1910 I:
67, II: 339; Hodge, Hammond and Rey 1945: 303; hereafter referred to as H, H & R), and on the face of it, Querecho seems
more likely to be *-kerésh* rendered in Spanish orthography than
the more specific *Keretsâ*. Hodge also collected the Jémez generic
for the Apacheans, which is *Tâgúgála* (Mooney 1898*b*: 245).
Since the researcher was the same in both cases, the differences
between the Pecos and Jémez forms probably reflect differences
between the two dialects and/or between informants.

J. P. Harrington, who used his own private phonetic orthog-
raphy and never adopted the phonemic approach (Stirling and
Glemser 1963: 373), has dealt with Jémez terms for Southern
Athabascans as follows:

> The Jemez name for Navaho or Athapascan is *K̂ʃâlă*, plu. *K̂ʃâ-
> lăʃ*; also *K̂ʃâlătsâ'â*, plu. *K̂ʃâlătsâ'âʃ* (*tsâ'â* 'person'). The Pecos
> name was presumably the same, and this explains the "Quer-
> echos" "Quereches", [*sic*] "Guerechos" of Coronado. The
> Jemez, and presumably the Pecos also, call the Apache
> *Togökʃâlă*, plu. *Togökʃâlăʃ* 'east Navaho' 'east Athapascan'
> (*togö* 'east'; *k̂ʃâlă*² as above). This is sometimes abbreviated to
> *Togö*, plu. *Togöʃ* (ʃ plu. postfix) [all parentheses appear in
> original]. (Harrington 1916: 573)

Since Harrington's [*K̂ʃ*] approximates [Ky] and his [ʃ] is
[sh] (Harrington 1916: 39–40), he renders (roughly) as *-kyala*
(plural *-kyalash*) what Hodge represented as *-gala*. In 1959 the
present author obtained at Jémez, a form that could be rendered
in standard English orthography as *gyelésh* or *kyelésh*, with "e"
as in "led." Thus, the vowel in the modern Jémez form can come
close to that in Pecos *-kerésh*.³

Actually, after differences in orthography are reconciled,
Hodge and Harrington are not far apart in consonants, and the

2 Here "kʃala" should obviously be "k̂ʃala." This may be a printer's error.
3 Two Jémez informants I consulted in 1970 confirmed the version collected in
1959.

differing vowel sounds obtained by various researchers may reflect not only differences in their own powers of perception but also differences in the renditions of their informants, it being possible that some Jémez vowel phonemes wander over a broad sound spectrum. If the lateral consonants [l] and [r] are confused in Towa, this fact may account for the different medial consonants in the Pecos and Jémez forms. In any case, Harrington's indication that [sh] is the sign of the plural suggests that Coronado's followers took the already plural Pecos -*kerésh* and added to it Spanish masculine singular and plural endings.

Years after his initial work at Jémez, Harrington provided further support for the identification of the Teyas as Apacheans when he commented:

> My discovery that Teya is the Pecos-Jemez word for eastern Apache, that is, Lipanan, proves that at least the Teya band mentioned by Castañeda was Lipanan and makes it probable that the Querecho band was also Lipanan.[4] (Harrington 1940: 512)

From this statement it is apparent that Harrington considered the form Teya to be the equivalent of his own *Togö*, in which case it is also equivalent to Hodge's *Tagu-*.

On the basis of materials published by Hodge and Harrington, it has been previously suggested (D. Gunnerson 1956: 351–52) not only that *Tagu*=*Teya*=Eastern Apacheans but also that *kerésh*=*Querecho*=Western Apacheans. This idea represented a departure from previous thinking in that Harrington believed the Querechos, as well as the Teyas, might be Eastern Apacheans, while Hodge apparently never identified the Teyas as Apacheans at all. Other types of evidence supporting this identification, which carries with it the implication that the Western Apacheans were originally plains bison hunters, have been presented elsewhere (D. Gunnerson 1956).

Fortunately, because of the soldier Castañeda's curiosity about some ruined pueblos in what is now called the Galisteo Basin, we have a year date for the initial appearance of the Apacheans in the Pueblo area that is, interestingly, compatible with approxi-

4 It is important to note that Harrington's use of "Lipanan" is not restricted to the Lipan Apache tribe but refers to all the Eastern Apacheans.

mate dates suggested by other lines of evidence (D. Gunnerson 1956). The information providing the year date was obtained from Pueblo informants sometime between 1540 and 1542 and subsequently included in the account of Castañeda, who says:

> All I was able to find out . . . was that, sixteen years before, some people called Teyas, had come to this country in great numbers and had destroyed these villages. They had besieged Cicuye [Pecos] but had not been able to capture it, because it was strong, and when they left the region, they had made peace with the whole country. (Winship 1896: 524)

In brief, the Teya Apacheans first appeared among the New Mexico Pueblos about 1525 and quickly exhibited the adaptability that has characterized the Southern Athabascans throughout historic times by establishing friendship with the village Indians, whom (contrary to the exponents of the enemy people theory) they could not conquer.

Although Castañeda describes the Querechos as well as the Teyas elsewhere in his narrative, indicating that both groups were dog-nomads living exactly alike, it is not apparent from his evidence that the Querechos took part in the ca. 1525 invasion he describes. That Querechos were also involved in that incursion is, however, suggested by traditions of Keresan-speaking Pueblo people. In the 1880s Bandelier heard at Cochití a "folk tale" then current at Santo Domingo, part of which follows:

> A long time ago, and before the Spaniards came to New Mexico, some wild tribe from the plains made a sudden irruption into the valley of the Rio Grande. They were called the Kirauash, and they seriously threatened Santo Domingo, or (as it was then called) [parentheses in original] Gi-pu-y. ["Wicked sorcerers" of Santo Domingo plotted with the Kirauash to help them capture the pueblo, but the conspiracy was discovered.] The savages, seeing their plan frustrated, made a desperate attack upon the neighboring village of Cochiti, which was repulsed. Enraged at their failure, they withdrew toward the plains. Their retreat carried them past the most southerly pueblos of the Tanos, which they were able to surprise and utterly destroy. (Bandelier 1890–1892 II: 116, 117)

Bandelier noted the similarity between the names "Kirauash" and "Querecho" and commented on the resemblance of his Santo

Domingo folk tale to Castañeda's much earlier account that
identified the invaders as Teyas. In spite of the fact that the
Coronado narratives linked the Querechos and Teyas in several
contexts, it apparently did not occur to Bandelier that both
groups might have been involved in the assault on the Pueblos.
Rather, he decided that Castañeda had been wrong and that the
Querechos, not the Teyas, had been the aggressors (Bandelier
1890–1892 II: 117–20). Such a conclusion does not do justice to
the fact that Castañeda's information was obtained when the invasion was still a quite recent event, fresh in the memories of the
Pueblo people he questioned. Since one specific act, the destruction of Tano Pueblos in the Galisteo Basin, is attributed to Querechos by Keres and to Teyas by Pecos people, both of these
plains groups may have been involved in the initial invasion of
Pueblo territory; and if both were Apacheans, as the positive
evidence seems to indicate, this is not at all unlikely.

Actually, later consideration of the discrepancies between the
Castañeda and Bandelier versions seems to show that the differences may be merely a reflection of the relative richness of the
Keresan and Towa vocabularies relating to Apacheans. Towa
has separate terms for Eastern and Western Apacheans, that is,
the linguistic means to differentiate; and it may well be that Castañeda's informants (who were probably Pecos Indians) were
being precise when they said the invaders were Teyas. And it
may be that the Keresans called the same invaders Kirauash
(Querechos) simply because they, like some other groups, not-
ably the Tewas and Kiowas, ordinarily use only one term to
designate all Apacheans. Although the Tewas have interacted
extensively with both Eastern and Western Apacheans, at the
turn of this century they ordinarily applied a single term, *Sabe*,
to all Southern Athabascans indiscriminately (Harrington 1916:
573).

Kiowa usage is of even greater interest, not only because this
tribe has just one term for all Apacheans but also because that
term closely resembles the Pecos-Jémez name for Eastern Apacheans specifically. Mooney (1898*b*: 245) gives the Kiowa form
as *Tagui* or as *Tagu'i* (1896: 1081), which is similar to the Pecos

and Jémez forms collected by Hodge. In 1884, Ten Kate (Hodge 1907–1910 I: 67) rendered the Kiowa term as *Tokuwe*, which resembles Harrington's version of the Jémez form. Although Kiowa is related to Tanoan and presumed Jémez-Kiowa cognates have been listed (Hale 1962: 1–5), the reason for the close resemblance in form and usage between Jémez *Tagu-(Togö)* meaning "east" and "Eastern Apachean," and the Kiowa *Tagui* (*Tokuwe*) meaning "Apachean" is not clarified by the known history of the Kiowa.

Neither Hodge nor Harrington gives the etymology of Towa *-kerésh* (*kyala, -gala*) beyond its use to designate Southern Athabascans, but Jaramillo's statement, previously cited, suggests that the term had something to do with the buffalo. As purely descriptive terms, both Querecho ("Buffalo hunter?") and Teya ("Easterner?") could have been appropriately applied to both peoples, since both lived on and among the buffalo and both were located to the east of the Pueblos, although the Teyas apparently lived farther east or southeast than the Querechos.

One way to describe the location of these groups in 1541 is to determine the points at which Coronado's army met them on the Plains, a difficult undertaking because ambiguities in the narratives of the expedition have provided latitude for a number of different reconstructions of his route. It is safe to generalize that the Querechos and Teyas lived most of the year where the main buffalo herds were, but their well-trained pack dogs made it possible for them to transport surplus meat and hides to permanent settlements on the peripheries of the Buffalo Plains. Here, as trade-friends of the village people, they could live through the winter in sheltered places and trade products of the buffalo for corn and other commodities (H & R 1940: 261–62, 310).

The Querechos and the Teyas were the only Indians met by Coronado's men on the Buffalo Plains, and the skin tent and the pack dog were the distinguishing characteristics of these Indians (H & R 1940: passim). Considering the several descriptions of these "wild tribes" of the Plains in the narratives of the Coronado expedition, it seems significant that although Coronado's men visited Zuñi, Hopiland and Acoma, Taos and Jémez, they did not report wild tribes in the vicinity of these pueblos. Bandelier (1892: 7) and Harrington (1940: 510) assume that there were Apaches in the vicinity of Zuñi who were merely hiding out here during Coronado's time. However, the fact that Coronado's men spent nearly two years among the Pueblos and questioned the inhabitants specifically about the country and its peoples without obtaining information on any wild tribes except those on the Plains is a strong argument against the presence of wild tribes within the Pueblo area west of the Río Grande in 1540–1542. Actually, Castañeda stated explicitly that "between them [the Pueblos] there are no villages or houses, but, on the contrary, the land is all uninhabited" (H & R 1940: 259). The fact that the Pueblos did not complain of wandering predatory tribes is emphasized by their complaints concerning one another, and the stories of inter-Pueblo conflict heard by Fray Marcos were substantially augmented by what the Pueblo people themselves told Coronado. The most reasonable conclusion to be drawn from these facts is that at the time of Coronado's *entrada*, wild tribes were not a threat to the pueblos; these towns threatened one another.

Coronado's sojourn in New Mexico apparently had little effect on inter-Pueblo relations in that region. Since he did not use any Pueblo group against another to serve his own ends nor deliberately increase the hostility that various Pueblo peoples already felt for one another, he can scarcely be charged with upsetting the native balance of power. However, his two-year stay in New Mexico may have had a significant effect on relations among the Pueblo peoples and the Apacheans. The various Pueblo groups must have been thoroughly disturbed by the possibility that other Spanish expeditions would follow Coronado's. It has already been shown that there was trade and communication between Mexican Indians and Zuñi before Coronado's journey north. Moreover, Spanish slavers were operating in Sinaloa and southern Sonora in the early 1530s, and it was Spaniards involved in a slave-hunting expedition that Cabeza de Vaca and his companions fell in with in 1536 (Bandelier 1890: 13–14, 44–45). News of this kind of activity may have accounted in part for the treatment given the Negro Esteban at Zuñi.

After Fray Marcos returned to Mexico City, Viceroy Mendoza sent Melchior Díaz, commander of the Spanish outpost at Culiacán, to verify the friar's reports (Winship 1896: 383–84). Penetrating as far as northern Sonora, Díaz learned that

> the inhabitants of Cibola have sent word to those of this village and of the surrounding country, warning them not to receive the Christians if they should come, but to kill them . . . if they do not dare to kill them, they request them to send word, that they may come and do it. (Bandelier 1892: 10)

News of the northward advance of the Spanish frontier in Mexico after 1542, which was accompanied by bloody wars between Spaniards and Indians and also by Spanish slave-raiding expeditions beyond the frontier (Forbes 1960: 29–48), undoubtedly intensified Pueblo apprehension. However, the records show that their solution to the potential problem was not the formation of a league among themselves for mutual protection; on the contrary, it is entirely possible that each band of plains Querechos that appeared west of the Río Grande after 1542 was encouraged by a Pueblo or group of Pueblos to take up residence in its neighborhood to serve, if needed, as allies against the Spaniards if they should return. Furthermore, it is even possible that these Apache allies were used against other Pueblo groups in the meanwhile or even occasionally used by one faction of a Pueblo against another. Nearly a century later Benavides wrote of the "continuous civil wars" of the Pueblo people caused by factionalism between "warriors" and "sorcerers" (Ayer 1916: 30–31), and the Santo Domingo folk tale concerning the original incursion of the Kirauash (Querecho Apaches) obtained by Bandelier actually included the statement that "wicked sorcerers" of Santo Domingo had "entered into negotiations with the Kirauash for the purpose of delivering the pueblo into their hands" (Bandelier 1890–1892 II: 116–17).

The symbiotic trade relationships that grew up between western Apachean groups and such western Pueblo peoples as the

Zuñis, Acomas, and Hopis may have developed because once the Apaches had infiltrated the Pueblo area and entrenched themselves in the mountains that contained most of the game, these Pueblo dwellers no longer dared venture far from their homes. In such case, they would have had to depend heavily on their Apache allies for meat, hides, and salt (Bandelier 1890–1892 I: 38). The ambivalent attitude of the Pueblo peoples toward the Apacheans, which can still be detected today, was well described by Castañeda in his account of Teya-Pueblo relations at the time of Coronado's *entrada*.

> These [the Teyas] knew the people in the settlements, and were friendly with them, and they went there to spend the winter under the wings of the settlements. The inhabitants do not dare to let them come inside, because they cannot trust them. Although they are received as friends, and trade with them, they do not stay in the villages over night, but outside under the wings. The villages are guarded by sentinels with trumpets, who call to one another just as in the fortresses of Spain. (Winship 1896: 524)

The actual westward movement of the Apaches after 1542 is undocumented, but the presence of Apaches called Querechos near Acoma and the Hopi Pueblos was an accomplished fact by 1582, and the relations between at least the Acomas and their Querecho neighbors followed the pattern of Teya-Pueblo relations described by Castañeda. As for the years between, the only references to Querechos living west of the Río Grande occur in connection with Ibarra's expedition into territory that became northern Chihuahua, and these references are questionable.

Ibarra in Northern Mexico
1565

The northward venture of Francisco Ibarra in 1565 (H & R 1928) did not reach the area that came to be known as New Mexico, yet this expedition, and other enterprises of the Ibarra family, are of interest here. Baltasár de Obregón, a member of the expedition and its principal chronicler, called tribes that the party heard of and met in northern Mexico, "Querechos." Since in all other cases people called Querechos by Spanish explorers can be identified (by convincing circumstantial evidence) as Apaches, it becomes important to consider Obregón's use of the term in some detail.

It is not altogether impossible that by 1565 there should have been buffalo-hunting Apaches on what Sauer (1932: 46) calls "the high grassy steppes" of northern Chihuahua, especially since that area may by then have been inhabited at least marginally and seasonally by bison (H & R 1928: 202, 215). And if some Apacheans could move within a few decades (after 1542 and before 1582) from the Buffalo Plains as far as the Hopi country, others might have been able to penetrate what is now Chihuahua. The weight of evidence and scholarly opinion, however, is thus far against the identification of Obregón's "Querechos" as Apacheans. No other exploring party found Querechos in northern Mexico. Apaches as such are not reported there until the late 1600s, and there are other historic tribes with whom Obregón's "Querechos" can more reasonably be identified.

Ibarra's men and other Iberian adventurers of the middle and late 1500s undoubtedly got the term Querecho from written reports of the Coronado expedition and probably even more frequently from verbal accounts by the numerous survivors of that *entrada*. Castañeda, for example, did not actually write out his narrative until "more than twenty years" after he returned with Coronado from Cíbola (New Mexico) in 1542. In his manuscript, however, he indicated that in the interim he had been asked all too often to relate his experiences verbally and that discussion of the land traversed by Coronado's army, including debate as to its merits, had never ceased in New Spain. Of those things that he thought might strain the credulity of his readers, Castañeda says, "I dare to write of them because I am writing at a time when many men are still living who saw them and will vouch for my account" (Winship 1896: 470–72, 541–42). These old comrades-in-arms, in turn, had undoubtedly been repeating their own versions of the event, maintaining an oral history of the journey (e.g., Hackett 1923–1937 I: 59). As raconteurs, they probably contributed, for the most part anonymously, those bits of information that do not appear in the recorded accounts of individual participants but have nevertheless found their way into general histories such as that of Obregón, who indicates that he interviewed veterans of Coronado's army (H & R 1928: 24, 26).

Now Castañeda is easily the key witness so far as information on the early Plains Apacheans is concerned, and the career of Francisco de Ibarra (Mecham 1968), considered in the light of what is known of Castañeda's life, yields new insights into the history of the search for the Northern Mystery (of which the Apacheans were incidentally a part). Scrutiny reveals that the accounts of the various expeditions northward overlap in their chronological coverage, forming continuous links in a chain of information. It appears that "New Mexico" and the plains beyond were never really "forgotten" (cf. H & R 1966: 8); there were only lulls in *known* exploring activity as a result of Indian wars or as those with the power to implement exploration were disappointed in the results, died, ran out of funds, or were replaced by others unversed in the lore of New Spain.

Pedro de Castañeda de Nájera was an "early settler" of the town of Culiacán on the west coast of Mexico. He may well have been with Nuño de Guzmán, who founded this settlement in 1531 during an expedition that included the earliest attempt to find the fabulous "Seven Cities." In any case, Castañeda is one of the authorities on Guzmán's motives and actions (Winship 1896: 472–73; Bandelier 1890: 11–13; Bancroft 1884: 36–38). Culiacán, in the province known as Nueva Galicia (Mecham 1968: 35) and in the state known now as Sinaloa, was long the northernmost Spanish outpost on the west coast of Mexico. To this small frontier community which owed its very existence to the Northern Mystery, Cabeza de Vaca and his companions, having made contact with Spanish slave raiders, were brought in 1536. They stayed there for fifteen days, exciting the citizens with new hearsay stories of cities to the north (Mecham 1968: 22–25, 27; Winship 1896: 474; Bandelier 1890: 47–48). Likewise, Culiacán was the launching point for the expeditions that Cabeza de Vaca's stories triggered—the journeys of Fray Marcos de Niza, Melchior Díaz, and finally, Coronado. Four early settlers of

Culiacán, including Castañeda and Pedro de Tovar, who later became *alcalde mayor* of the town, joined Coronado's forces, and Castañeda stopped off again at Culiacán when Coronado passed through on his return journey in 1542. He apparently remained at Culiacán permanently, for it was there he wrote his narrative, probably not long after 1562 (H & R 1940: 191*n*, 196*n*, 278).

During Coronado's absence in the north, the rise of the Ibarra family in New Spain began. Captain Miguel Ibarra served with distinction during various Mexican Indian uprisings and in 1542 was appointed a *regidor* of the *cabildo* of Guadalajara. In 1546 he outfitted, and hence acquired an interest in, the expedition that discovered the rich silver mines of Zacatecas. Miguel's nephew, Diego Ibarra, had served under his uncle during the Indian rebellions, losing a leg as a result of one encounter. After the discovery of the Zacatecas mines, Diego became one of four partners who undertook to exploit the mineral wealth of the mines and found a town near by. His position was further strengthened by his marriage to the daughter of Luís de Velasco, second viceroy of New Spain. Being physically handicapped and having no children of his own, Diego became a kind of foster-father of *his* nephew, Francisco Ibarra, who came to the New World from Spain as a young boy and was eventually made a page in the court of the viceroy in Mexico City (Mecham 1968: 1–43 passim).

Velasco arrived in Mexico in 1550 and his predecessor, Mendoza, departed in 1551. In the interim Mendoza briefed Velasco on the affairs of New Spain. According to Obregón:

> Among the things discussed, he (Mendoza)[5] particularly emphasized the means appropriate for new conquests which he (Velasco) ought to adopt, especially for the discovery and explanation of the stock, root, and coming of the ancient Mexican Culguas to conquer this empire and the provinces of Mexico. (He pointed out) methods of shortening long and difficult roads, unnecessary expenses, and advised that the route should be through level lands suitable for the journey. Likewise he ex-

---

5 To avoid confusion or misinterpretation, brackets used in the original quotations have been changed to parentheses; my interpolations are noted in brackets. This system has been used throughout the book.

> plained the recent good news which had just come from persons
> who had been in the localities and places where it was suspected
> the Mexican nation had its origin. (H & R 1928: 41)

What this "recent good news" was and who brought it is not
clear. It may have resulted from prospecting that had been inspired by the discoveries at Zacatecas or from the *visita* or general inspection of Nueva Galicia conducted by La Marcha
between 3 December 1549 and 7 December 1550. The news may
have been rumors emanating from slavers carrying out "isolated,
illegal raiding excursions" beyond Zacatecas (Mecham 1968:
46, 50 ff., 57). In any case (according to Obregón),

> The Viceroy Don Luís de Velasco was very much pleased
> with these warnings and was bent on putting the discovery into
> practise with the greatest order possible. Accordingly he put it
> into effect later. He inquired of all the explorers of new lands
> about the reports which they had received and what they knew
> of New Mexico. (H & R 1928: 41)

Meanwhile, the province of Nueva Galicia, especially the silver
mines at Zacatecas, yielded great wealth for Diego Ibarra
(Mecham 1968: 40–47), and Viceroy Velasco was apparently
indeed interested in the north, for in 1554 he gave young Francisco Ibarra the right to explore in that direction, implying that
Coronado's efforts had been inadequate. Ibarra used Zacatecas as
his base of operations. His preliminary activities brought him into
prolonged direct contact with one of Coronado's most outstanding officers, for more than once he derived vital assistance from
Pedro de Tovar in Culiacán (Mecham 1968: esp. 134–35; 140,
58–59). Ibarra and his men stayed in Culiacán at times and got
to know the settlers (H & R 1928: 75–76, 105–7, 111, 132–33).
Also, in Zacatecas in 1559, Juan Jaramillo, author of a firsthand
account of the Coronado expedition second in value only to that
of Castañeda, recruited men for the Florida expedition of Tris-
tán de Luna y Arrellano, still another of Coronado's captains
(Hackett 1923–1937 I: 49; Priestley 1928 I: xiv, xxv–xxvi, xxx).
Thus, while Ibarra was extending the frontiers of New Spain by
exploring and founding the district to be known as Nueva Vizcaya, he had an opportunity to become acquainted with several

veterans of Coronado's *entrada*—Castañeda among them. And when he set out in 1565 on what was to be his final, most ambitious effort to reach whatever it was that constituted the Northern Mystery, he not only stopped first in Culiacán to obtain essential equipment (Mecham 1968: 162–63), but he apparently also took with him both an Indian interpreter who had served Coronado, and a former member of Coronado's army, Francisco de Caravajal (H & R 1928: 83, 212–13).

Some seven months later, after innumerable hardships, Ibarra returned to his own district, having terminated his *entrada* at Paquimé, a large ruined pueblo that was almost certainly the archeological site in northern Chihuahua now called Casas Grandes. He had failed to reach Coronado's Cíbola with its inhabited pueblos and hence failed to cast any new light on the northern lands (Mecham 1968: 159–86). Had he attained his goal he could only have verified Coronado's findings.

In fact with so many survivors of Coronado's army still active on the north-Mexican frontier, it is impossible that Ibarra and later adventurers could have been unaware of Coronado's journey and its disappointing results. How, then, could Ibarra have hoped to find "another famous and rich Mexico" (H & R 1928: 91)? The discovery of truly rich mines on the northern frontier after Coronado's return could understandably have strengthened the hope of finding more beyond. As for the possibility of finding settlements of wealthy and civilized people, soldiers of fortune preferred to believe that Coronado had given up too soon—that greater efforts would lead to greater discoveries. Such a belief is more than implied in Viceroy Velasco's charge to Ibarra to "explore those lands which Coronado had scarely seen," and it seems improbable that he was referring here to the Pueblo country of New Mexico called Cíbola, where Coronado's army had stayed for nearly two years. Rather, he may have had in mind the "Plains of Cíbola" and "Quivira," which Coronado had not fully explored, much to the disappointment of some of his soldiers. Among these was Castañeda, who strongly intimates that it was in the prairie land of Quivira—or beyond—that promise lay.

Here it is desirable to consider why, after more than twenty

years, Castañeda committed his narrative to writing. Authors of
such accounts usually hoped to gain some reward for past
services or permission to undertake some new and hopefully
profitable enterprise. Castañeda's explicit reason was to correct
misconceptions of the land covered by Coronado. He may have
hoped to gain something from the publication of the work itself,
since he asks that it be sponsored by the anonymous personage to
whom it is addressed (H & R 1940: 193).

In one place Castañeda expresses his opinion that it was the
Lord's will that further exploration of Quivira should await other
people and that "those of us who went thither should be satisfied
with telling that we were the first to discover it and gain information of it" (H & R 1940: 264). Yet elsewhere he says of
Coronado's army:

> Since, after they returned here from the land which they had
> conquered and abandoned, time has made clear to them the na-
> ture and location of the region they reached, and the beginning
> of a fine land they had in their grasp, their hearts bemoan the
> fact that they lost such an opportune occasion . . . I believe
> that some of those who came from there would today be glad if
> they could go back and try to recover what they lost. (H & R
> 1940: 194)

Further, Castañeda indicated that he and others who had remained
in Culiacán had fallen into "poverty and privation" in "pacifying
and holding" that land (H & R 1940: 278), a type of statement
that often accompanied requests for consideration from high
officials. And, finally, the comments in his last chapter on the
most feasible routes for those who might undertake to return to
the lands discovered by Coronado suggest that he knew plans for
fresh expeditions were in the making (H & R 1940: 281–83).
Perhaps he also meant to imply that he would be a desirable
guide.

Whatever Castañeda's basic reason for writing his narrative, he
apparently prepared it soon after 1562, the year in which, after
unavoidable delays, the viceroy granted Francisco Ibarra his
commission as governor of the new district to be called Nueva
Vizcaya, with the right to look for the settlements said to exist

beyond known territory. The anonymous person to whom Castañeda presented his manuscript, addressed only as "your Lordship," may have been Viceroy Velasco, Diego de Ibarra, Pedro
de Tovar, or even the newly appointed Governor Francisco
Ibarra himself. For between 1562 and 1565 Ibarra extended his
jurisdiction, or at least his influence, over Castañeda's home area
of Culiacán (H & R 1928: 75–76; Mecham 1968: 192), and
hence Castañeda might have felt himself to be Ibarra's "vassal."
Ibarra may have read Castañeda's account or at least talked to its
author, for Obregón refers to Ibarra's 1565 journey as "the expedition to the plains in search of new lands" and elsewhere suggests more than once that the main destination of the exploring
party was the Buffalo Plains (H & R 1928: 145, 147, 152, 153,
162), which Castañeda describes more vividly than any other
author. Although the extent to which Pedro Castañeda de Nájera
and Francisco Ibarra interacted, if at all, will probably remain a
matter for speculation, Obregón's *General History*, for better or
worse, links the results of Coronado's expedition to that of Ibarra
and to the explorations that followed both.

Obregón's *History*, like that of Castañeda, was written some
twenty years after those events in which the author actually participated. What is more, by the time Obregón finished writing in
April 1584, he had access to and included along with his description of Ibarra's 1565 journey, information on two still later expeditions to New Mexico—that of Rodríguez and Chamuscado
in 1581 and that of Espejo in 1582–1583 (H & R 1966).

Obregón sent his manuscript to the king of Spain and in a letter to the monarch says that he served in the conquests of Cíbola
and New Mexico (H & R 1928: xxviii). The reasoning behind
this statement finally comes out in the narrative itself, where
Obregón reveals that he considered Paquimé (Casas Grandes),
though in ruins, to be the southernmost of the New Mexico
Pueblos.

> According to the second explorers who went with Antonio de
> Espejo, we came within two days' march of the last inhabited
> part of this region [New Mexico]. . . . We may rightfully af-

firm that we saw the walls of its enclosures and towns, and had
we gone ahead it would have been discovered, subdued, controlled and placed under the royal crown of your majesty.
(H & R 1928: 199, 213–14)

Although Obregón's evaluation of the accomplishments of
various explorers is at times confusing and contradictory, he
seems to have realized that Coronado had discovered most, if not
all, of the inhabited pueblos and that Chamuscado and Espejo
had at best only extended his discoveries (H & R 1928: 216). But
Obregón also seems to have clung to the possibility that Coronado had not adequately followed up leads to rich kingdoms that
he got in Quivira (H & R 1928: 217) and to have thought that
the ruins of Paquimé (Casas Grandes), containing buildings that
resembled those constructed by the ancient Romans, warranted
great expectations (H & R 1928: 205) of finding people more
civilized than the Pueblo Indians of New Mexico. Hence, while
Obregón appeared to be bidding for the right to lead a colonizing
expedition to the Pueblo country—a right finally granted to
Juan de Oñate (H & R 1953)—he already had his eye on more
remote regions. Offering his *General History* as evidence that he
was well-informed concerning the new lands, he volunteered to
explore six hundred leagues *beyond* New Mexico (H & R 1928:
xxviii, 205).

As stated previously, Obregón's account is of importance for
this study primarily because of his comments on Indians he called
Querechos. If, in 1565, members of Ibarra's party actually
thought the nomadic Indians they saw were Querechos, it is
possible that Casas Grandes provided the stimulus. These explorers would have known that some of the inhabited pueblos
of New Mexico were near the Plains and that the Querechos
known to Coronado's men visited these settlements. Hence, when
they found Casas Grandes near what appeared to be the beginnings of the Plains, they might reasonably have supposed that
they were in or near New Mexico and that the wild and roaming people they met near by were the same as Coronado's Querechos. Obregón wrote twenty years after Ibarra's expedition,
however, and obviously after long reflection on the lands and

peoples seen by various explorers who had penetrated farther north. The name Querechos was apparently applied to nomadic people by Ibarra's men in 1565 (Paso y Troncoso 1939–1940 X: 152), but Obregón's comments on these Indians in part reflect later events.

When, for example, Obregón digresses from a preliminary account of Coronado's expedition to describe the plains Querechos as "coarse, vile and wicked" (H & R 1928: 19–20), it indicates that he was mixing information from two different time periods and two different areas. All the known primary accounts of the Coronado expedition speak well of the plains Querechos, and Obregón himself was favorably impressed by the "Querechos" he had seen. The chronicles of Espejo's later expedition are not only the first primary narratives to mention Querechos in the *mountains* of New Mexico but also the first to describe conflict between Spaniards and Querechos. Therefore, it may be accounts of Espejo's experiences with mountain Querechos that are reflected in Obregón's description and cause Obregón's opinions about them to sound contradictory. Sauer, who found Obregón's account unsatisfactory in many respects, comments on that author's tendency to let "one event suggest another which happened in another place or at another time" (Sauer 1932: 38–39).

It would seem from Obregón's history that Ibarra and his men seldom knew where they were on their journey in 1565, nor where they were going. For example, they "rediscovered" the valley of Corazones, where Coronado had previously tried to found a settlement. Their interpreter, who had also served Coronado, knew the customs and languages of the natives only that far. Yet for some reason, Obregón says Corazones was "near the plains of the cattle" (H & R 1928: 83, 162), although Ibarra's party struggled far beyond this valley and still never reached the true Plains.

Beyond Corazones, Ibarra reached the town of Guaraspi, which Hammond and Rey (1928: 173, *n*251) locate in the Yaqui Valley. Obregón says of the people there that they were

> greedy, thievish, careful, and very skillful and versed in the art and practice of war. This is due to the fact that they are neigh-

bors of the most valiant and daring people in those provinces. These are the Querechos, who follow the cattle. (H & R 1928: 174)

Of the people of Cumupa, five days from Guaraspi, he says: "They are a warlike people as was to be expected from neighbors of the Querechos" (H & R 1928: 174–75).

Still farther on, Ibarra's party reached "the stronghold of Çaguaripa":

> This valley and town of Çaguaripa is on the frontier of the Indians of the plains. These people are very skilful, warlike, and better versed in the use and practise of war than all other people in the provinces as far as the vaqueros, called Querechos. (H & R 1928: 179)

Later, according to Obregón, the explorers

> went into the lands of the Querechos, who are neighbors of the people in the plains of the cattle, their enemies. Their habitat extends two journeys from the plains. (H & R 1928: 194)

From this and other statements it seems that Obregón distinguished between the "Querechos" of the intermontane grasslands, the only "Querechos" he saw, and those of the true Plains. Unfortunately, when the explorers finally made contact with a band of "Querechos" near Casas Grandes, they had no interpreter who could speak to them and so had to communicate by means of signs (H & R 1928: 198). There is nothing in Obregón's description of these Indians that would confirm or disprove their identity as Apacheans. They had dogs, although he does not say that these were used as pack animals, and the explorers did not see their dwellings.

> There came to the camp three hundred Querechos with their women and children. . . . The men are lively, of noble disposition, friendly, brave and able-bodied; the women and children are attractive. They came singing and dancing around the camp and showed great joy and merriment at seeing us. They made strange faces toward the sky which are ceremonies they employ in their worship of the sun. . . . [They gave] the information by means of signs, that Cíbola was three days' march from there and the cattle four journeys toward the north. . . . These people are enemies of the Querechos who live among the cattle.

They have droves of dogs. They are well built, lively and warlike. They eat all sorts of wild reptiles; some corn, acorns, and
walnuts, Castile prunes, and all kinds of game. They are more
friendly, loyal, and valiant than those we had met before. They
possess hides from the cattle; they do not have salt. We could not
see what sort of habitations or houses they had because the army
passed at a distance from their town. (H & R 1928: 201–2, 203)

Sauer (1932: 38–39, 46) suggests that these Indians of the Chihuahua steppes were, in Ibarra's time, Sumas.

Although Obregón probably did not see Apacheans in 1565,
he seems to have been the first author to apply the Old-World
Spanish word *"vaquero,"* meaning cowherd, to the Indians who
followed the New-World *"vacas"* (cattle) or buffalo on foot.
He thus anticipated, and perhaps provided the basis for, the later
use of the term to designate the Plains Apaches specifically in
documents relating to the colonization of New Mexico (1598–
1634). Obregón's source for the term *vaquero* as a name for
nomadic buffalo hunters is not evident. The word itself was
probably imported from Spain in its usual context, along with
domesticated cattle. It does not occur in contemporary accounts
of the Coronado expedition, as does Querecho, and if *vaquero*
came to be used as a Spanish equivalent for Querecho in the verbal discussions of the Plains of Cíbola that followed, this is not
evident in Castañeda's belated manuscript of ca. 1562. Neither
does the term occur in firsthand accounts of the Chamuscado and
Espejo expeditions, although Obregón, in his secondary descriptions, uses it as an alternative designation for the Querechos met
by both Coronado and Chamuscado (H & R 1928: 19–20, 302).
Interestingly enough, still another member of Ibarra's expedition,
Antonio Ruíz, is credited with an account that refers indirectly
to the Plains dog-nomads met by Coronado as *baqueros* or querechos. The document itself, however, dates from the early seventeenth century (Sauer 1932: 51, 53, 54).

If we can rely on Garcilaso de la Vega's secondary account,
the men of de Soto's expedition used the term in 1542, calling
an area (probably west of the Trinity River in Texas) where
they found fresh buffalo meat and hides *la provincia de los
vaqueros,* although they never saw any live buffalo (Garcilaso

de la Vega 1605: 279; Varner and Varner 1951: 516; hereafter referred to as V & V). Unfortunately, none of the firsthand accounts of de Soto's expedition corroborates Garcilaso, who did not publish until 1605, twenty years after Obregón's manuscript was sent to Spain. And by 1605 the *Vaquero* Apaches had been mentioned in numerous documents originating in New Mexico and in Mexico City as well. However, the survivors of de Soto's expedition did go to Mexico in 1543, and some of them stayed there (Swanton 1946: 59), leading Pichardo, who apparently accepted Garcilaso's statement, to speculate nearly three centuries later as to whether they had introduced the term *vaquero* to New Spain (Hackett 1931–1946 III: 90–91).

The interest expressed here in the extension of *vaquero* to designate buffalo-hunting Indians is more than a digression; this example suggests the manner in which this and other relevant New-World words, including perhaps the name "Apache" itself, were spread from one center for Spanish conquest to another by soldiers of fortune, with local variations and derivatives developing in different parts of Latin America.

As for Francisco Ibarra, his failing health was finally broken by the hardships of his 1565 journey; the Ibarra family fortune was depleted, and the politico-legal problems of organizing an exploring expedition had increased. Further long-range expeditions, except for illegal and undocumented slave raids, had to await the emergence of leaders with strength, wealth, political influence, or boldness—or better yet, a combination of these. Meanwhile, however, Ibarra was far from inactive. Under his orders, the frontiers of Nueva Vizcaya were extended northward by his followers, notable among the advances being the founding in 1567 of mining settlements first at Indé and then Santa Bárbara (figure 2) by Rodrigo del Río de Losa, his trusted lieutenant (H & R 1966: 4).

Just as Zacatecas had served as a base for the expeditions of Ibarra himself (with auxiliary support from Culiacán), his town of Santa Bárbara became

> the focus of sixteenth-century adventurers in northern Mexico, the "end of the line" for layman, soldier, or priest, and the home

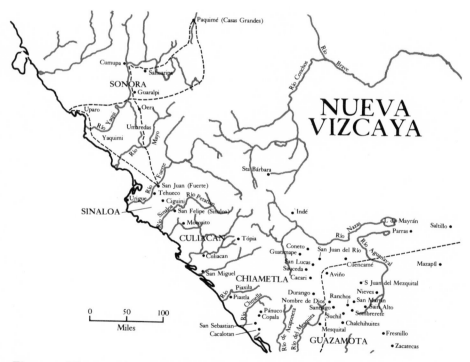

Figure 2. The frontiers of Northern New Spain in Francisco Ibarra's time (1563–1575).

base or point of concentration for fitting out new prospecting ventures. Here the expeditions of Chamuscado and Espejo, hopeful of finding "another Mexico," were conceived and launched. Probably no other center on Mexico's northern frontier so completely nourished and fed the little groups that were to go still farther into the unknown interior. (H & R 1966: 5)

Francisco Ibarra died in 1575 (Mecham 1968: 222–23), but it seems more than reasonable that, just as he and his men must have heard and been influenced by the stories of Coronado's veterans, later adventurers were stimulated by the unfulfilled but still smoldering ambitions of the Ibarra family and its followers. For the Ibarras retained control of Nueva Vizcaya for years to come. Francisco's brother Juan was appointed governor but died before he could leave Spain. The title with all its privileges finally came to Diego Ibarra himself (Mecham 1968: 239), who governed, often from Mexico City, through two relatives. The first of these was Martín López de Ibarra, who seems to have been Francisco's cousin and to have accompanied him on his expeditions after 1562. The second was a Juan de Ibarra, another of Diego's nephews (H & R 1928: 45; Hackett 1923–1937 I: 115). With these men and other veterans of frontier expansion, such as Rodrigo del Río de Losa, still active, it seems incredible that the next adventurers to set out for the north could leave Santa Bárbara unacquainted with the history of those who had gone before (cf. H & R 1966: 8).

The Rodríguez-Chamuscado Expedition
1581–1582

The documents bearing on the next two expeditions to New Mexico show renewed rivalry among aspiring *conquistadores* for the right to explore that territory. They also suggest a struggle between the Ibarras, other officials of New Spain, and viceregal authority to control access to lands north of the settled frontier of Nueva Vizcaya. In the contest that took place between 1580 and 1583 the Ibarras scored a victory, and it was north-Mexican silver, transmuted into Ibarra power, that first indirectly and then directly paved a new trail to New Mexico via the Conchos River and the Río Grande.

Both the Rodríguez-Chamuscado expedition and that of Espejo, which followed, should be re-evaluated in light of the contemporary political conditions and social networks which were inextricably intertwined. The earlier territorial expansion of the Ibarras, made possible by the favor of Diego Ibarra's father-in-law, Luís de Velasco I, second viceroy of New Spain, had been bitterly opposed by some government officials, especially members of northern provincial *audiencias* (Mecham 1968: 187–203). Velasco I had died in 1564 (Bancroft 1883 II: 589–90), but his son, Luís de Velasco II, Diego Ibarra's brother-in-law and later eighth viceroy of New Spain, had thus far survived the political tempests that followed his father's regime (Bancroft 1883 II: passim). By October 1580, when the term of Don Lorenzo Suárez de Mendoza y Figueroa, count of Coruña, began, corruption in high places had become notorious. With the advent of this fifth viceroy, matters worsened. "Taking advantage of the viceroy's weakness, government servants became more bold; public funds were misappropriated, and the venality of the judges was without precedent" (Bancroft 1883 II: 739). In such a setting the first would-be discoverers, since young Francisco Ibarra, set out for the north.

The real story of the Rodríguez-Chamuscado expedition may never be known. Neither of the principals lived to tell it, and Gallegos, the soldier who furnished the most detailed account, strongly desired a royal commission to become the "founder" of the new area (H & R 1966: 147–48). Only very belatedly did Suárez de Mendoza report the affair to the king of Spain, and to the careful reader his report is ambiguous. According to the viceroy's version, dated 1 November 1582,[6] Fray Agustín Rodríguez had come to him two years before in November 1580, say-

---

6 This date and the date of a letter from the king to Coruña (20 April 1583) controverts the prevalent idea that the count died or ceased to rule in June 1582 (H & R 1966: 67n2; Bancroft 1883 II: 739, 740n3), and lends weight to the statement of Chavero that Coruña died on 19 June 1583 (Riva Palacio 1967 II: 436).

ing "that he ardently wished to go into the interior to preach the
holy gospel in the region beyond the Santa Bárbara mines in New
Vizcaya" (H & R 1966: 123). The friar's exact destination was
thus unspecified. The viceroy continued:

> I granted him permission to do so and to take along some other
> friars and up to twenty men who might volunteer to go with him
> as protectors and companions. I also authorized them to take
> along some articles for trading, but I did not permit a greater
> number of people to join them, since your Majesty had given
> instructions that no new expeditions into the interior should be
> undertaken without your express authorization. And I ordered
> that whoever was designated by the friar should act as leader
> and be obeyed by the rest, so that there would be no disorderly
> conduct. (H & R 1966: 123)

The substance of the viceroy's letter suggests that he had behaved in keeping with the character attributed to him by Bancroft (1883 II: 738–39) i.e., a good but weak and inefficient
man. It would appear that he had yielded too easily to persuasion
in granting permission to undertake the journey. Then he had
delayed two years before giving any report of his action to the
king, waiting not merely until some six months after the survivors
of the expedition returned but until after news had reached him
that at least one and probably two friars had been killed by Indians in New Mexico, an event that could not, perhaps, be ignored. When the viceroy did report, he may have attempted to
justify his actions by indicating that he had given primary
authorization for the journey to a friar for missionary purposes
and that he had given the friar authority to appoint a lay leader.
Coruña appears to believe that the group did not constitute an
"expedition," because of its small size and hence did not fall
under the king's mandate. Finally, the viceroy is strangely vague
with regard to the specific, authorized destination of the party.
He implies that the group had permission to go to Indians living
along the Conchos River and that they found more civilized
people only incidentally, without saying why or how far they
ventured beyond the Conchos.

Close perusal of accounts given by the surviving soldiers, especially the voluntary "Relation" of Hernán Gallegos (H & R

1966: 67–114) as opposed to his later, sworn "Testimony" (H & R 1966: 133–38) evokes a different interpretation. These statements indicate that the viceroy was eager to sponsor important discoveries during his administration and connived to ignore the rights of exploration that belonged to Diego Ibarra as governor of Nueva Vizcaya. From the accounts of the soldiers it appears that the military leader Francisco Sánchez Chamuscado obtained the primary commission to make the journey (H & R 1966: 121), that the layman "took along" the friars, who played a subordinate role (H & R 1966: 69), and that the party intended to go to the Pueblos of "New Mexico" from the beginning (H & R 1966: 67).

Had Fray Agustín and Chamuscado survived to give their versions, the picture might have been different, but as the records stand, Gallegos emerges as the boldest spirit involved in the undertaking, finally declaring that he himself had led the expedition (H & R 1966: 147). This soldier's "Relation" is full of flattery that might have swayed the kind of person the count of Coruña is supposed to have been. And it could have been dangerous for Gallegos to minimize the role of the missionaries if he was lying, and to be so blatantly defiant of the Ibarras if he could not count on powerful support.

Whatever the circumstances, after long planning, the second expedition to reach New Mexico and the Buffalo Plains to the east consisted of three friars, including Fray Agustín, and eight or nine soldiers headed by Francisco Chamuscado. They left Santa Bárbara on 6 June 1581, very probably without the knowledge and consent of the Ibarras or their local representatives. Hammond and Rey have said of this expedition:

> These servants of King Philip, soldiers and friars, motivated by different forces, were destined to become the real discoverers of New Mexico. Completely unaware, apparently, of Coronado's exploration of 1540–1542, which was not strange in an era when there were almost no printed books except for religious tracts, these men set out on their mission into the unknown wilderness. (H & R 1966: 8)

However, statements of the explorers themselves controvert this idea. Hernán Gallegos, notary of the expedition, in submitting his account of events to the viceroy, says he does so

since your Excellency has such a great part in the enterprise under discussion: for it was by your support and during your term
in office that the discovery, *so greatly desired by our predecessors* [italics mine], was achieved. (H & R 1966: 69)

And in another place Gallegos says the returning explorers were
well-received in Mexico City because they had carried out an

enterprise on which his Majesty and his subjects had previously
spent much money, but without success . . . where five hundred men had failed to discover or explore, eight men had succeeded at their own cost. (H & R 1966: 114)

The "five hundred men" he mentions had to be Coronado's
army. Moreover, Gallegos had knowledge of Ibarra's later *entrada*. In 1583, calling himself "discoverer of New Mexico," he
offered to "pacify" that land "subject to the same terms and
conditions which your majesty granted to Francisco de Ibarra"
(H & R 1966: 147).

The members of the Rodríguez–Chamuscado expedition did
not become aware of previous explorations only after returning
from their own. Pedro de Bustamante, one of the soldiers, said
that he and the friar Agustín Rodríguez had been planning the
expedition for more than two years, having been influenced by
the report of an Indian and by Cabeza de Vaca's book about his
travels (H & R 1966: 128).

However, with an oral history of northward exploration still
alive and with the Ibarra family and its followers still very much
concerned with affairs on the frontier where the 1581 expedition
originated, there seems little likelihood that Chamuscado, Rodríguez, and their companions could have been ignorant of their
predecessors. Further statements of Gallegos clinch the matter.

We were also influenced by the accounts of those who had gone
inland to explore, and who had written chronicles, copies of
which we had with us. These accounts informed us that the said
settled people were very brave and numerous; but that did not
discourage us from going ahead. . . .
    Before this time numerous Spaniards with ample commissions
from the viceroys of New Spain had entered the land in an
attempt to discover this settlement, and they had not found it.
Thus we concluded that our project was directed by the hand

of God. . . . We therefore went ahead very happily and joy-
fully. (H & R 1966: 77, 83)

The chronicles they had with them could well have included
handwritten copies of Castañeda's narrative and that of Jaramillo.
Such documents were often copied and recopied as they were
transmitted from one official to another, and if the viceroy did
have a deep interest in their venture, as Gallegos asserts, it seems
unlikely that he would have allowed them to undertake it without as much preliminary knowledge as he could provide. The
second paragraph of the quotation indicates that they were well
aware of previous explorations while they were conducting their
own.

In a letter to the king, dated 10 November 1582, Diego de
Ibarra briefly described the Rodríguez–Chamuscado expedition
and claimed the lands it had visited as part of his district.

> I only wish to inform your majesty that, according to the ter-
> ritory that the district of Nueva Vizcaya is known to cover, the
> jurisdiction of this discovery appears to belong to it, for it is
> known that persons of this district had news of it many days
> [years?] ago, and the soldiers who just went with the said re-
> ligious were from the company of Governor Martín López de
> Ibarra, my deputy. (Hackett 1923–1937 I: 113, 115)

Actually, the adventurers who went to New Mexico in 1581
added little to the information obtained in 1540–1542. These later
explorers, like Coronado and his men, learned early of inter-
Pueblo hostilities. The Piros, whom they reached first, were at
war with another group that lived farther on, and Gallegos commented that when the Pueblo Indians retired at night they pulled
up their ladders to protect themselves against enemies, "since they
are at war with one another" (H & R 1966: 82, 84–85).[7]

From people at a pueblo (which may have been San Marcos)
in the Galisteo Basin, the explorers obtained information about
the buffalo and the nomadic people who lived on the Buffalo
Plains.

7 In 1957 Tesuque Indians volunteered the information that originally their
pueblo had no doors at ground level because the Pueblos fought among themselves. It would be interesting to determine whether such a tradition still exists
at other pueblos.

They indicated to us that the inhabitants of the buffalo region were not striped; that they lived by hunting and ate nothing but buffalo meat during the winter; that during the rainy season they would go to the areas of the prickly pear and yucca; that they were enemies of our informants, but nevertheless came to the pueblos of the latter in order to trade such articles as deerskins and buffalo hides for making footwear, and a large amount of meat, in exchange for corn and blankets; and that in this way, by communicating with one another, each nation had come to understand the other's language. (H & R 1966: 87)

In reply to further questions

the natives stated that the buffalo were two days' journey away. We asked them why they lived so far from the herds, and they replied that it was on account of their cornfields and cultivated lands, so that the buffalo would not eat the crops, for during certain seasons of the year the buffalo came within eight leagues of the settlement. They also said that the Indians who followed these herds were very brave, fine hunters with bow and arrow who would kill us. (H & R 1966: 87)

None of the Pueblo Indians wanted to accompany the Spaniards to the Plains "because the Indians who followed the buffalo were enemies and very cunning; and that the two peoples would kill each other and start trouble" (H & R 1966: 88).

In 1581–1582, then, Pueblos and groups of Pueblos were avowedly hostile toward one another, the cleavage apparently being largely, but not entirely, along linguistic lines. The attitude of the Pueblo people toward the Plains nomads was still ambivalent. They tolerated them for purposes of trade but did not trust them.

When the members of the Rodríguez party finally saw the Plains nomads for themselves, they were impressed by and described exactly the same traits dwelt on earlier by Coronado and his men—the ability of these people to live on the buffalo, their skin tents, and the manner in which they used dogs as beasts of burden (H & R 1966: 90; 1928: 305).

The records of the expedition also indicate that the northward advance of Iberians in Mexico had cast a shadow well beyond the frontier. Mexican Indians met along the Conchos and on the lower Río Grande were afraid of the explorers because the Indians had been victims of slave hunters sent out, according to

Gallegos (a prejudiced witness), by Francisco and Diego Ibarra (H & R 1928: 273, 276, 278; 1966: 71–72, 73). The Plains Indians, too, met the Spaniards armed and ready for battle (H & R 1928: 303; 1966: 89). Perhaps they had also encountered or heard of the slaving expeditions operating out of north-Mexican settlements. Accounts of the Rodríguez–Chamuscado expedition do not mention wild tribes living near the western Pueblos, although their visits to Acoma and Zuñi were brief, and they did not reach the Hopi towns (H & R 1966: 107–8).

These adventurers returned to the mining town of Santa Bárbara without their spiritual leader Fray Agustín, who remained behind and was martyred by Pueblo Indians, and without their military leader Francisco Chamuscado, who died on the way home (H & R 1966: 112, 221). Moreover, the survivors had to face the local officials, all apparently loyal adherents of the Ibarras. As the explorers must have expected, the settlers and authorities of Santa Bárbara attempted to arrest them, gain custody of records made on the journey, and claim the new land for Diego de Ibarra. But three of the returned soldiers got away from the town and reported to their sponsor, the viceroy in Mexico City, while the others remained "to ward off penetration into the land we had discovered." On their journey the three bound for Mexico City went through Zacatecas, where the official in charge, Rodrigo del Río de Losa probably tried to circumvent them. One of the three was forced to go back with reports to Santa Bárbara, but the other two went on to the capital where the viceroy helpfully sent instructions back to the frontier that no one should be allowed to enter New Mexico except by his order (H & R 1966: 113–14). A modest follow-up expedition was in the planning stage[8] when news came to the viceroy (before 1 November 1582)

---

8 The capable and much respected Rodrigo del Río de Losa (Powell 1969: passim), who had risen to positions of influence while serving the Ibarras and was probably in sympathy with their interests, was "staying" in Mexico City about this time. Whether he had gone there as a result of the Rodríguez-Chamuscado affair or was actually already in the city is not clear. The viceroy consulted him concerning follow-up expeditions to New Mexico (H & R 1966: 123–24), perhaps first because it would have been awkward to avoid doing so and later because the situation was out of control, and the viceroy needed to diffuse the responsibility for decisions.

that the friars who had remained in New Mexico had been killed by Pueblo Indians. It then appeared that a major expedition might be required if the territory were to be re-entered, and the matter therefore had to be referred to the king, with all the attendant delays (H & R 1966: 123–24).

Meanwhile, in allowing friars to remain in New Mexico, the Rodríguez–Chamuscado expedition had provided a credible pretext for a rival group to set forth "urgently impelled by a most pious and benevolent motive" (H & R 1966: 233). Antonio de Espejo, a wealthy fugitive from justice who needed to stay beyond the reach of authorities and also find a means to redeem himself, agreed to go to New Mexico with friars anxious to find and, if necessary, rescue those who had stayed in the pueblos. Strangely enough, the records of this expedition suggest that when it set out from Santa Bárbara on 10 November 1582, the death of these friars was not known in Santa Bárbara, although news of it had apparently reached Mexico City before 1 November.

It is evident that Espejo's "relief" expedition went with the knowledge and assistance of Juan de Ibarra, lieutenant governor of Nueva Vizcaya, leaving the vicinity of Santa Bárbara on the very day that his uncle Diego wrote the king from Mexico City that he would await a royal decision on jurisdiction over the new lands. The *entrada* was in part, of course, a commercial venture. Obregón says that Father Pedro de Heredia, a member of the group, had a commission from Juan de Ibarra "by which he was given authority to penetrate and explore . . . and which bound the magistrate of the jurisdiction to aid and support him." Apparently the authorities of Santa Bárbara "likewise invested money and helped the expedition as much as possible, each according to his means" (H & R 1928: 316–17; 1966: 154, 155). It is interesting, also, that one of the soldiers enlisted was a Juan López de Ibarra, according to Obregón, a native of Biscay and according to Luxán, from the town of Ybar (H & R 1928: 316; 1966: 199). He may well have been a relative of the governors of

Nueva Vizcaya, but the fact is not evident from a check of the published information on the Ibarra family.

Espejo's Expedition
1582–1583

The third expedition into New Mexico, led by Antonio de Espejo in 1582–1583, did not attempt to make contact with Plains dog-nomads but encountered mountain Querechos at both Acoma and the Hopi Pueblos. Espejo himself in discussing Acoma says:

> The mountains thereabout apparently give promise of mines and other riches, but we did not go to see them as the people from there were many and warlike. The mountain people come to aid those of the settlements, who call the mountain people Quere-chos. They carry on trade with those of the settlements, taking to them salt, game, such as deer, rabbits, and hares, tanned deer-skins, and other things, to trade for cotton *mantas* and other things, with which the [Pueblo] government pays them. (Bolton 1916: 183)

Luxán, a member of Espejo's party, said of Acoma: "Because of its conflict with the Querechos Indians, who are like the Chichi-mecos, it is built on a high and rocky cliff" (H & R 1966: 182). Since the archeological record shows that Acoma has been oc-cupied for at least a thousand years (Stubbs 1950: 87), the Querechos had nothing to do with the original choice of location. However, it is very likely that the Acoma Indians either had the same ambivalent attitude toward the Querechos shown by the eastern Pueblos or that they were friends of some Querecho bands and enemies of others.

There were also Querechos among the Hopis in 1582–1583. According to Luxán, as the Spaniards approached the Hopi Pueblos they met some friendly Zuñi Indians who told them that the two largest Hopi Pueblos had determined to fight the ex-plorers and "that for this purpose there was a great gathering of wild and warlike people to oppose us" (H & R 1966: 187). Luxán also says of Hopiland that there were "many Chichimecos, who are called Corechos" (H & R 1966: 189). In the end, the Hopis decided to be friendly and gave many gifts to the Spaniards, who returned from the Hopi Pueblos by way of Acoma. Said Luxán:

> The people of Acoma and the neighboring mountain people rebelled . . . and kept shouting at us from the hills night and day. When we reached the cieneguilla de los Curechos with the camp and saw the impudence of the Indians, we decided to give them a surprise that morning. (H & R 1966: 200–201)

During the ensuing fight, the Spaniards set fire to the "shacks" of the *ranchería* and destroyed "a very fine field of corn belonging to the natives, something they felt a great deal" (H & R 1966: 201). Later there were peace parleys with the Querechos, and the details suggest a relationship between the Querechos at Hopi and those at Acoma. Among the gifts that the Hopis had given the Spaniards were some Querecho women. During the battle near Acoma just described, one of these women had escaped to the Querechos there. These Querechos agreed to return her to the Spaniards if the Spaniards would return a woman just captured from them. But the Querechos near Acoma had already sent the Querecho woman from the Hopi country back to her own land, so they attempted a ruse, and there was more fighting before the Spaniards left (H & R 1966: 201–2).

Obregón, who apparently got his version of the Espejo expedition from still another member of the party, Bernaldo de Luna, does not mention wild tribes in connection with the first visit of the party to Acoma (H & R 1928: 324–25). He says of the Hopis, who had decided not to fight Espejo after all,

> they changed their minds and sent away the warriors that had been assembled in the mountains. These people are called the Querechos. They go about naked and the people of this town had enlisted their aid. (H & R 1928: 328)

Of the fight near Acoma, Obregón says:

> From this pueblo of Acacolma [Acoma] they went to the Cieneguilla del Rosal belonging to the Querechos. There are numberless roses of Castile here. . . . These people do not wear clothes; they are hostile and warlike. They use the same kind of weapons as the other natives. (H & R 1928: 332–33)

Hammond and Rey (1928: 332) cite Hodge to the effect that the *cieneguilla* where Espejo's men fought the Querechos was identical with present Acomita, a farming village of the Acoma Indians themselves. These authors point out that Alvarado, one of Coronado's men, saw fields there in 1540. Possibly the Querecho allies of the Acomas were housed there temporarily because they gave seasonal help to the Acoma Indians in tending their crops. Such a practice is known to have existed in other cases where a Pueblo had symbiotic relations with less settled tribes. On the other hand, in 1582–1583, the Querechos may have been in possession of the farming village by "squatters' rights." Father Morfi, in 1782, said that the Acoma Indians were not then using their best land, at De Cuero, five leagues west of La Laguna and irrigated by the spring of El Gallo, because the Gila Apaches had killed many of their people there and run off many herds (Thomas 1932: 105). Although the Acoma Indians and the Querechos were allies in 1582–1583, the Acomas may still have preferred the comparative safety of their mesa. The Querechos near Acoma in 1583 were probably Navajos or another Apachean group, for close relations between Acoma and Apacheans, including Navajos, existed later. Obviously, Acomita and its vicinity hold promise for archeologists seeking pre-1600 Navajo village sites.

So far as inter-Pueblo relations were concerned, the reports of the Espejo expedition indicate that the Zuñi-Hopi hostility present in 1540 still existed. Zuñi Indians not only warned Espejo that the Hopis were preparing to fight him, but he was able to recruit a substantial number of Zuñis willing to help him fight the Hopis. This fact becomes more significant when one considers that, after Coronado's treatment of the Zuñis, they themselves had reason to be hostile toward Spaniards. Apparently their antagonism toward the Hopis was even stronger.

Espejo returned to the vicinity of Santa Bárbara on 20 September 1583, and his reports intensified rivalry for the commission to explore (and exploit) the new lands he had visited. As for the name of the coveted territory, even before Espejo's departure Gallegos had referred to the Pueblo country as "New

Mexico." Moreover, before the return of Espejo's party, Gallegos had declared himself "discoverer of New Mexico" and had petitioned the king for the privilege of "conquest and pacification of that land." The Council of the Indies and the king were also using this name for the Pueblo country before the return of Espejo, who proposed to call it Nueva Andalusia, after his native district in Spain (H & R 1966: 67, 145, 147, 150, 232, but cf. p. 12). Espejo himself was not slow to request the right to colonize and explore the lands he had visited, and in the next year (1584) Baltasár de Obregón, the veteran of Ibarra's 1565 *entrada*, offered his *General History* to the king with the same purpose in mind. But there were several contenders, the details of the competition being too involved to present here, and it was actually not until January 1598 that a legal colonizing expedition got under way for New Mexico. Meanwhile, however, there were two unauthorized attempts that failed.

The Expedition of Castaño de Sosa
1590[9]

In 1590 Castaño de Sosa took a chance on the strength of his privileges as lieutenant governor of the new and sparsely settled province of Nuevo León. Motivated by personal ambition that had been thwarted by the dwindling mineral resources of his locality, and depending, no doubt, on the likelihood that success, if he could achieve it, would soften official displeasure, he uprooted the entire population of the town of Almadén (present Monclova, in Coahuila) and set out to colonize New Mexico. The legality of his enterprise has been dated elsewhere (Schroeder

9 Hakluyt (1598–1600 III: 396–97) includes a letter by a Batholomew Cano dated 30 May 1590 in Mexico, that was destined for Seville but intercepted by the English. Cano says, among other things, "There are departed out of Mexico and other townes hereabout by the commaundement of the Viceroy 500. souldiers Spaniards, under the cõduct of Rodorigo del Rio the gouernour of Nueva Biscaia which are gone to win a great city called Cibola." If such an *entrada* took place, it seems otherwise undocumented. Cano may have confused the activities of Castaño, whose attempts to organize an expedition were known to the viceroy before the group started out in July 1590, with Rodrigo del Río de Losa's role in helping settle over 900 friendly Tlaxcalan Indians at frontier outposts threatened by hostile tribes (Powell 1969: 194–97).

and Matson 1965; hereafter referred to as S & M; H & R 1966). Of interest here is the fact that Castaño's party, on a laborious journey that followed the Pecos River for much of the way, came upon Indians using pack dogs near that river, probably well below the present Texas–New Mexico line. These Indians were Plains Apaches, distinguished from other tribes farther south by their use of pack dogs, as is shown by the comments of the expedition's chronicler.

> These people had with them many loaded dogs, as is the custom in those regions, and we saw them loaded, a thing new to us, never before seen. [Some of these Indians who had been captured and released went away] . . . with a dog laden with two hides tied to his *reata* (rope), breast harness (*pretal*) (and) crupper (*taharria*) [all parentheses appear in original], which all were delighted to see, as it was a new thing. (S & M 1965: 56)

Castaño's party was apparently the first to engage in battle with the Plains Apaches, who had stolen some of their cattle, and Indians were killed in the fight (S & M 1965: 56–57, and Map 3).

Before meeting the group of Plains Apaches, Castaño's people had seen "many recently built *rancherias*" and slept in some old ones, "where there were many flies." After encountering the Apaches, too, they found near the river "a recently constructed *rancheria* which could have held a great number of people, as it occupied a very large area" (S & M 1965: 55, 58). Since the structures had been "built," these sites were not merely the remains of tipi camps. Since some had been built recently, and it was November, they may well have been winter villages of pole and brush shelters located near the river where firewood was available.

Later, at one of the Pueblos (thought by Schroeder and Matson to have been Picurís and by Hammond and Rey to have been San Juan), the explorers found huts "a long arquebus shot" away where some Indians were staying who had either come to trade at the pueblo or had sought refuge there (S & M 1965: 124–28; H & R 1966: 284). It was mid-January, and the snow was three feet deep. This situation is reminiscent of Castañeda's statements that the Plains nomads traded and wintered at the Pueblos and is

compatible with the relatively recent Taos practice of quarter-
ing such visitors as the Jicarilla Apaches in specific areas outside
the pueblo.

The expedition of Castaño de Sosa ended when Captain Juan
Morlete was sent by the viceroy to force his return to Mexico.
Although Castaño's only major battle with Indians on this journey was that with the inhabitants of Pecos Pueblo, the arrival
of a colonizing expedition must have given the Pueblo Indians an
inkling of the permanent trouble that was to come. On the other
hand, Castaño's brush with southern Apaches was only a fore-
taste of what Spanish colonists were to suffer from Apacheans living in that same general area in the future.

The Humaña Expedition
1593

Francisco de Leyva Bonilla and Antonio Gutiérrez de Humaña
(or Umaña) left Santa Bárbara in 1593 on an unauthorized expedition. This group was in the Pueblo area for about a year, after
which it went to the Plains via Pecos, beyond which it encountered Vaquero Indians. Somewhere on the Plains, Humaña killed
Leyva after a dispute. So much is known because an Indian servant, Jusepe Gutiérrez of Culhuacán in Mexico, was frightened
by the murder and ran away before the main body of the expedition met whatever fate befell it—probably death at the hands of
the Quivira Indians (H & R 1953: 5, 403, 416–19, 842).

Jusepe was either captured or rescued by the Plains Apaches
and "remained . . . for a year with the Apache and Vaquero
Indians." He ran away again and finally reached the Pueblos,
where he made contact with Oñate's people in 1598. In relating
his experiences, he said that the Humaña expedition had come
upon Indian *rancherías* in the buffalo country, some of them
abandoned (H & R 1953: 416–18, 852). In this same testimony,
given on 16 February 1599, Jusepe described a large Plains settlement of houses built on a frame of poles and having straw roofs
(H & R 1966: 323–26). Although Jusepe himself does not at-
tribute this settlement to the Vaquero Apaches, Oñate, in a letter

written to the viceroy on 2 March of the same year, does (H & R 1953: 485), thus leading to confusion. However, from the account of Oñate's expedition to Quivira in 1601 it becomes apparent that the large settlement of straw-roofed houses seen by Jusepe was a settlement of the Quivira (Wichita) Indians (H & R 1953: 754).

Jusepe's captivity among the Plains Apaches had beneficial consequences for Oñate. The Mexican Indian had learned to speak the Apache language and was thus able to help the Spaniards communicate not only with Apaches but with other groups such as the Escanxaques and Quivirans, who had learned the language of the Apaches through association with them.

Don Juan de Oñate in New Mexico
1598–1609

From among those who sought the appointment to explore and colonize New Mexico, Don Juan de Oñate was finally chosen— after the winds of officialdom had blown alternately hot and cold on his candidacy for several trying years. With Oñate's appointment, the Ibarra influence that had been so strong a factor in the "rediscoveries" of New Mexico may have ended, or the commission granted Oñate may have been a further result of Ibarra power—a power that has gone hitherto unnoticed because Diego Ibarra lacked a direct male heir to bear his name.

Historians have already pointed out that Juan de Oñate's success in obtaining the right to colonize New Mexico was due finally to the influence of powerful friends (Hackett 1923–1937 I: 202, 204–5; H & R 1953: 6, 12). Most important of these was Viceroy Don Luís Velasco II, brother-in-law of Diego Ibarra. This viceroy's son, Francisco, married Diego Ibarra's only daughter, Mariana (Mecham 1968: 43), and the union had resulted in at least one grandchild, Luís Velasco y Ibarra, who was named as the viceroy's heir (Paso y Troncoso 1939–1940 XIV: 365). As for the Ibarras and the Oñates, the fortunes of these two Basque families had been early bound together. Cristóbal de Oñate, Juan's father, and Diego Ibarra had been two of four

original developers of Zacatecas and its silver mines, which were
to help finance Juan Oñate's colonization of New Mexico just
as they had financed young Francisco Ibarra's unsuccessful explorations many years before. And still powerful on the frontier
was Rodrigo del Río de Losa, Francisco's trusted associate to
whom Juan de Oñate turned for advice. Diego Ibarra himself
lived until 1600, long enough to see New Mexico controlled by
the son of his partner. How much he or his relatives and friends
did to help decide this issue in Oñate's favor when the cause
seemed lost would be an interesting subject for detailed inquiry.[10]

Juan de Oñate was the son-in-law of still a third partner in the
Zacatecas venture of 1546—Juan de Tolosa, another Basque and
the actual discoverer of the mine. Tolosa had married a grand-
daughter of the Aztec ruler Montezuma; in marrying Tolosa's
daughter Oñate had thus married the great-granddaughter of
Montezuma. In fact, many descendants of the *conquistadores*
were bound together by complex ties of blood, marriage, business, and politics; and it was a massing of resources that made it
possible for Juan de Oñate to colonize New Mexico "at his own
expense" (Mecham 1968: 39–49; G. Espinosa 1933: 72–75).
Various relatives of *conquistadores* appear on Oñate's muster roll,
and among the men who enlisted was apparently the son of
Baltasár Obregón (H & R 1953: 159), whose *General History*
provides continuity in the names applied to the Southern Athabascan dog-nomads whom Oñate was finally to call Apaches.

Oñate's caravan of colonists, soldiers, and priests reached San
Juan Pueblo on 11 July 1598 (H & R 1953: 320), making this
upper Río Grande village their headquarters for a few months.
Then the Spaniards moved to a pueblo which they called San
Gabriel, at the confluence of the Chama and the Río Grande
(H & R 1953: 17). Oñate had been obtaining information on the
country along the way, and before August he had explored the

---

10 Villagrá, in his history of New Mexico, says that Viceroy Velasco II, after
granting Oñate the right of colonization in 1595, advised him to confer with
Rodrigo del Río and with "Diego Fernández de Velasco, governor of Nueva
Vizcaya," which Oñate did (G. Espinosa 1933: 74; Bancroft 1889: 116–17). The
relationship of this Diego Fernández de Velasco to the viceroy and/or to Diego
Ibarra, if any, is not indicated.

Río Grande Valley as far north as Taos, and had been to Picurís and Pecos. Early in August, Jémez was visited (H & R 1953: 318–23). Oñate must have received information about the nomadic tribes of the area—the mountain tribes around the Pueblos as well as the Vaqueros on the Plains—within his first two months in New Mexico, for on 9 September 1598, he mentions some of them in assigning the Franciscan friars to mission posts.

> To Father Fray de San Miguel, the province of Pecos with the seven pueblos of the ciénaga to the east and all of the Vaquero Indians of that range as far as the Sierra Nevada.
>
> To Father Fray Francisco de Zamora, the province of the Picuríes, together with all the Apaches from the Sierra Nevada toward the north and east, and the province of Taos, with its neighboring pueblos and those that border upon it and those of that cordillera of the bank of the Río del Norte.
>
> To Father Fray Alonzo de Lugo, the province of Emmes [Jémez] . . . and, in addition, all of the Apaches and Cocoyes of the neighboring sierras and settlements. (H & R 1953: 345)

Thus, the first known reference to Apaches by that name locates them in mountains near Picurís and near Jémez, and these mountain Apaches are distinguished from the Vaqueros of the Plains. The "Apaches from the Sierra Nevada toward the north and east" of Picurís are of particular interest for this study, for it is the first mention of Apaches in the area where the Jicarillas emerge into history in 1700.[11]

Previously, there seems to have been general acceptance of the idea that "Apache" was derived from a Zuñi word meaning "enemy" (Hodge 1907–1910 I: 63), although Harrington (1940: 512–13) thought that the word came from Yavapai. However, Santamaria's dictionary of New-World Indian words incorporated into Spanish ("Americanismos") contains a number of terms similar to "apache" with a wide distribution in Latin America (Santamaria 1942 I: 109–10). These pose the question

11 Unless Castañeda's Pueblo of Acha, "forty leagues to the north or east" of Coronado's headquarters at Tiguex is a reference to the mountain Apaches later called "Achos," a name which should have been spelled "Hachos." Schroeder (1968) prefers to identify Castañeda's Acha with Hopi villages. I reserve judgment for the time being.

of whether Ibero-Americans and/or their Nahuatl-speaking servants did not bring the name Apache to New Mexico with them in 1598. In answer to a query on this possibility, Dr. Charles E. Dibble (letter 18 July 1969) pointed out that phonemically "apache" could be Nahuatl and that the Spanish word for raccoon (a New-World animal) was *mapache,* derived from Nahuatl "mapachtli."

Moreover, according to Santamaria (1942 I: 109), in Mexico "apache" is used, although rarely (now?) as a form of *mapache.* Various comments on apache, *mapache,* and related words (Santamaria 1942 I: 109–10; II: 237–38) indicate characteristics of the raccoon which might have caused the name to be applied to Southern Athabascans. In Mexico the animal lives chiefly by stealing maize from the cultivated fields, which mountain Athabascans, the first to be called Apaches, seem to have been doing in New Mexico even before Oñate's *entrada.* The raccoon has pack-rat tendencies, and various words related to apache refer to accumulating stones in cairns along trails—a form of trail-marker used by Southern Athabascans (Thomas 1935: 111). But if Apache actually is derived from the Nahuatl word for raccoon, the Apachean practice of painting the eyelids and orbital areas and sometimes even parts of the temples in a manner suggesting the raccoon's "mask" may have been part of the reason.

Castañeda said that the Plains dog-nomads "ahogolan los ojos," which Winship (1896: 442, 506) translated, "they decorate their eyes." The word "ahogolan" is difficult to interpret. It may mean extinguish or drown, and Castañeda may have used it to indicate that the Indians "blotted out" or completely surrounded their eyes with paint. On the other hand, "ahogolan" may also refer to the headpiece of a horse's bridle (Velasquez 1955: 20), and Castañeda may have extended it to mean something like blinders, since the eyes were involved.[12] A skin painting that depicts the massacre of a Spanish and Indian expedition led by Captain Villasur in 1720 (Thomas 1935: 162 ff.) shows Apache allies of

12 Perhaps the Plains Apaches painted the area around their eyes for the same reason that Eskimos use snow goggles and that skiers "paint" their cheeks—to reduce glare from the sun.

the Spaniards with painted facial decoration ranging from stripes resembling a "head stall" to coverage resembling a racoon-like mask (Hotz 1960: *Tafeln* 12, 13; 1970: Plates 12, 13). Moreover, photographs and descriptions of modern Jicarilla Apache males indicate that upon occasion they painted the entire orbital area.[13] If a Nahuatl origin for the name of the Apaches can be established, it will be only one of many instances in which Iberians carried Indian words from one part of the New World to another.

Oñate's followers found Apaches in various parts of the Southwest. The Pueblo of Acoma, which had had mountain Querecho allies in 1582–1583, had allies called Apaches in 1599. This information is contained incidentally in documents bearing on an episode of 4 December 1598, in which Oñate's nephew Juan de Zaldívar and twelve other Spaniards were killed at Acoma. On 12 January 1599, Juan de Zaldívar's brother Vicente took seventy men to punish the Acoma Indians for this massacre (H & R 1953: 325–26). Among them was Captain Gaspar Pérez de Villagrá, who in 1609 wrote or finished a history of New Mexico in verse, most of which is devoted to the battle at Acoma in which he took active part (G. Espinosa 1933). Villagrá tells of Gicombo, an Acoma captain who did not favor war with the Spaniards and who had been away during the massacre of 4 December. When he learned of it, he realized that his pueblo would suffer for its rashness.

> After considering the matter, Gicombo sent Buzcoico as messenger to the Apache nation, a foreign tribe which lived far from his people and who were strangers to them. He sent a message there to his faithful friend Bempol, an Apache war-captain of renown, requesting him to meet at Acoma when six suns had passed, that he might discuss with him matters of great importance. (G. Espinosa 1933: 213)

Bempol came to Acoma and remained to help his friend Gicombo. After the punitive expedition had laid siege to Acoma, and a small party of Spaniards, Villagrá among them, had succeeded in scal-

---

13 See Collier (1962: 146). Moreover, in the tribal museum of the Jicarillas at Dulce, New Mexico, there was on exhibit in 1969 an old photograph of boys with bows and arrows in which one boy had painted eyes.

ing the rocks, Gicombo sent Bempol with four hundred of his warriors (whether Apache or Acoma warriors is not clear) to repel the invaders (G. Espinosa 1933: 234). When it was obvious that Acoma would be conquered, Bempol the Apache, preferring death to capture, took in his arms his small daughter, who had been living at Acoma for some years, and leaped from the mesa top (G. Espinosa 1933: 257–58), as did many natives of the pueblo.

The story of Bempol may have been introduced by Villagrá to adorn his tale; certainly it contains a surprising amount of information. Yet Villagrá had been in a position to get such detail. He was one of the Spaniards who had undertaken to scale the mesa wall. These men had climbed a rock, separated from the main part of the mesa by a fissure, and had brought along a wooden beam to bridge the gulf. Villagrá leaped across to the main rock in the face of the approaching enemy in order to place the beam so that the others could cross. So, according to Villagrá's epic, he would have been one of those who fought the Apache leader face to face. When Acoma surrendered, the Indians were brought to trial, and in keeping with Spanish legal procedure, a defense attorney was appointed to represent the Acoma Indians. Villagrá was assigned to see that the attorney performed to the best of his ability. "Should he fail to do so, Villagrá, as his guarantor, accepted as his own this obligation and pledged to satisfy it with his own person and property" (H & R 1953: 463).

Thus, Villagrá had a good opportunity to learn from the Indians things which he could not have observed personally. The testimony of Spaniards and Acoma Indians alike (H & R 1953: 428–79) bears out most of Villagrá's account except that no one else mentions the presence of the Apache war-captain at Acoma. Yet the summoning of an Apache for assistance in 1598 fits in very well with the behavior of the Acomas in 1583, when they and the Hopis as well, sent for Querechos to use them against Espejo's party. Moreover, the personal friendship between Gicombo and Bempol suggests the person-to-person and family-to-family guest-friend and trade-friend relationship by means of which Apache groups maintained friendly relations with Pueblo peoples and other groups in modern times (Hill 1948: 388–90; Kluckhohn and Leighton 1946: 75–76; Goodwin 1942: 63–69).

The Acoma Indians were convicted, since in their own testimony they admitted the actions with which they were charged. The sentence imposed by Oñate on 12 February 1599 was extremely severe. One portion of it is of special interest here.

> The old men and women [of Acoma] disabled in the war, I ordered freed and entrusted to the Indians of the province of the Querechos that they may support them and may not allow them to leave their pueblos. (H & R 1953: 478)

Villagrá was appointed a member of the council of war charged with carrying out the punishment of the Acoma Indians (G. Espinosa 1933: 286–87), and in a letter dated 30 May 1599, Oñate addresses Villagrá as "Governor of Acoma" (G. Espinosa 1933: 288).

Well before the Spaniards were killed at Acoma, Vicente de Zaldívar, one of Oñate's officers, had set out on 15 September 1598 to explore the Buffalo Plains. Eleven leagues beyond Pecos Pueblo he began to meet Plains Indians with well-made skin tents and dogs as beasts of burden. When he reached a river that has been identified as the Canadian, he met Plains Indians who had been to trade at Taos and Picurís, adding these northernmost villages, separated from the Plains by high mountains, to the list of pueblos to which the Plains Apaches took their trains of pack dogs. He returned to San Juan on 8 November 1598, but his report (H & R 1953: 398–405) in which he refers to the Plains Indians as Vaqueros was delayed until 23 February 1599, perhaps by the absence of Governor Oñate and then by the emergency created by the Acoma rebellion.

Although Jusepe, the Indian servant from the Humaña expedition, was already known to the Spaniards and had accompanied Zaldívar to the Buffalo Plains as guide and interpreter, it was not until 16 February 1599, that Oñate took Jusepe's sworn deposition in which he told of having lived for a year with the Apache and Vaquero Indians (H & R 1953: 418). This, the first reference to Plains Indians as Apaches, was recorded several

months after Oñate first referred to mountain Indians as Apaches
on 9 September 1598.

The use of "and" in Jusepe's statement can scarcely mean that
he was distinguishing between Plains Apaches and Vaqueros
since the evidence of subsequent documents makes it certain that
the Plains Indians called Vaqueros in the Spanish documents
were Apaches. Rather, the phrase "Apache and Vaquero" was
meant to indicate that the Plains Indians were Apaches who lived
as Vaqueros or buffalo hunters (literally cowherds). This explanation for the compound name is explicitly corroborated by
the declaration of Marcos Leandro, who stated in 1601 that the
Pueblo people traded with

> a nation of Indians . . . who are called Apaches and also are
> called the Vaqueros by the Spaniards since they live in the plains
> of Civola (Cíbola) where they say there is a great number of
> ganado civoleno (buffalo). (Forbes 1960: 99)

Oñate had not yet been to the plains himself when, in a letter
to the viceroy of New Spain dated 2 March 1599, he reported:

> We have seen other nations, such as the Querechos or Vaqueros,
> who live among the Cíbola cattle in tents of tanned hides. The
> Apaches, some of whom we also saw, are extremely numerous.
> Although I was told that they lived in rancherías, in recent days
> I have learned that they live in pueblos the same as the people
> here. They have a pueblo eighteen leagues from here with fifteen
> plazas. They are a people that has not yet publicly rendered
> obedience to his majesty, as I had the other provinces do. (H & R
> 1953: 484)

And elsewhere in this letter Oñate speaks of the Plains Indians
known to the Indian interpreter Jusepe as Vaqueros (H & R
1953: 485).

In equating Vaqueros and plains Querechos, Oñate provided a
link between the terminology used by the Spaniards during his
administration and that used by earlier explorers. His reason for
differentiating Apaches from Vaqueros in his letter of 2 March
1599 is not obvious. Such usage may merely represent an early
tendency, seemingly apparent in the missionary assignments of
9 September 1598, to speak of mountain bands as Apaches. If
Oñate was restricting the term Apache to mountain dwellers at

this time, Jusepe's application of the term to Plains people had had little influence. Moreover, although the missionary assignments made it clear that the Spaniards knew of Apaches in mountain areas, there are no actual references to meetings with them prior to the date of Oñate's letter. The first reported interaction between Oñate's followers and mountain Apaches took place in July 1599 but did not become a matter of record until 18 August 1602. It was then that Vicente Zaldívar, pleading Oñate's cause before the royal *audiencia* in Mexico City and incidentally enumerating his own achievements, said:

> During the month of July, 1599, I went, by order of the governor, to explore the land toward the west with only twenty-five men and traveled more than two hundred leagues inland, traversing many nations of warlike people, such as the Apaches, who are very numerous and extend for more than two hundred leagues, judging by what I have seen, and . . . I left them all at peace and friendly. (H & R 1953: 814)

Unfortunately, no diary of Zaldívar's trip to the west seems to be extant, but some of his fellow soldiers and a friar corroborated his statement that he made such a journey and commented on it (H & R 1953: 821, 828–29, 833).

Oñate himself crossed the plains to Quivira in 1601, taking Jusepe as guide and interpreter. Concerning this trip, he reported on 14 December of that year:

> Occasionally we found rancherías inhabited by people of the Apache nation, who are the masters of the plains. They have no permanent settlements or homes, but follow the cattle as they roam about. We had no trouble with them, even though we crossed their land, nor was there an Indian who ventured to harm us in the least. (H & R 1953: 749)

Oñate's reference to the plains buffalo hunters as "people of the Apache nation" indicates that by 1601 the Spaniards were using Apache as a generic term for related groups of unsettled people living both on the Plains and in mountains around the Pueblos.

An increasing tendency of the Spaniards to refer to the nomads of the Plains as Apaches is evident even in documents of preceding months. In July of 1601, which Oñate was absent from New Mexico on his trip to Quivira, some of his soldiers who carried reports and letters to Mexico City were interrogated there by authorities concerning conditions in New Mexico. Two of these witnesses refer to the Plains Indians as "Vaqueros" (H & R 1953: 628, 636); one designates them as "Apaches," or "Vaqueros" (H & R 1953: 647, and one calls them first "Vaqueros" and later "Vaquero Apaches" (H & R 1953: 660).

During another official inquiry concerning New Mexico, held on 22 April 1602 after Oñate had returned from Quivira and had referred to the Plains Indians as belonging to the "Apache nation," all the witnesses referred to these Indians as either Apaches or Vaquero Apaches (H & R 1953: 838, 841, 852, 854, 864, 869). Thus in a few years, judging from the published documents, the term Vaquero used alone gave way to Apache or the typically qualified Vaquero Apache.

There can be little doubt that the Spaniards began to use Apache as a generic name for groups scattered throughout the Pueblo area and over the Plains because they came to realize that these bands spoke mutually intelligible dialects of the same language. The strong probability that linguistic similarities were the criteria that led to the lumping of these bands as one "nation" minimizes the possibility, favored by some writers, that the term Apache was used to refer to just any roving tribe. The Apaches dominated the buffalo country ca. 1600, and the documents dating from Oñate's administration and later clearly differentiate Apaches from tribes who bordered their domain.

For example, the Vaqueros (Apaches) met by Vicente de Zaldívar in 1598 asked him through his interpreter Jusepe for aid against "the Xumanas, which is the name they gave to a nation of Indians who are striped like the Chichimecos" (H & R 1953: 399–400). It is impossible to identify these particular Xumanas of 1598 because no additional information concerning them was recorded, and apparently the name "Jumano" in various forms was a descriptive term used to designate people who either painted or tattooed themselves and was thus applied to groups differing in culture and in language (Scholes and Mera 1940). The fact that Indians called Jumanos are always differentiated from Apaches in other Spanish documents, however, minimizes the probability that those referred to in Zaldívar's report were Southern Athabascans.

In 1601 the Spaniards also differentiated the Plains Apaches from the Escanxaques, a roving group whom Oñate met on the eastern border of the Buffalo Plains about twenty leagues from Quivira (H & R 1953: 854). The Escanxaques followed the buffalo as the Apaches did, but most of their houses were made of branches. They had a few skin-covered pole frames which resembled Apache tents in shape, but they apparently had neither the sewn skin tent nor pack dogs. They were dirty, which the Apaches were not, and they were *habitually* painted or tattooed, a trait never ascribed to the Plains Apaches in the Oñate documents (H & R 1953: 841, 854, 865).

There were two or three Apaches living among the Escanxaques, and through these Apaches the Spaniards were able to communicate with the Escanxaques, for Jusepe, whom Oñate (like Zaldívar) used as guide and interpreter, could speak with the Apaches, and the Apaches could speak with the Escanxaques. If the Escanxaques had spoken a Plains Apache dialect in 1601, Jusepe should have been able to speak directly to them. (H & R 1953: 841, 865). From these facts, it can be seen that during Oñate's administration the Spaniards did not call all "barbarous" groups Apaches; they could and did distinguish between Apaches and other "wild" tribes.

Zárate-Salmerón's account, written in 1626, indicates that ca. 1600 the Quivira (Wichita) Indians understood the Apache language also. This friar relates (as do other chroniclers) that Oñate was accompanied to the Quivira villages by the Escanxaques, enemies of the Quivirans, and that the Escanxaques began to burn and loot. The Spaniards made them stop, and as a result the Escanxaques attacked the Spaniards, who killed many Escanxaques before the battle was over. When the Quivirans who had fled returned to their village, they realized that the Spaniards did not mean to harm them, therefore (and this event is narrated only by Zárate-Salmerón) they sent an ambassador with six hundred men to New Mexico to gain the friendship of the Spaniards and ask their aid against enemies. The Quivirans and the Spaniards held all their conversation in the Apache language, which the Quivirans understood very well (Zárate-Salmerón 1899–1900 XII: 44–47; Milich 1966: 62).

In 1629 when Father Benavides wished to contact the hostile Navajo Apaches in order to begin their conversion, he sent as ambassador some Indians of Santa Clara Pueblo who spoke the Apache language (H, H & R 1945: 86). Thus, Southern Athabascans seems to have been an important medium for communication on both the Plains and in the Pueblo area from 1598 through the early 1600s. Considering the volume of trade which Apaches carried on with other groups such as the Pueblo Indians, the Quivirans, and people living in the direction of "Florida" (H & R 1940: 261), it is not surprising that Apaches could communicate with Indians of diverse linguistic stocks. It has already been mentioned that Pueblo Indians (probably living in the Galisteo Basin) told members of the Rodríguez expedition of 1581 that through trading with the Plains nomads they had learned their language (H & R 1927: 267).

As for the attitude of Apaches toward other groups in this period, Oñate's followers like those of Coronado, found the Plains dog-nomads friendly. To Castaño de Sosa, who encountered them farther south, they were hostile, perhaps because Spanish slavers or stories of slave raids had already penetrated their territory. Humaña's party apparently traveled through Vaquero country without harm. Humaña killed Leyva and Jusepe ran away, after which most of the party were probably killed by the Indians of Quivira. The Plains Apaches did not trouble Vicente de Zaldívar, Oñate's lieutenant, who went among them in 1598, and in the Zaldívar Inquiry of 1602, Alférez Leonís Tremiño de Bañuelos stated:

> More than a year after the return of the sargento mayor from this trip [to the Plains], while this witness was with him at a pueblo named San Marcos, he saw that a Vaquero chief came with more than two hundred Indian archers under his command to visit Vicente de Zaldívar and with great joy gave him a piece of buffalo meat, and other things, and through an Indian interpreter explained that he and his nation were our friends. (H & R 1953: 827)

This description of the visit of the Vaquero chief to Zaldívar
fits well with later accounts of similar episodes and is important
because it may document the beginnings of the direct trade between Plains Apaches and the Spaniards themselves, which was
later to become so important for the colonists. As for Oñate's
expedition to the Plains in 1601, the members found the Plains
Apaches friendly and helpful both on their journey to and return
from Quivira.

Concerning the Apaches in the mountains west of the Río
Grande, Zaldívar says that on his journey in July 1599, he left
all the war-like tribes, including the Apaches, "at peace and
friendly." He goes on to say (although it is not clear whether he
speaks specifically of Apaches):

> I went up the sierra with a lone companion, endangering my life,
> so that they could see that we intended them no harm, but
> treated them affectionately, presented them with gifts, and re-
> assured them so that they served us as guides and gave us native
> blackberries. (H & R 1953: 814–15)

During the Valverde investigation of conditions in New
Mexico held in Mexico City in 1601, Marcelo de Espinosa, one
of Oñate's men lately come from New Mexico, after describing
the Pueblo Indians says:

> This province, aside from the places mentioned [the pueblos], is
> uninhabited, and there are no other pueblos except that in the
> uninhabited areas there are Indians who roam like nomads, with-
> out a fixed place of residence and without other possessions than
> their bows and arrows. They do not plant or harvest. They live
> by hunting. At planting time, before the towns and villages
> came under the favor and protection of the Spaniards, and after
> the harvest, they fought the Indians of the pueblos for their prod-
> ucts, leaving their women and children in the sierra. (H & R
> 1953: 639)

These nomadic Indians were apparently those living in the basin-
range country around the Pueblos rather than those on the
Plains, for the record continues: "Asked what information there
was of other provinces, the witness said that he went on the trip
to the buffalo where he saw rancherías of thirty or forty tents."

And Bañuelos says that Zaldívar's westward expedition of 1599, marched inland

> more than two hundred leagues, meeting many Indian nations, Apaches, Cruzados, and Tepeguanes, all able fighters. The sargento mayor left them at peace through good treatment and gifts, and to this day they have remained peaceful and done no harm. (H & R 1953: 829)

If the nomads of the mountains constituted more of a threat to the Pueblos ca. 1600 than did those of the Plains, there is a plausible reason. The Plains Apaches had access to the great bison herds from which they not only obtained a living for themselves but enough surplus products to assure themselves a welcome as trade-friends at the eastern Pueblos. The mountain nomads, on the other hand, had to compete with Pueblo hunters for game, which was probably least plentiful at times when drought decreased the surplus of corn which the Pueblos had to trade. Having less in the way of surplus to trade than the Plains Apaches, the mountain nomads may have early resorted to robbery in desperation. The seeming discrepancies in Spanish statements, which as early as Espejo's *entrada* in 1583 speak of mountain Querechos both as allies and as enemies of Pueblo people, are probably attributable to the fact that each band of Querechos (like the later Apaches) had at least one Pueblo with which it traded and always kept the peace, while other Querecho bands might be attacking it. Such paired relationships between specific Apache Bands and specific Pueblos are demonstrable from later documents. Whether or not any of the Pueblos used Apache allies against other Pueblos is an interesting question. If the Hopis and Acomas could muster Apache allies against the Spaniards, as they did in 1582–1583, they may have been able to use them against their Pueblo enemies. In fact, the records of the Spanish colony's earliest years, while they certainly indicate conflict between the Pueblos and mountain nomads, contain as much or more evidence of conflict between Pueblos themselves, with the Apaches sometimes involved. On 21 January 1599, when the Spaniards went to subdue the rebellious Acomas, these Indians hurled insults, saying that they were ready for battle and after killing the Spaniards would kill "the Indians at the Pueblos of Zía, Santo Domingo and San Juan Bautista because they had failed to kill the Spaniards" (H & R 1953: 470). Thus the presence of Oñate's colonists was specified as a stimulus to already existing inter-Pueblo tensions.

The colonists who had come with Oñate, like the explorers who had preceded them, were disappointed upon their arrival by the lack of obvious riches in New Mexico, and the difficulty of getting even a bare living from the area was a further discouragement. The group was early divided into two factions—those loyal to Oñate, who wanted to stay, and those who wanted to return to Mexico. Since their arrival, the Spaniards had been forced to exact a tribute of food and clothing from the Pueblo Indians to keep from starving and freezing. In 1601 a state of famine must have existed, for many of the Pueblo Indians themselves were dying of hunger. The faction wishing to leave took advantage of Oñate's absence on the Buffalo Plains to desert. With them went some of the friars, who felt that the methods of extortion the Spaniards practiced upon the Pueblo Indians were so cruel that missionary efforts could make no headway. Even they, however, recognized that dire necessity drove the Spaniards (like the mountain Apaches) to prey upon the Pueblos (H & R 1953: 672–700). Fray Juan de Escalona said in a letter to the viceroy of New Spain, dated 1 October 1601:

> Because of this situation and because the Spaniards asked the natives for blankets as tribute, even before teaching them the meaning of God, the Indians began to get restless, abandon their pueblos, and take to the mountains. (H & R 1953: 692)

Apparently even in 1601, then, some of the Pueblo people felt more secure in the country occupied by mountain Indians than within reach of the Spaniards.

The loyal colonists who chose to remain in New Mexico presented a more favorable picture of conditions there and defended the Spanish practice of exacting tribute from the Pueblo Indians. These citizens declared that the presence of Spaniards in the province was of benefit to the Pueblo people, who said that they had formerly fought bitter wars among themselves but were now at peace (H & R 1953: 704, 710, 715, 722). Here it is pertinent to call attention again to the inter-Pueblo hostility noted years before by Coronado's men and the exploring parties that followed them.

As an indirect result of Oñate's expedition to the Plains in 1601, additional light was cast on those Apaches living in the mountains east of Taos. Indeed, philological research has made it possible to link them specifically with the Jicarillas. When the group of Quivira Indians came to San Gabriel to ask Oñate's help against enemies, he was forced to refuse. Because many of the colonists left behind in New Mexico had deserted while he was on the Plains, he could not send soldiers back with the Quivira Indians at that time, but he finally promised to send six in the future. The Quiviran "ambassador" left two guides for the Spaniards, saying that on their previous journey to Quivira Oñate's men had traveled by a very roundabout way and that if they had gone straight toward the north they would have arrived quickly.

Zárate-Salmerón, writing in 1626, interpreted the advice of the Quivira Indians thus: "So that, according to what they said, one should go through Taos and through lands of the great Captain Quinia through those plains" (MS. Ayer 1274, listed in Butler 1937: 158).

Captain Quinia was the leader of the Quinia Apaches, as Benavides made clear in 1630 and 1634 (Ayer 1916: 41–42; H, H & R 1945: 89–91). The tribal name of these Apaches may well be preserved in a phonetically identical Southern Athabascan word still applied to the Jicarillas by the Mescalero Apaches. According to Mooney (Hodge 1907–1910 I: 632), the Mescaleros call the Jicarillas "kinya-inde." The form "-inde" is simply a variant of a pan-Athabascan word meaning people and can here be appropriately translated Apaches, so the name becomes "Kinya Apaches." In translating "kinya" it has been necessary to use Navajo dictionaries (there are none for other Apachean groups) and, with Carol Condie Stout of Albuquerque, New Mexico serving as intermediary, Navajo informants (because they were available). The Navajo form "kin" or "khin" means house— Pueblo house as opposed to hogan (Franciscan Fathers 1910: 133–36; Harrington 1916: 213, 521, 526). According to a reliable

Navajo informant,[14] "-ya" means up and the form "kinya" could refer either to a house (or houses) on a high place or to a high house (or houses) in the multistory sense.

The possibility, then, is that part of the modern Jicarillas were the Quinia Apaches, or "Apaches of the high houses," in the early 1600s and that they bore the name because then, as later, they were closely associated with Taos, "highest" of the Pueblos, and perhaps with Picurís, once also multistoried. Certainly, Zárate-Salmerón used Taos as a point of reference for locating the Quinia Apaches, whose lands were reached by going through Taos.

An interpretation that links the Quinia Apaches with Pueblos also gains strength from the fact that the name of a modern Navajo clan "kin-ya ni," translated high houses, was collected by Bourke, who says that these people "were so called because they lived near an old ruined pueblo." (Bloom 1933–1938 XI: 221). Moreover, the Navajo informant cited above says that this clan name is associated with Chaco Canyon, famous for its pueblo ruins.

Since Zárate-Salmerón did not arrive in New Mexico until 1621 (H, H & R 1945: 276), his account of the visit of Quivira Indians to New Mexico had to be based on hearsay. It is impossible to be sure from his comments whether the Apache named Quinia was already a great chief and known to the Spaniards in 1601, as in the 1620s, because this friar was describing the best route to Quivira in terms of the situation as he knew it in the 1620s. However, archeological sites that can be attributed to Jicarillas and/or related Apachean groups have been found in the eastern edge of the Sangre de Cristo Mountains, over the crest from Taos, in a locality where they would have been most easily reached from the Río Grande Valley by means of mountain passes beginning near Taos. Some of these sites date from the early 1600s; one may be as early as 1550 (J. Gunnerson 1969: esp. 37). Although Jicarillas themselves were living in multiroomed (but not multistoried) adobe houses ca. 1700, there is as yet no

14 Carol Stout, letter of 5 February 1971.

archeological evidence that they were doing so ca. 1600. Oñate's statement that some Apaches in 1598 were living in "pueblos" like those on the Río Grande, however, should cause archeologists to remain alert to the possibility.

While Oñate's followers had made general statements, apparently based on hearsay, that mountain tribes had been in the habit of attacking the Pueblos before 1598, the first references to specific attacks occur in documents pertaining to the career of Juan Martínez de Montoya, who was granted an *encomienda* or "living" at the Jémez pueblos. Before 6 October 1606 and again in 1606–1607, Montoya is certified to have taken part in various campaigns against Apaches, who in at least one case had attacked the Spanish settlement at San Gabriel itself (Scholes 1944: 340). It was the Navajo Apaches who in later years attacked the Tewa Pueblos of the upper Río Grande, and it was the Navajos who lived near Jémez, which, as *encomendero*, Montoya would have been obligated to protect. Hence, considering the area in which these early Apache attacks occurred, it was probably the Navajo who were responsible.

These and possibly other aggressions led to the order of Viceroy Velasco dated 6 March 1608—

> Whereas Father Fray Lázaro Ximénez, of the order of Saint Francis, who returned recently from the provinces of New Mexico and is now going back, has reported to me that the Spaniards and the Christian and peaceful natives in New Mexico are frequently harassed by attacks of the Apache Indians, who destroy and burn their pueblos, waylay and kill their people by treachery, steal their horses and cause other damages, and that, as a result of ineffective measures to remedy this situation, the teaching of the gospel, the Spaniards, and everything connected with them are despised by the natives and produce much scorn and criticism, wherefore the viceroy has asked me to send the governor of those provinces a number of armed soldiers to protect and defend the land; therefore, . . . I order that, in accordance with the number of people and arms available in the presidio in New Mexico, the governor must send out an adequate patrol to put a stop to the above outrages and to defend the friendly Indians and the horses. The ways and means to accomplish this we leave to his discretion. Mexico, March 6, 1608. Don Luis de Velasco. By order of the viceroy . . . (H & R 1953: 1059)

Apaches may have moved west of the Río Grande because they were encouraged to do so by Pueblos who hoped to use them as military allies against the Spaniards and possibly against other Pueblos. This hypothesis is supported only by circumstantial evidence. First, such Apache-Pueblo alliances did actually come into being apparently only after Coronado's army had given a two-year demonstration of what the Pueblo people might expect from a Spanish occupation, and second, certain Pueblos actually did call upon their Apache allies to aid them against the Spaniards before the sixteenth century ended. After the arrival of Oñate's colonists and the beginning of sustained missionary work, unconverted Pueblos often threatened to use Apache allies against the settlers and Christian Indians, and the Jémez actually did so on several documented occasions. It is entirely probable, also, that the numerous independent Navajo attacks on the Tewas were actively encouraged by the Jémez, with whom the Navajo have been so closely associated that the Tewa name for the Navajo means "Jémez Apache" (Harrington 1916: 575).

In summary, information gleaned from Spanish documents and supported by other lines of evidence suggests that the history of the Apaches in the Southwest begins in the early 1500s. They apparently first became known to the eastern Pueblo people in 1525 as Plains nomads called Teyas and Querechos who entered the Río Grande Valley from a northerly direction and attacked various Pueblos. According to Pueblo Indians, the nomadic buffalo hunters finally made friends with all the villages and returned to the Plains, where Coronado and his men observed them in 1541. Sometime after 1542 and before 1582 the Querechos moved permanently across the Río Grande. Various bands settled in mountainous areas near western Pueblos, possibly at the invitation of individual Pueblos with whom they formed military alliances and trade relationships. The Pueblo people may have made these alliances in anticipation of another invasion by the Spaniards. The alliances may also have been strategic moves in the warfare that the Pueblos had been waging against one another before the arrival of Spanish observers.

In any case, the Querechos or mountain Apaches, who seem to

have been the ancestors of part of the modern Western Apacheans, were attacking some Pueblos for loot before Oñate's colonists arrived in 1598. In contrast, the Plains Apaches, still known in the Pecos-Jémez dialect of the Towa language as Teyas or Eastern Apaches, remained friendly. In the mountains north and east of Picurís there were, by 1598, Apaches who almost certainly included the ancestors of the Jicarillas. Some of these Apaches may already have been living in houses like those of the Pueblo people. The Quinia Apaches, probably ancestors of the Jicarillas, apparently controlled country between Taos and the Quivira (Wichita) villages. Strangely enough, little more concerning these mountain Apaches living beyond Taos and Picurís is to be found in the records of the next one hundred years.

Chapter Three

Apaches and New Mexico
after Oñate, 1609–1680

The dissatisfaction of the New Mexico colonists had led Oñate to offer his resignation on 24 August 1607. It was accepted on 27 February 1608 (H & R 1953: 1042–45, 1048–49), and Don Pedro de Peralta was appointed to replace Oñate on 30 March 1609 (H & R 1953: 1084–86). Instructions of the same date enjoined Peralta "to subdue the enemy or drive him out" in order to maintain the prestige of the Spanish with both friends and foes. He was instructed to congregate the dispersed Pueblo people to facilitate administration and missionary work as well as protection. Moreover, it was noted that

> some of the pueblos and nations are on the frontiers of the Apaches, who are usually a refuge and shelter for our enemies, [anti-Spanish Pueblo people] and there they hold meetings and consultations, hatch their plots against the whole land, and set out to plunder and make war. (H & R 1953: 1089–90)

The implication, it seems, was that these border Pueblos should also be relocated.

The memorial of Father Velasco, 9 April 1609, is more specific concerning these alliances between unconverted Pueblos and Apaches.

> Since those [converted] Indians have shown so much friendship for the Spaniards, they have lost the good will of the Picuríes, Taos, Pecos, Apaches, and Vaqueros, who have formed a league among themselves and with other barbarous nations to exterminate our friends. . . . Many times these hostile natives have selfishly persuaded the peaceful Indians that the latter should throw off the heavy Spanish yoke because the hostile tribes believe that no benefit can come to the friendly natives from association with the Spaniards. (H & R 1953: 1094)

At this point, then, the aggressions of the Apaches, who had apparently been peaceful at the turn of the century, can be attributed partly to discord among the Pueblos, some of whom were using the Apaches as allies. For example,

> in a report on New Mexican affairs written by Fray Francisco Pérez Guerta about 1617 . . . it is stated that in the Spring of 1614 some Jemez Indians, together with some Apaches (Navahos?) [parentheses in original], killed an Indian of Cochiti. Several of the Jemez captains were brought to Santo Domingo, and there one was hanged. (Scholes 1938: 63)

The famous relation of Father Gerónimo de Zárate-Salmerón, who apparently worked in New Mexico between 1621 and 1626 (Scholes 1938: 64–65), reveals little concerning Apache-Pueblo relations in New Mexico at that time. Zárate-Salmerón was, however, the first to name and locate the Navajos, who, judging from his account, were living somewhere between the Chama River and the Colorado (Milich 1966: 94).

Zárate-Salmerón's relation seems to have been submitted in 1629 (Scholes 1938: 64), the year in which Fray Estévan de Perea probably wrote his report (Bloom 1933: 223). Perea, who apparently went to New Mexico with Governor Peralta in 1609, includes in his relation an incident important for the history of Hopi-Apache relations. Three Franciscans and twelve soldiers went to the Hopi Pueblos, then called the "province of Moqui," where an apostate Christian Indian had preceded them, alarming the Hopis with stories that the Spaniards were coming to burn their pueblos and behead their children. The apostate told the Hopis that if the Spaniards put water on their heads they would surely die. "This news so disturbed (*alteraron*) [parentheses in original] the Moquinos that they secretly summoned in their favor the neighboring Apaches, with whom at that time they had a truce" (Bloom 1933: 231). This episode is highly reminiscent of Espejo's experience at the Hopi Pueblos in 1583 when the Hopis summoned the neighboring Querechos to aid them against the Spaniards and supports the probability that those Querechos were Southern Athabascans.

Fray Alonso de Benavides, who had been in charge of the Franciscan missions in New Mexico from 1625–1629, presented his first *Memorial* concerning that province in Madrid, 1 August 1630, while his revised *Memorial* was presented to Pope Urban VIII on 12 February 1634 (H, H & R 1945: 5, 11). Although Benavides is known to have exaggerated his accounts where population statistics were concerned, his works provide considerable insight into human relations in the New Mexico of his time. He was the first to make explicit the close relationship of the Apache dialects: "And although, being one nation, it is all (of) one tongue, since it is so extensive there does not fail to be some variation, but no such matter that it cannot be very well understood" (Ayer 1916: 39–40). Surely, this linguistic similarity was the shared trait that enabled the Spaniards to recognize the relationship of the various Apachean groups. Moreover, the very fact that Benavides did recognize the relationship between widely scattered Apacheans and nevertheless listed separately such tribes as the Jumanos and Mansos, whom he and his friars also knew, seems reason enough to discount Forbes's (1959) identification of these and other north-Mexican tribes as Athabascans.[1]

In addition, Benavides stated from personal observation a fact that can also be deduced from scattered statements in earlier Spanish documents: the Apaches surrounded the Pueblos on all

---

1 See D. Gunnerson 1960: 315–16, for additional arguments against Forbes's identification.

sides. He described the branches of the "huge Apache nation" as they occurred in a circle around the Río Grande Pueblos (H, H & R 1945: 180–92). West of the Río Grande from south to north were the Xilas and the Navajos. Fifty leagues or more beyond the Navajos and between the Navajos and Taos Pueblo were the Apaches of Quinia. Although in one place Benavides indicates that the *rancherías* of the Apaches of Quinia were west of the Río Grande, he also says that their last settlements were near Taos (H, H & R 1945: 89, 91). Up and down the Plains to the east of the Río Grande were the Vaquero Apaches, and the Apaches of Perillo were in the mountains of the southeast corner of New Mexico. Some of the lands of the Quinia Apaches were apparently also east of Taos, since Zárate-Salmerón had said earlier that the most direct route to Quivira was by way of Taos and through the lands of Chief Quinia.

Other indications that the Quinia Apaches were near Taos are to be found in Benavides's statement concerning attempts to convert this group to Christianity. Before 1627, several friars had attempted to convert Chief Quinia, who was said to be "very famous in that country, very belligerent and valiant in war" (H, H & R 1945: 89). Because Chief Quinia was favorably disposed toward the friars, one of his own people had shot him with an arrow. Fray Pedro de Ortega, taking along a friar skilled in surgery, journeyed ten leagues to where Quinia was living in order to attend him. Father Ortega, who was apparently the first resident friar at Taos, served there from 1621 or 1622 until 1625 (H, H & R 1945: 283), and it may have been from Taos that he went to Chief Quinia ten leagues away. Having recovered from his wound, Quinia decided to become a Christian. Benavides says:

> In the year 1627, Captain Quinía came and asked me for baptism with great insistence. To console him, I went to his rancherías, *as he had retired farther inland* [italics mine], and planted there the first crosses. In the year 1628, Father Fray Pedro de Ortega baptized him and another famous captain, called Manases, who lived near his ranchería.
>
> The conversion of this tribe and province, in the year 1628, fell to the lot of Father Fray Bartolomé Romero, reader in theology, a friar of excellent virtues, who devoted himself to his

task with great and apostolic spirit. Captain Quinía came to meet him and escort him to his country, bringing along one of his sons whom Father Romero baptized in the city of Santa Fe, where he was. This was done with great solemnity, the Spanish governor honoring him highly by acting as godfather. At the same time a famous Indian warrior whom Quinía had captured in war and whom he greatly loved was baptized and they gave him the name of Bernardino. The Spanish governor and fifty Spanish soldiers accompanied the father to the ranchería. In one day they built a church of logs, which they hewed, and they plastered these walls on the outside. The governor himself and Father Romero carried the logs; emulating them, the Spanish soldiers and the Indians did likewise. Hence it was built in that one day amid great apostolic rejoicings.

After setting this good example, the governor departed, and Father Romero remained alone and instructed them with great fervor. But the devil perverted Captain Quinía, and now, hating our holy law, which he had so much desired to profess; he attempted to kill Father Romero. Abjuring baptism Quinía abandoned the ranchería and moved elsewhere to prevent anyone from being taught by the father, who never deserted his post. Only the valiant Indian Bernardino remained with Father Romero and, as a good Christian, defended and protected him on many ocassions when they attempted to kill him. Thus, finding himself alone, the friar was obliged to abandon the post. Nevertheless, Captain Quinía repented of his sin, but from shame he did not dare to put in an appearance, and when I left New Mexico he was endeavoring to submit himself to our holy Catholic faith once more. (H, H & R 1945: 90; see also Bloom 1933: 226)

These comments of Father Benavides indicate that Quinia moved his *rancherías* occasionally, and it is possible that he lived at times west of the Río Grande, perhaps seeking the protection of the Navajos as the Jicarillas sometimes did later, or that he dominated territory on both sides of the river. Quinia's ambivalent attitude toward Christianity resembles that of the Jicarillas after 1700, and if the Quinia Apaches were the ancestors of the Jicarillas, their more or less friendly interaction with the Spaniards as early as the first part of the seventeenth century may help explain why the later Jicarillas were usually friendly to the Spaniards of New Mexico and why they, even more than the Navajos, were influenced by Spanish and/or Pueblo culture.

Before 1629, the friars had also attempted to convert the Va-

quero Apaches of the Plains, who were extremely important to
the economy of colonial New Mexico because they furnished the
skins used by both Pueblo Indians and Spaniards for clothing and
other items.

> With these hides they trade through all the land and gain their
> living. And it is the general dress as well among Indians as Span-
> iards, who use it as well for service as bags, tents, cuirasses, shoes
> (*calçado*), and everything that is needed. . . . When these In-
> dians go to trade and traffic, the entire rancherias go, with their
> wives and children, who live in tents made of these skins of
> buffalo (*síbola*), very thin and tanned; and the tents they carry
> loaded on pack-trains (*requas*) of dogs, harnessed up with their
> little pack-saddles; and the dogs are medium sized. And they
> are accustomed to take five hundred dogs in one pack-train, one
> in front of the other; and the people carry their merchandise
> (thus) loaded, which they barter for cotton cloth and for other
> things which they lack. (Ayer 1916: 55–56)

The Vaqueros are of special importance for this study because
they undoubtedly included the Plains Apaches of Kansas and
Nebraska, later to become known as Cuartelejos and Palomas—
groups which in turn seem to have become the Llanero Band of
the modern Jicarillas.

Benavides says of the Vaqueros:

> The beginning of the conversion of this tribe was brought
> about by the continuous intercourse which they have had with
> the friars in the Christian pueblos, where the Indians came to sell
> dressed síbola hides, and the friars always talked to them of God.
> (H, H & R 1945: 91)

And according to Benavides, "an attempt was made to establish
a large settlement on a site chosen by them" (H, H & R 1945:
92). However, the governor of New Mexico at that time, probably Felipe Sotelo (or Zotylo) sent another group of Indians out
to take as many Apache slaves as possible; these slave raiders attacked the Vaquero Band whose leader was most interested in
baptism, and this Vaquero chief was killed in the battle. The
friars and settlers were shocked, and the Vaqueros were alienated;
but, according to Benavides, in 1629 the Vaqueros who had been
victims of the raid again wanted to become Christians (H, H & R
1945: 91–92; Ayer 1916: 271–72).

Missionary efforts to the west also cast some light on Apaches. As mentioned previously, the Hopi Indians called on their Apache neighbors to help them repel the advances of missionaries, including Fray Francisco de Porras, whom they finally killed. While Fray Martín de Arvide was working at Jémez, Benavides sent him on a missionary expedition to the Navajo Apaches (H, H & R 1945: 79, 96). Arvide worked in the same area where Father Porras had served, among the Hopis (H, H & R 1945: 76–77, 79). Thus it would appear that the Apaches mentioned by both Perea and Benavides as neighbors of the Hopis ca. 1629 were Navajos, and this early identification of Navajos in that area strengthens the possibility that the Querechos who lived there in 1583 were specifically Navajo Apaches.

The Xila Apaches were said to be living only fourteen leagues from the Piro Pueblo of Senecú "where their chief captain, called Sanaba, oftentimes comes to gamble. After he had heard me preach to the Piros several times, he became inclined to our holy Catholic faith." According to Benavides, Sanaba and all the Xilas of his *ranchería* became converted. "With this good start, I founded that conversion in their pueblo of Xila, placing it in charge of Father Fray Martín del Espíritu Santo, who administered it with great courage during the year 1628" (H, H & R 1945: 82–83). Although the Xilas did not remain converts for long, their culture was apparently affected in at least one important respect as a result of Spanish missionary activity. In his first memorial (1630), Benavides says that the Xilas formerly did not plant and lived by hunting but that "today we have broken land for them and taught them to plant" (Ayer 1916: 44).

Apparently the Perillo Apaches also frequented the Piro Pueblo of Senecú, for they, too, according to Benavides, heard him preach there and as a result asked for baptism. "As proof of the joy with which they became converted to our holy Catholic faith, they established firm friendship with the Piros, with whom they were not on very good terms" (H, H & R 1945: 84–85).

In an attempt to convert the Navajos, Benavides went to live at Santa Clara, a Tewa pueblo on the Navajo frontier where those Apaches waged war and killed people every day. He sent out a group of Santa Clara Indians who spoke the Apache language well to make contact with the Navajos (H, H & R 1945: 85–89). A Navajo chief came in to Santa Clara to parley.

> And to confirm this peace, he wished to bring all the women and small children of those neighboring rancherias, with many dressed deerskins and rock alum (*piedra alumbre*), to make a big fair, which should last three days, and they would contract great friendship. (Ayer 1916: 52)

Although there seem to be no references to specific raids by Southern Athabascans between the first decade of the 1600s and the period in which Benavides worked in New Mexico, that informant represents the Apaches as a constant threat. Speaking of them in general he says: "It is a nation so bellicose, all of it, that it has been the crucible for the courage of the Spaniards." Yet the only Apaches that he accuses specifically are the Navajos, of whom he says at one point: "This province is the most bellicose of all the Apache nation, and (is) where the Spaniards have well shown their valor" (Ayer 1916: 41, 44).

The Xilas and the Perillo Apaches seem to have been at peace in Benavides's time. Chief Quinia's Apaches had once turned against the priest assigned to them but were otherwise apparently friendly to the Spaniards. The Vaquero Apaches had extended their trade in meat, salt, and buffalo hides to include the Spanish settlers, trade with New Mexico being so important to the Vaqueros that even the slave raids organized by Spanish governors against the Plains Apaches failed to stop their commerce for long. There is no indication, for example, that the Vaqueros attacked by Sotelo's slave raiders even retaliated.

Benavides, like earlier writers, makes it clear that Apache hostility was not the only source of conflict in New Mexico. He states that the Jémez Indians had previously been exceedingly hostile to the "Christian" Tewas (H, H & R 1945: 70). Of the Pueblo people in general he says that in the past "there were between them continuous civil wars, so great that they killed each other (off) and laid waste whole pueblos" (Ayer 1916: 31). Whereas earlier accounts indicate that before Oñate's time animosity among Pueblo peoples was a matter of one Pueblo or one group of linguistically-related Pueblos against others, Benavides attributes Pueblo warfare to some kind of general rivalry between military and religious leaders.

> All these folk and nations were in their gentilism divided into two factions, warriors and sorcerers. The warriors tried, in opposition to the sorcerers, to bring all the people under their (own) dominion and authority; and the sorcerers, with the same opposition, persuaded all that *they* made the rain fall and the earth yield good crops, and other things at which the warriors sneered. (Ayer 1916: 30–31)

Since factionalism within individual Pueblos has proved highly disruptive in more recent times, it is entirely possible that in prehistoric times intramural schisms, if extended by extramural alliances and counteralliances, could indeed have resulted in widespread warfare.

Actually, the advent of the Spaniards and their religion, by means of which they hoped to render the natives docile, occasioned the most bitter factional resentments and eventually the greatest inter-Pueblo violence in historic times. Moreover, if there was any hope of making the Pueblo people into peaceful Christians in the 1600s, it was soon shattered by a factional dispute between Spanish soldiers and priests rivaling that said to have existed formerly between Pueblo warriors and sorcerers.

Ironically, the Spaniards themselves used Indians against one another during a long and bitter struggle between the Franciscan friars and civil authority as it was represented by one governor after another, the conflict apparently stemming from the determination of both factions to control the labor and goods of the Pueblo Indians. Each faction (most blatantly those led by some of the governors) incited the Pueblo Indians against the other in order to gain its own ends. What is more, both Spanish factions were guilty of conniving with the dreaded common enemy, the Apaches, thus using tactics that the Spaniards denounced as barbarous when they were employed by the Indians.

At the root of the situation was the inability of the New Mexico colonists to get a living by their own efforts or to be satisfied with the standard of living that could be so attained. It

should be said in their defense, however, that the hostility of the
Pueblo people and their Apache allies made it difficult for the
few settlers to expand beyond the military post of Santa Fé, itself poorly armed, and exploit what lands were available for farming and stock raising. This situation made them dependent to a
large extent upon what tribute they could collect from the
"Christian" Pueblos close enough to be dominated by force.
While the amount of the tribute that could be legally exacted
under the *encomienda* system—thirty-three inches of woven cloth
and one *fanega* of corn from each Pueblo household per year—
does not seem ruinous, much more was apparently extorted. In
years of crop failure, the situation of the Pueblo farmers was desperate. Unable to maintain themselves adequately, they still had
to deal with the demands of the equally desperate Spaniards and
ward off attacks of neighboring Apaches made more aggressive
than usual by the failure of their own crops. The anxieties of the
Pueblo people were undoubtedly heightened in such periods
when they could not meet the expectations of the normally
friendly Plains Apaches who came to trade (see Kelley 1952).

Even after those of Oñate's colonists who remained in New
Mexico had accepted the fact that it was not a rich country, the
idea that enterprising individuals could become wealthy there
must have persisted in Mexico and Spain. There was never a lack
of candidates for the post of governor of the province, although
the position carried with it only a poor salary, and some governors actually purchased their appointments (Bandelier 1892:
104). Obviously they expected to prosper through private enterprise, a hope which was almost certainly stimulated in the early
1600s by reports of missionaries which exaggerated the mineral
resources of New Mexico and especially their richness. Glowing
accounts of mineral wealth in Benavides's published and widely
circulated *Memorial* of 1630 may well have helped attract to New
Mexico the governors whose avarice so offended the Franciscans
(Ayer 1916: 18–19; H, H & R 1945: 39, 227–29).

Arriving in New Mexico with an insatiable desire to become
rich, the governors found that they could not do so without
illegally exploiting the Indians (Forbes 1960: 131). France

Scholes, the foremost authority on New Mexico in the seventeenth century, has generalized:

> The governors violated the laws forbidding them to engage in trade; they exploited the Indians to the limit; they organized slave raids against the nomadic tribes of the plains,—in short, they sought every means to enrich themselves at the expense of the province. (Scholes 1936–1937 XI: 25)

But the friars also were not beyond reproach.

> The frequent accusations made by the clergy that the Spaniards were guilty of acts of cruelty and demoralizing social conduct in their ordinary relations with the Indians were countered by an increasing number of complaints concerning the harsh discipline enforced by the clergy on their wards and the moral laxness of an unfortunately large number of the mission priests. (Scholes 1936–1937 XI: 22)

It is, therefore, from the petitions and memorials of priests, from the testimony offered in trials and investigations of governors, in short, from the charges and countercharges made in the struggle between church and civil authorities for power and self-justification that specific items bearing on intergroup relations can be gleaned.

The serious trouble between representatives of church and crown in New Mexico began about 1620 (Bancroft 1889: 159), but the first major offense against peaceful Apaches recorded by the Franciscans was the slave raid launched against a band of Vaqueros by Governor Sotelo.

> In order to obtain slaves to sell in New Spain, the governor sent a brave Indian captain . . . to bring back as many captives as he could. This infernal minister happened to go to the village of the chief captain, who had promised the Virgin that he would become a Christian, together with all his people. He fought with the captain and killed him, as well as many of his people, for he had taken a great many Indian warriors along with him. As the slain captain was wearing about his neck a rosary I had given him, he held it out in front of him, beseeching his assailant for its sake and for the sake of the Mother of God not to kill him; but this did not suffice to keep the tyrant from venting his cruelty. Some captives were brought back to the governor. Though he refused to accept them on account of the tumult this event had occasioned, and though he wanted to hang the one he had sent on the mission, nevertheless his greed was quite apparent. This

provoked a revolt throughout this entire province, although once more, thank God, we are succeeding in pacifying it, and the Indians already know who is to blame [Benavides]. (Forrestal 1954: 55–56)

Governor Francisco de Sylva, who succeeded Sotelo in 1629, actively assisted the friars in their attempt to convert the Quinia Apaches, but like his predecessor, he was accused of hostility to the church (H, H & R 1945: 2–4, 90, 212). The next two governors, who ruled consecutively between 1632 and 1637, were "virtually at cold war with the Franciscans" and one, Francisco de la Mora, was accused of abusing the Pueblo Indians (Forbes 1960: 129).

Since the Spaniards had learned of at least one mountain pass via Taos early in the 1600s, slave raiders and adventurers probably used it from time to time, as well as the route via Pecos. There seem to have been various expeditions that went as far as Quivira before 1680, although the references to these are all too ambiguous. Father Alonso Posada, writing in 1686, says:

> In the year 1634, Captain Alonso Vaca with some soldiers left the city of Santa Fé traveling along the eastern rather than the southern course as he did on the other journeys. After having gone almost three hundred leagues in this direction, he arrived at the River *Grande* [Arkansas] and wanted to cross over, but the friendly Indians in his company warned him not to, because on the other bank was the Quivira nation. (Tyler and Taylor 1958: 298; hereafter referred to as T & T)

Since Father Posada apparently did not arrive in New Mexico until 1650 (T & T 1958: 285), his information may have been hearsay; but if such an expedition did cross the Plains, it went through Apache territory.

During the term of the next governor, Luís de Rosas, the conflict between the clergy and the government came to a climax, precipitating events that indirectly made it an important period in the culture history of the Southern Athabascans. In Rosas's administration civil war broke out between the Franciscans and the governor's faction, and early in 1640 the friars abandoned all of the Pueblos and missions, withdrawing for sixteen months to the Pueblo of Santo Domingo where they were joined by those of the settlers who sympathized with their cause. This group built defensive structures from which they sent out raiding parties to steal livestock and horses of the governor and his supporters. They seem also to have raided the Pueblos (Forbes 1960: 135–36).

In the conflicts that preceded this drastic action, the governor had ordered the Pueblos not to obey the friars, and at Taos he complained about the priests in front of the Indians. As a result, both the Taos and the Jémez revolted, killing their priests and others (Forbes 1960: 134; H, H & R 1945: 284). The Jémez rebels were allied with Apaches (Scholes 1938: 94–96), probably Navajos. The Taos fled to the Plains in 1639 or 1640, where they lived among Apaches who already inhabited the area. No contemporary account of their flight has been discovered, but well over a century later, in 1778, a few details concerning the incident were included in a brief history of New Mexico written by Father Silvestre Vélex de Escalante at the request of his superior, Father Morfi. This information on the flight of the Taos was apparently derived from local New Mexico tradition in 1778, for few or no written records of the period before 1680 existed in New Mexico in Escalante's time (Twitchell 1914 II: 268).

> In the middle of the last century some families of Christian Indians of the nation and pueblo of Taos rebelled, withdrew to the buffalo plains and fortified themselves at a place which afterward on this account was called *El Cuartelejo*. And they were there until Don Juan de Archuleta, by order of the governor, went with twenty soldiers and some Indian auxiliaries and brought them back to Taos. He found in the possession of these rebellious Taos Indians some casques and other pieces of copper and tin, and when he asked them whence they had gotten these they replied 'from the Quivira pueblos,' to which they had journeyed from the Cuartelejo. This caused great joy and content for all the Spaniards and priests of the kingdom, as they believed these casques and other pieces were made in Quivira, and from this they inferred that it was a much advanced and rich kingdom. (Twitchell 1914 II: 279–80)

Escalante's explanation of the name "El Cuartelejo" may or may not be accurate, but it is all too possible that the impoverished settlers, whose descendants still dream of improbable treasure troves, thought again of Quivira as a source of riches.

Other Indians besides the Taos and Jémez seem to have revolted in 1639, and large herds of livestock were stolen from the missions. Apparently Governor Rosas made no effort to punish the Pueblo rebels or to campaign against Apache raiders; instead he consented to Apaches' raiding the missions, or at least permitted the raids, and the Apaches took full advantage of the opportunity to kill mission Indians and acquire herds of horses and mares. Meanwhile, Rosas's men were engaged in "robbing the various pueblos, taking from both priests and Indians" (Forbes 1960: 133–34).

Among the numerous crimes of which Rosas was accused, the following were said to have been committed in 1638–1639:

> *Item:* that he went loaded with knives to the pueblo of Pecos to barter with a number of Apache Indians, friends of the baptized natives, pretending that he went to serve His Majesty; and as he did not find any trading he became angry and rash to such a degree with the priest (of Pecos) that he carried him a captive to the *villa* (Santa Fe).

> *Item:* that in a journey that was made by order of the said governor to Quivira they (the Spaniards) killed a great number of the said friendly Apaches, and these killings were done in company with many infidel enemies of the said Apaches, an action prohibited by *cédula* of His Majesty . . . and they captured them (Apaches) in this unjust war, and they took them to sell in *tierra de paz* (in Nueva Vizcaya).

> The Christian natives of the pueblo of Pecos have made a great demonstration of feeling in regard to this, because they were living with them (the Apaches) and with them they had their commerce, by means of which they clothed themselves and paid their tributes.

> *Item:* that because of the above-mentioned war the same Apache nation remained with hatred and enmity towards the Spaniards. (Forbes 1960: 132, Scholes 1936–1937 XI: 302, 328 *n*14)

These charges reveal that at ca. 1640, as in 1540, Plains Apaches were not only still trading at Pecos but were still living there at times, probably during the winter. Moreover, trade with the Apaches had become important to the Pecos Indians for a new reason. They were using items obtained from the Apaches in barter to pay their tributes to the Spaniards. It is possible that the Spaniards had by 1640 so disrupted relations among native groups, who did not all weave cotton, that some Pueblos no longer had access to the cloth that was part of the established tribute. Each effort of the conquerors to gain wealth from a new source apparently further complicated relationships among the Indians and thus seriously inhibited the very activities by which the Pueblos attempted to fulfill the obligations imposed on them by the Spaniards. Some of the captive Plains Apaches referred to in the accusations quoted above were impressed, along with Christian Indians, as laborers in a weaving shop that Rosas had set up for himself in Santa Fé (Scholes 1936–1937 XI: 300–301), and this situation no doubt gave the Plains Athabascans an increasingly intimate view of Spanish affairs in the garrison town.

There is no indication that the expedition made to Quivira during Rosas's administration was connected with the flight of the Taos Indians to the Plains, described later by Escalante. Yet it seems a coincidence that the two events should have occurred so close together, and the expedition could have been one undertaken immediately after the Taos revolt to bring the rebels back. The Apaches, undoubtedly Cuartelejos, might have been killed as a punishment for harboring the Taos Indians or in the process of defending those refugees.

A new governor, Juan Flores de Sierra y Valdés, arrived in Santa Fé in 1641 and began an investigation of the conflict between Rosas and the Franciscans. But Flores died before he could resolve the problem, whereupon the Franciscans gained control of the government and put ex-Governor Rosas in prison. There he was murdered, if not through an actual plot by the Franciscan faction at least with its acquiescence. However, the next governor, Alonzo Pacheco de Heredia, after re-establishing civil government, tried and executed for treason eight pro-Franciscan captains of the Santa Fé garrison. Among them was a Juan de Archuleta, assumed to have been the one credited by Escalante with leading the expedition that went to El Cuartelejo and brought back Taos refugees. It has been suggested that this

Archuleta undertook the journey at a time when Governor
Pacheco was keeping the pro-Franciscan captains busy by sending them off on campaigns until he strengthened his own position. In any case, Archuleta could not have made the journey
after 21 July 1643, since he was executed for treason on that
date (Forbes 1960: 135–38).

The years in which the Taos Indians went to the Plains and
were brought back are important because the sojourn of a substantial number of Pueblo Indians among Plains Apaches could
be expected to have a greater impact on Vaquero culture than had
the visits of these Plains nomads to the Pueblos. Specifically, it
has been thought by some that the Cuartelejo Apaches and related bands adopted a semi-sedentary way of life, including horticulture with irrigation and pottery making, under the influence
of the Taos refugees. In evaluating these possibilities it would be
helpful to know how early the influence of the Pueblo migrants
began to be exerted and how long it persisted. Fortunately, evidence was presented later in the century that casts light on this
problem.

Meanwhile, the Taos were not the only Pueblo Indians who
fled to the protection of Apaches in this period. Father Juan de
Prada, in 1638, after stating that the Apaches "who live in
rancherías in the environs of the converted pueblos" continually
attack them, later says:

> Upon the slightest occasion of annoyance with the soldiers some
> of the baptized Indians, fleeing from their pueblo, have gone
> over to the heathen, believing that they enjoy greater happiness
> with them, since they live according to their whims and in com-
> plete freedom. (Hackett 1923–1937 III: 110–11)

The Apaches probably harbored still more refugees during the
rule of Governor Pacheco, who intensified the problems of the
Pueblo Indians in many ways. He decreed, for example, that they
could not travel from one pueblo to another without a license, in
a period when some of the villages were without food and had to
seek it elsewhere. Even before Pacheco, tribute had apparently
been increased; it was being collected every four or five months
instead of once a year as in Benavides's time. Pacheco, however,

attempted to collect the same amount of goods from each individual that had formerly been demanded of each household. Those Spaniards who opposed this measure did so because they feared that it would cause all the Pueblo Indians to flee to the Apaches (Forbes 1960: 139). Conflict between the Franciscans and the government again reached a climax in Pacheco's administration, and in September 1644, twenty-one friars gathered at their headquarters in the Pueblo of Santo Domingo to sign a protest against the rule of bad governors. During the same period the Zuñis and Picurís may have revolted and been punished.

Pacheco's successor, Fernando de Argüello, cooperated with the Franciscans, helping them re-establish control over the Río Grande Pueblos and severely punishing Indians for idolatry (Forbes 1960: 142). The Jémez remained as rebellious as ever, and sometime between 1644 and 1647, again in league with Apaches, they revolted and killed another Spaniard. Several of their leaders were hanged, some were whipped, and still others condemned to servitude (Scholes 1938: 94–96).

A document bearing what appears to be a forged signature of Governor Luís de Guzmán y Figueroa may nevertheless contain a valid statement concerning mountain Apaches in the Taos-Picurís-Pecos area at almost the time he took office. Attempting to gain royal favor in the 1680s and 1690s, a soldier named Juan Domínguez de Mendoza submitted a series of testimonials concerning his services in New Mexico earlier in the century. Although various discrepancies in these documents strongly suggest that signatures, at least, were forged, it is possible that the contents are not entirely fabrications. This soldier, born in Mexico City, had come to New Mexico about the middle of the century. In 1646 he was either twelve or seventeen years old (Chávez 1954: 24, 25–26), so that he could conceivably have taken part in a campaign against the "Apaches del Acho," who were said to have made war on Taos and Picurís and threatened Pecos in April 1646 (Forbes 1960: 143, 146). These Achos, considering their location, could have been the Apaches of Chief Quinia under a new or alternative name. They are not mentioned again, however, until 1680 when they were allied with the Taos

Indians in the Pueblo Rebellion. There were undoubtedly Apaches in the mountains of northeastern New Mexico in 1646 but whether they were called Achos at that time remains uncertain. It is always possible that the name Acho, familiar by 1680, was projected back to the 1640s by Domínguez de Mendoza.

In 1650, "all of the Apaches" were said to be involved in the most general plot against the Spaniards conceived up to that time. As part of the plan, Christian Indians guarding Spanish livestock turned it over to the conspirators, claiming later that it had been stolen by Apaches. The natives were to make a concerted attack in all districts on Holy Thursday, at a time when the Spaniards would be gathered together in observance of the day. When this plot was discovered, Hernando de Ugarte y la Concha, then governor, hanged nine leaders from the Pueblos of Isleta, Alameda, San Felipe, Cochití, and Jémez, and sold many other inhabitants of these villages into servitude for ten years. Again, in the early 1650s, a military force that penetrated the Navajo country found Christian Indians consorting with these Apaches (Forbes 1960: 144–45).

Another event of importance to historians of the period took place in 1650, for it was apparently in that year that Father Alonso Posada, who in 1686 was to write one of the most important accounts of New Mexico, arrived to begin work as a missionary. Although his observations were not recorded until after the Pueblo Rebellion, they apply to the period between 1650 and 1665 when he was active in New Mexico (T & T 1958: 285, 289).

Few details survive from the administration of Governor Juan Manso de Contreras (1656–1659), but in a controversy stemming from his attempt to acquire Apache slaves it was discovered that some Picurís Indians had joined with Spaniards in a slave raid against Apaches (Forbes 1960: 149). Such behavior represented a departure from the friendly relations that the Picurís usually maintained with Apaches, and it may have been such an incident that provoked the Achos in 1646, if they actually did attack the border pueblos.

Of the decades following the scandals of the Rosas administration, Scholes has generalized, "Expeditions were constantly being organized for the purpose of seizing Apache captives to be sold as slaves in New Spain" (Scholes 1936–1937 XI: 99), and the situation was no better under Governor López de Mendizabal, who took office in 1659. Technically, only Apaches taken during wars of reprisal were considered legitimate booty, but Spaniards often deliberately provoked trouble on trading expeditions so they could seize such "legitimate" captives. Sometimes, when Apacheans came to pueblos to trade or to seek food during drought and famine, unlawful seizures were made. López apparently specialized in such tactics.

> According to a complaint presented by Capt. Andrés Hurtado during López' *residencia*, the governor caused an unprovoked attack to be made on Apaches who came in peace to the pueblo of Jémez. Several were killed and more than thirty women and children were taken captive. As a result of this unjustified action, the Apaches raided the frontier pueblos, killed more than twenty Christian Indians, and carried off more than 300 head of livestock. (Scholes 1937–1941 XII: 398)

Mountain Apaches living near Taos were also seized when they entered that pueblo in peace. To provide justification for such acts López drew up about ninety decrees legalizing the capture of Apaches (Forbes 1960: 154). Another expedition that went out on a slave raid in Governor López's time brought in seventy Apache captives, but while this trading party of forty colonists and eight hundred Indians was away on the Plains, Apaches from other areas raided the settlements—killing, stealing, and taking captives for themselves (Scholes 1937–1941 XII: 163).

Apaches taken during the wars of reprisal were assigned for service for a period of years during which they were to be civilized and taught the Christian faith; however,

> for all practical purposes, these captives were slaves and were freely bought and sold. The price of a strong Apache boy or girl ten or twelve years of age was thirty to forty pesos. The Pueblos frequently acquired Plains Indians in this manner but they usually sold them to the colonists for horses and cattle. There were few Hispanic households that did not have one or more of these servants, and the governors also held a fairly large number. There was also an active trade in these captives with the mining

and ranching centers of New Spain, and occasionally the governors or private individuals sent them as gifts to friends in Mexico
City. (Scholes 1937–1941 XII: 397)

Governor López kept as servants

negro slaves brought from New Spain, Indians from the pueblos,
and captive Apaches. They were forever quarreling, and at
night they slipped out to carouse with the townspeople. Thiev-
ing was a frequent occurrence. The governor and his wife tried
to maintain discipline by flogging offenders or dismissing the
worst of them, but these measures had little effect. The servants
spied on their masters, noted what books they read, watched
every little act and gesture, and then spread all manner of
rumors, even concerning the intimate details of their lives.
(Scholes 1937–1941 XII: 393)

Moreover, Governor López was apparently guilty of improper
conduct with his household servants, including unconverted
Apache women (Scholes 1937: 392). With their own people in
such close contact with the Spaniards, able to observe at first
hand the quarrels between the friars and the civil authorities as
well as between the factions in each of these groups, neither the
Pueblo Indians nor the Apaches should have been ignorant of
the state of Spanish affairs in New Mexico. Thus, although the
administration of the province became more peaceful after 1664,
the Spanish had already earned the contempt of the Indians, and
Apache-Pueblo-Spanish relations worsened.

While the Plains Apaches continued to trade in New Mexico,
these nomads had given up the practice of bringing their dog
trains, women, and children into the Río Grande Valley well
before López's term. Instead they carried on trade at border
Pueblos, especially Pecos, or Spanish traders sought them out on
the Plains. And like the "squaw men" of the American West,
these Spanish traders apparently sometimes found it desirable to
take an Indian wife for the duration of their stay (Forbes 1960:
153–55).

In 1659 there occurred an incident that probably influenced
the nature of Apache-Pueblo trade and, indirectly, changed relationships between Plains Apaches and their Caddoan neighbors
to the east.

In 1658 a famine had occurred, and the Apaches suffered so severely from it that they came in to the pueblos in 1659 to sell all of their slaves and their own children in exchange for food. The Franciscans purchased many of these Indians on the grounds that they could convert them. López, however, took advantage of the famine by seizing men, women, and children who had come in peace. The governor charged, however, that these seizures were made before his time and that the priests themselves had sold forty-three Indians at Parral. (Forbes 1960: 151)

Before this time, the most important commodities brought to the Pueblos by Plains Apaches on regular trading expeditions had been hides, meat, and salt. Although they probably bartered a few captives taken from other Plains tribes or brought them to their Pueblo trade-friends as gifts, trade in slaves had not been emphasized. While Father Alonso de Posada was serving as priest at Pecos, "a camp of Apache Indians entered the town to sell hides of antelope and leather and brought with them some captive Indian children from Quivira to trade for horses" (T & T 1958: 301). Posada served at Pecos before 1661, but the exact date is unknown. Later in the century and in the 1700s, possibly because the Franciscans showed willingness to purchase captives brought in by Apaches in 1659, there are an increasing number of references to Plains Apaches as traders in slaves, and the seasonal trade "fairs" in New Mexico even came to be called "ransomings." The Plains Apaches seem to have obtained most of their slaves from Caddoan tribes, which may account for the enmity between these two groups revealed in later documents. It appears, likewise, that after the Plains Apaches themselves became important suppliers of slaves to the New Mexico market, Spanish slave raids against these Apaches decreased and that "genízaros," or converted non-Athabascan, non-Pueblo Plains Indians, formed an increasingly large element in the population of the province.

Even the Hopis, once allied with the Navajos in their neighborhood, did some trading in Apaches in 1661. A Captain Trujillo testified that the Indians of Walpi, "having captured nine Apaches, gave one to their friar and one to him as *alcalde mayor*, and offered to trade the others for things they could use" (Scholes 1937–1941 XII: 414). Whether these Apaches had been captured in war or whether the Hopis had betrayed them in order to buy Spanish favor is not indicated. In any case, although captives were used for menial purposes in prehistoric times, the Spanish made trading in slaves a lucrative business for Indians and white men alike in the Southwest.

Diego de Peñalosa, who took office in 1661, admitted in 1665 to having so many Apache slaves that he had given away more than a hundred (Forbes 1960: 156). Some of these may have been acquired by a force that he sent far into the Plains, for at the trial of this governor in 1665 it was said that about 1662 he

> caused to be reduced . . . the Taos Indians who had been in revolt for twenty-two years, and were living as heathen among the people of El Cuartelejo, on the frontier of La Quivira. He reduced thirty-three, . . . having caused El Cuartelejo to be laid waste for more than 200 leagues beyond New Mexico. (Hackett 1923–1937 III: 263–64)

This document is the first primary source to mention El Cuartelejo. The statement that the Taos refugees had been in revolt for twenty-two years before Peñalosa's expedition "reduced" them definitely associates their original flight with the Taos Rebellion of 1639, as Hodge supposed. The testimony given in 1665 also indicates that by the 1660s the name of El Cuartelejo was not confined to the specific place where the Taos refugees had "fortified" themselves but was rather applied to a region that at its eastern extremity bordered on Quivira. The witness apparently applied the term El Cuartelejo to all the Apache settlements between New Mexico and the place where the Taos had settled, so that it might well have included the lands of the mountain Apaches living east and northeast of Taos.

The expedition sent out in Peñalosa's term may have been the last official penetration of Apache country beyond Taos before the Pueblo Rebellion, and the destruction wrought by Peñalosa's men could well account for the anxiety shown by the foothills Apaches when Ulibarri later entered their lands in 1706. But Peñalosa's expedition may not have been the first that went out to gather up the Taos apostates. Forbes's supposition that part of the Taos refugees were brought back in or before 1643 is based on the assumption that Juan de Archuleta, named by Escalante in 1778 as leader of the expedition, was the captain executed by Governor Pacheco for treason. However, there was another Juan de Archuleta who was active in New Mexico affairs in the 1660s. Father Angélico Chávez, who provides interesting material on the history of the Archuleta family in New Mexico, says of this man:

> Juan de Archuleta II, presumably the son of the preceding Juan, was thirty-eight years old in 1664 and a resident of La Cañada. . . . As a Río Arriba leader, he was a sort of lackey to Governor Peñalosa. Before this, in 1661, he had acted in the same capacity to Governor Mendizábal. Around this time, or later, he was sent to the bison plains to bring back the Taos Indians, who had fled from their pueblo. (Chávez 1954: 6)

Although Chávez's last statement is based on Escalante, who did not himself know the date of the expedition, it is probably the most reasonable interpretation of the evidence. Given the facts that an expedition was actually made to El Cuartelejo about 1662 and that there was a Juan Archuleta extant at the time who would have been an appropriate leader, and considering the lack of direct evidence for an earlier expedition, it seems reasonable that either (1) the 1662 expedition was the one of which Escalante wrote, or (2) two different journeys were undertaken, both of which could have been led by Archuletas. The thirty-three Taos Indians retrieved ca. 1662 probably did not represent all that fled originally, but whether some had been returned earlier or whether it was simply impossible to round them all up in 1662 remains a question.

The testimony given at Peñalosa's trial makes it clear that the Taos refugees were indeed living among the people of El Cuartelejo. It indicates, moreover, that what may have started out as the name of a structure or group of structures built by the Taos became the name of a region and the natives of that region. Although neither the 1665 document nor Escalante's letter of 1778 identifies the people of El Cuartelejo as Apaches, Spanish accounts of the early 1700s provide ample evidence that they were. The specific consequences of Taos-Apache contacts in El Cuar-

telejo between ca. 1639 and ca. 1662 are not yet clear, but it can
be assumed that interaction over a period representing more than
a generation would have affected both groups concerned. Inter-
marriage undoubtedly took place; perhaps children with a mixed
linguistic and cultural heritage were born and grew to adult-
hood. If the time spent by Taos Indians among the Cuartelejo
Apaches did nothing else, it probably reinforced with bonds of
kinship the existing bonds of friendship.

A famine began in 1666 that lasted until at least 1671 (Forbes
1960: 160). A vivid description of the disasters that befell the
province and their results is contained in Fray Francisco de
Ayeta's petition for aid from the viceroy, dated 10 May 1679.

> In the year 1670 there was a very great famine in those prov-
> inces, which compelled the Spanish inhabitants and the Indians
> alike to eat the hides that they had and the straps of the carts,
> preparing them for food by soaking them and washing them and
> toasting them in the fire with maize, and boiling them with
> herbs and roots. By this means, almost half the people in the said
> provinces escaped (starvation) [parentheses in original]. There
> followed in the next year of 1671 a great pestilence, which also
> carried off many people and cattle; and shortly thereafter, in the
> year of 1672, the hostile Apaches who were then at peace, re-
> belled and rose up, and the said province was totally sacked and
> robbed by their attacks and outrages, especially of all the cattle
> and sheep, of which it had previously been very productive.
> They killed, stole, and carried off all except a few small flocks of
> sheep. (Hackett 1923–1937 III: 302)

The Pueblo Indians, who died of starvation by the hundreds,
again made plans to revolt, and they enlisted the aid of Apaches.
Again, all the colonists were to be killed on Holy Thursday, but
again the plot was discovered and a leader hanged. Alliances
shifted rapidly in this period. For example, the Piros and Tom-
piros, with Apache help, at long last rose against the Spaniards.
But their rebellion was crushed, and they were forced into Spanish service as auxiliaries to fight their former Apache allies. With
the Spanish-dominated Pueblos a source of manpower to be
used against them, the nature of Apache aggressions changed.
Their occasional raids became all-out attacks whose aim was
total destruction (Forbes 1960: 161–64).

The Apaches chiefly involved seem to have been, as usual, mountain bands to the west, south, and southeast of the Pueblo area, but in 1675 a Plains Band was named among the hostiles. These were the Faraons, first mentioned in this year as the "Apaches called Paraonez" (Forbes 1960: 171). They were special friends of the Pecos Indians but by the 1700s were to be the scourge of New Mexico, raiding the peaceful foothills Apaches as well as Spaniards and Pueblos.

In 1675, also, came the prelude to the Pueblo Rebellion when the Tewas, over whom the Spaniards had had the greatest control, began actively to defy Spanish religious authority. Juan Francisco Treviño, then governor, arrested the Indian leaders, burned their kivas, and seized their religious paraphernalia. Three Tewas were hanged; and forty-three were lashed, imprisoned, and sentenced to be sold into slavery (Forbes 1960: 171–72). However, in an unprecedented display of courage

> a large squad of Tewa warriors descended on Santa Fe, and seventy of them actually entered the Governor's rooms in the palace, where they demanded the release of prisoners. In an act symbolizing the declining Hispanic hold upon New Mexico, Governor Treviño acquiesced to the Indians' demands, and the captives, including Popé, future leader of the revolt of 1680, were freed. Treviño, it seems, could not afford to face a rebellion of the Tewas and their allies at the same time that the Spanish soldiers were continually being kept busy by the Apaches. (Forbes 1960: 172)

In the next few years, Apaches in southeastern New Mexico harassed the Salinas Pueblos and extended their attacks to the El Paso area. On the west the Spaniards were engaged in major conflicts with the Navajos, who suffered heavy losses in the exchange of hostilities (Forbes 1960: 172–75). However, if Apaches of the plains and mountains northeast of New Mexico attacked in those years, the fact has not been recorded. At last this period of turmoil reached a climax, and on the morning of 10 August 1680, the Pueblos successfully revolted, freeing themselves of Spanish rule for more than a decade.

Chapter Four

The Apaches in the Pueblo Rebellion and in the Hiatus in Spanish Rule, 1680-1692

Fortunately for the Spaniards, Governor Otermín received advance warning of the rebellion from loyal Pueblo chiefs, and this first word of impending violence indicated that the Apaches were in league with the Pueblo rebels (Hackett 1942 I: 4). Most of the statements concerning Apaches in the documents bearing on the revolt of 1680 consist of general references to this Apache-Pueblo alliance or express the fear that it will take place. The only Southern Athabascans mentioned specifically were the Acho Apaches of northeastern New Mexico, who were said to have joined with the Indians of Taos and Picurís in killing the Spanish residents in that area (Hackett 1942 I: 98).

The Indians from Pecos and other Pueblos southeast of Santa

Fé came to attack the Spanish capital expecting reinforcements who were to include Tewas, Taos, and Picurís Indians and their Apache allies (Hackett 1942 I: 13). Moreover, a leader of the Pueblo Indians who beseiged the town demanded among other things that "all the Apache men and women whom the Spaniards had captured in war be turned over to them" (Hackett 1942 I: 99). Otermín did not think any Apaches were involved and probably not many were, for a few days later the attackers were still "expecting" help from the Apaches (Hackett 1942 I: 99, 102). However, when the Spaniards finally managed to regain control of Santa Fé, some Apaches were apparently found among the dead besiegers (Forbes 1960: 180).

Forced to retreat to El Paso, the remnants of the New Mexico colony thought they were being watched constantly by Apache spies en route. In fact, Governor Otermín declared that the Apaches were responsible for the loss of New Mexico because they had long tried to persuade the Pueblo Indians to rebel and had weakened Spanish domination through their own constant attacks (Forbes 1960: 182). At El Paso, Otermín's charges, forbidden to desert the colony, settled down to a dreary life that was made difficult by crop failures and also became dangerous as the Apaches shifted their attacks to that area—because of their hatred for the Spaniards or because the El Paso area had, with the arrival of the New Mexico colony, become a more profitable source of loot (Forbes 1960: 185, 190).

Another reason for the southward shift of Apache activity came out in the testimony of a Jumano slave who escaped to the Spaniards in 1682. He said that large numbers of Plains Apaches who lived as much as 200 leagues to the east were raiding for horses on the frontiers of Sonora and also obtaining them from the Gila Apaches in trade. Apparently these Plain Apaches had formerly traded with the Spaniards in New Mexico for horses, which had become essential to them for warfare and hunting, but with the departure of the New Mexico colony they had been forced to find another source of supply (Forbes 1960: 191). The Plains Apaches referred to may well have been the Faraons, who by 1692 were ranging as far west as Acoma.

The years following 1680 saw the efforts of the displaced colonists directed alternately toward circumventing Apache depredations in the northern provinces of New Spain and toward reconquering the lost kingdom of New Mexico. In the south, as they had in the north, the Apaches entered into anti-Spanish conspiracies with other native groups, including so-called Mexican border tribes such as the Mansos, Sumas, Janos, and Jocomes (Forbes 1960: 190–235), eventually becoming so closely allied and intermarried with these people that the Spaniards, in referring to them, sometimes used compound names such as "Apache Mansos," leading some authors to conclude erroneously that the Mexican border tribes were themselves Athabascans (cf. D. Gunnerson 1960: 315–16). As for the situation in the north, the Spaniards based their hope of reclaiming New Mexico on the possibility that the Apaches would so harass the Pueblos that the latter would welcome the return of the Europeans as a lesser evil.

Fray Francisco de Ayeta had the opinion that even with the Spaniards in control and in times of peace, the Pueblo Indians were virtually the slaves of the Apaches, who mistreated them "by word and deed" if the Pueblos did not give the Apaches what they wanted. He said the Pueblo Indians were afraid to complain to the officials for fear the Apaches would come back and kill them (Hackett 1942 II: 307). The Spaniards fully expected that after their departure the Apaches would totally destroy the Pueblos.

Apaches did give some Pueblos trouble before Otermín's return, apparently harassing those least active in the revolt, so that Indians from such villages "denounced the leaders of the rebellion, saying that when the Spaniards were among them they lived in security and quiet, and afterwards with much uneasiness" (Hackett 1942 II: 240). A Piro Indian who had lived at Socorro testified that the Apaches had "ambushed" it twice while he was there (Hackett 1942 II: 243).

When Otermín attempted to reconquer New Mexico in 1681, the Pueblo groups he encountered emphasized their fear of Apaches whenever it served their purposes, but apparently the Apaches had done little actual harm. At Isleta the Indians gave battle, but seeing they could not win, they surrendered. "They excused themselves for having taken up arms by saying that they had believed themselves ambushed by the Apaches" (Hackett 1942 II: 208). They also stated that rebels from the more north-ern Pueblos were plotting to kill the Isleta men and give the women and children to Apaches as gifts of friendship (Hackett 1942 II: 330).

Otermín sent out an advance party which encountered a large number of the Indian rebels on a hill near the Pueblo of Cochití. They asked for peace, and the Spanish granted it.

> As for their arms, they did not give them up, saying, I believe maliciously, that in the sierras they were in great fear of the Apache enemies; and so that they might not be stirred up, I did not ask for them. On the other hand, I learned afterwards that some of them had asked for powder so that the Apaches might not harm them. (Hackett 1942 II: 263)

Actually, further events proved that the rebels had no intention of making peace or abiding by the terms of surrender that they had agreed to, so their fear of the Apaches had been merely an excuse to retain their arms and get more powder to use against the Spaniards.

Finding himself still unable to cope with the Pueblo rebels in 1681, Otermín withdrew once more to El Paso. The observations of those who had accompanied him to New Mexico are well stated by Father Ayeta.

> It has been experienced and seen that the Apaches have not de-stroyed any pueblo or even damaged one seriously. It happened that, although during the discussions of peace to which the apostates invited them they spent some months in dances, fiestas, and entertainments, in the end the Apaches were unwilling to accept it and left, still at war, as in fact they are at present; and it is seen that this notwithstanding, they [the Pueblo tribes] . . . have maintained themselves without the Spaniards. (Hack-ett 1942 II: 308)

But there was plenty of violence in New Mexico during the *hiatus* in Spanish rule, as Father Escalante indicated in his con-cise history of 1778.

The rebellious pueblos of New Mexico became inflamed one against the other and began to wage war. The Queres, Taos, and Pecos fought against the Tehuas and Tanos. . . . The Apaches were at peace with some of these pueblos, and in others inflicted all the damage they could. The Yutas, when they heard of the misfortune of the Spaniards (1680) [parentheses in original] waged unceasing war upon the Jemez, Taos, and Picuriés; and even with greater vigor upon the Tehuas, among whom they made formidable incursions. Not alone with this and with their civil wars were all the apostates afflicted but also by famine and pestilence. The Queres and Jemez finished off the Piros and Tihuas who remained after the invasion by Otermín because they considered them friendly to the Spaniards. Of the Tihuas there only escaped some families which retired to the province of Aloqui (*Moqui*) [parentheses in original]; of the Piros none whatever. (Twitchell 1914 II: 276–77)

After 1680, their repressed resentments against one another having mounted steadily for nearly a century, the Pueblo Indians were free to express overtly hostilities that had existed in latent form as far back as Spanish records on New Mexico are available. And if the internecine Pueblo warfare of the 1680s is used as a basis for comparison, Apache aggressiveness does not present nearly so marked a contrast.

With the Spaniards gone from New Mexico, the near-hiatus in contemporary records of activity there allows time out to consider how much the Spaniards knew of the country where the Jicarilla Apaches and allied bands were later found during or shortly after the Reconquest. Zárate-Salmerón and others in his time (1626) had known that there was a pass to the Plains by way of Taos and through the lands of the Quinia Apaches. In 1630 Benavides said that the Apaches extended to the north so far that the Spaniards had not found the end of them, and that the Vaqueros, or Plains Apaches, extended to the east more than a hundred leagues (Ayer 1916: 41, 56). Moreover, Benavides enumerates some culture traits, in addition to language, that were apparently common to all Apache bands by 1630. Among these traits, significantly, was small-scale horticulture.

They do not dwell in settlements, nor in houses, but in tents and huts, forasmuch as they move from mountain range to range, seeking game, which is their sustenance. However, each hut of a principal or individual has its recognized land on which they plant corn and other seeds. They go clad in *gamuzas*, which are the skins of deer, very well tanned and adorned in their fashion, and the women gallantly and honestly clad. They have no more idolatry than that of the Sun, and even that is not general to all of (them); and they scoff much at the other nations which have idols. They are wont to have the (as many) wives as they can support; and upon her whom they take in adultery they irremissably execute their law, which is to cut off her ears and nose; and they repudiate her. They are very obedient to their elders (*mayores;* also superiors) and hold them in great respect. They teach and chastise their children (which is a) difference from the other nations, who have no chastisement whatever. They pride themselves much on speaking the truth, and hold for dishonored him whom they catch in a lie. (Ayer 1916: 40; see also H, H & R 1945: 80–81)

Later, beginning with the exploration of La Salle in 1680, French activities along the Mississippi River and on the Gulf coast began to trouble Spanish authorities. When, in addition, Diego de Peñalosa, the notorious ex-governor of New Mexico, persisted in trying to sell himself and his knowledge of the interior provinces to the French, the Council of the Indies requested information on the lands beyond New Mexico. The man who prepared the desired report was Fray Alonso de Posada, who had served in New Mexico from 1650 to 1665 and had acquired information about the lands from the "infidel Indians" (T & T 1958: 288), who were probably mainly Apaches.

Fray Alonso's report indicates that before 1665, expeditions had crossed the Plains from New Mexico to the lands of the Texas or Caddo Indians on the southeast and to the land of Quivira on the northeast. Posada knew something of the nature and extent of the mountains northeast of Santa Fé (see Hackett 1931–1946 IV: 381), and he knew that Apaches lived "along" at least part of these mountains, which he called the Sierra Blancas, as well as on the Plains. Since the friar seemed to be including the northern part of the present Sangre de Cristo Range in the Sierra Blancas, he must have known of the proto-Jicarillas as well as of the Carlana or Sierra Blanca Apaches in the mountains of southeastern Colorado.

The Spaniards still did not know the details of the river systems between the Rocky Mountains and the Mississippi nor were the relationships of some of these streams to be straightened out until the nineteenth century. However, Posada's comments on the country to the northeast and the east, along with his comments on the Apaches of that area and their neighbors, fill to some extent the gap resulting from the destruction of seventeenth-century documents, set the stage onto which the Eastern Apaches emerge after the Reconquest, and reinforce beyond question the indications given by Benavides that the Southern Athabascans were different from various tribes with whom they have been confused.

Posada used Santa Fé as a point of reference for giving directions and distances. He located Santa Fé, "the center of New Mexico," at thirty-seven degrees north latitude (it is actually at about thirty-six). He stated that "north of Santa Fé, at thirty-eight and thirty-nine degrees there are some mountain ranges from which rivers flow both east and west. . . . Of course, those which flow east are the larger and longer." Again he said that "in a northerly direction from Santa Fé," beyond some "hills" located at thirty-eight or thirty-nine degrees,

> at a distance of thirty to forty leagues, is a very high mountain range called *Sierra Blanca*, and farther on in the same direction at fifty-four degrees there are some high and inaccessible mountains which are covered with perpetual snows and are therefore called the *Sierras Nevadas*. . . . They are very wide on the eastern end and come almost to those settlements of foreign nations that are northeast of Florida. . . . The *Sierra Blanca* . . . is between the *Sierras Nevadas* and the eastern region. (T & T 1958: 297–98)

Posada's distances were probably more accurate than his latitudes. At 2.6 to 2.7 miles per league, his "Sierra Blanca" would have begun about eighty miles northeast of Santa Fé, at or beyond present Cimarrón, and would have continued on into the Ratón-Trinidad area, where the main range of the Rockies still bore the name "Sierra Blanca" past the mid-1800s. The Spaniards had evidently noted the marked northeastward trend of the mountains that begins south of Cimarrón, and at Ratón continues, although in attenuated form, as far eastward as the eastern boundary of New Mexico, along the Colorado–New Mexico line.

This low, east-west running mountain spur was specifically identified as part of the Sierra Blanca in eighteenth-century documents to be discussed later.

Posada's comments on the Apaches, which were not improved
upon as a summary statement until the late 1700s, if then, are too
important to be paraphrased.

> So that it may be seen that there can be some trustworthy in-
> formation it should be noted that the Apacha nation possesses
> and controls all the plains of *sibola*. The Indians of this nation
> are so haughty and arrogant and so proud as warriors that they
> are the common enemy of all the tribes below the northern re-
> gions (immediately surrounding New Mexico). They have
> struck fear to all other tribes and have overrun, ruined and cast
> most of them out of their own lands. This tribe occupies, de-
> fends and considers itself owner of four hundred leagues of land
> east and west and two hundred leagues north and south. In some
> places along their borders they claim even more territory. Its
> center (that of the Apacha nation) is the plains of Sibola. This
> nation is confined on the east by the Quiviras (in southern Kan-
> sas) with whom they are now and have been continually at war.
> In the same region (the Apacha nation) also borders on the
> Texas nation with whom they have always had war. Although
> the Quivira and Texas nations are wide and have many people,
> the Apacha nation in the interior (around Santa Fé) bordering
> these nations along two hundred leagues as mentioned, has not
> only kept it boundaries (inviolate) but has invaded those of the
> other nations.

> When your informant (Posada) was Minister in the town of
> Pecos a camp of Apacha Indians entered the town to sell hides
> of antelope and leather and brought with them some captive
> Indian children from Quivira to trade for horses. When they
> were asked several different times if they had ever gotten some
> earrings or bracelets of gold and silver (they always wear these
> adornments on the left arm) [parentheses in original] on raids
> in Quivira or Texas, they agreed to a man that while they had
> killed important captains and many ordinary Indians too, who
> were from these nations, none had found on the bodies any such
> things (adornments). They said they had found many buffalo
> skins, elk and antelope hides, maize and fruits. They also said that
> all the inhabitants of those lands, the women as well as the men,
> dressed in skins (*gamuza*). From these reports one sees that there
> isn't as much gold and silver as is reported.

> From the east to the west through the southern region, the
> Apacha nation borders the following: after the Texas, the Ahi-
> jados, the Cuytoas and the Escanjaques in a fifty league district

(in southeastern New Mexico and Texas). Since these are the ones that live along the *Nueces* River the Apacha nation has caused them to retreat to the district of the *Río del Norte,* a district of little less than one hundred leagues. After these nations there comes the Jumana tribe and the others mentioned at the *Junta de los Ríos Norte* and *Conchos.* These also (the Apaches have) dispossessed from their lands by the *Nueces* River and cornered in said spot due to the hostility of war. They also sustain a war with the Desumanas, Sumas, Mansos and others that are living between the Junction of the *Norte* and *Conchos* rivers on the banks of the *Río del Norte* to the Mission of Our Lady of Guadalupe (present *Ciudad Juárez*). They also keep the Spanish garrison there very busy and in the same region all the tribes toward Sonora, such as the Jamos and the Carretas, whom they also have dispossessed, and toward Sonora they attack them right from the mountains, however they do it even more from the area about fifty leagues to the north. The Apacha nation has some very fertile and pleasant parcels of land and meadows where many Apachas live. This is in the *Sierra Azul,* a range renowned for its riches because its metals have been shown so many times but never taken (that is, fully explored and extracted) because of our neglect and luke-warm attitude.

In the same region the Apacha nation wars against and greatly harms the Sipias nation, which nation is located north of Sinaloa and Sonora and south of the Apachas. The Mission of Our Lady of Guadalupe must be one hundred leagues to the east of *el Cuartelejo.* . . . From there the Apacha nation continues on the said east-west trail in the southern region, to the nation of Coninas. This Coninas tribe is completely subjugated to the Apachas. Passing from south to north about seventy leagues along the river called the Grande (where it has been said there are metals and quicksilver) [parentheses in original] behind the towns of Moquy, looking eastward a distance of twenty leagues one comes to the Yutas nation, which comes before Teguayo.

The Yutas nation reaches near the South Sea (Pacific Ocean). These Indians are fond of the Spaniard, are well built, brave and energetic, for only these (Yutas) carry on campaigns against the valiant Apachas with a courage equal (to the courage of the Apachas). They are so steady in battle that through diligent persistence and to maintain their honorable reputation they do not retreat without winning or dying. The *Grande* River (here the San Juan and Colorado) divides Yuta and Apacha. This river guided Don Juan de Oñate to the South Sea (Pacific).

The Apacha nation continues along the Sierra Blanca, *which is farther on, in the mountains north of New Mexico* [italics mine]. Continuing from west to east in a northerly direction these (Apachas) are bordered by the Quivira nation at a distance of fifty leagues. These (the Quivira) are on the other side of that *Grande* River (here the Arkansas) which rises in the *Sierras Nevadas*. On this as well as the other side of the river the Quivira Nation expands greatly. The Apachas are also at war along the frontier they share with the Quiviras.

All the mountain ranges which are within and surrounding New Mexican provinces are considered by the Apachas as their property. The Apachas are so constantly at war with them that usually the Spaniards carry arms. They attack the Indian pueblos from previously prepared ambushes killing the men atrociously and carrying off the women and children as legitimate captives of war. They usually destroy their enemies' corn fields and steal Spanish horses day and night wreaking all other damages their fierce pride can plot. The Indians of this nation who live in the eastern province of New Mexico have and have always had particular care in maintaining peace with the Spaniards in order that they might have commerce with them, having an outlet for their dressed skins and hides. In other areas these same Indians who inhabit said mountains surrounding New Mexico are continually at war with the Spaniards.

This nation, as already mentioned, is the owner and possessor of all the plains of *sibola*, and the center of the above-mentioned nations. It is not governed by chiefs or hereditary princes, but rather by those who give proof in war of being the bravest. They use no (idols?) or other base superstitions and only adore the sun with the veneration of a father, for they say they are the children of the sun. They clothe themselves in dressed skins, always wearing shoes, boots and jackets which they take pride in keeping clean. On their travels they carry only bows and arrows. The arrows are sharp and well made and the bows are well proportioned after the Turkish manner. The very sight of such arms distinguishes this tribe from the others. They have wives that they hold in especial esteem and when a woman is caught in adultery they cut her nose to mark her as an adulteress. (T & T 1958: 300–303)

It is of special interest that Posada used the word "cuartelejo" in 1686 (T & T 1958: 306) to describe, apparently, an area containing settlements of huts belonging to Indians who lived far southwest of Santa Fé. Such usage suggests that the term El Cuartelejo, which was applied to the Apache country on the plains bordering Quivira in 1662, could have been used because the Apaches who lived in that area had semi-permanent villages of huts at the time.

Unlike such missionaries as Zárate-Salmerón and Benavides, Posada pointed out honestly that there was no evidence to support the notion that silver and gold were to be found in New Mexico or beyond it in Quivira. Hence, it was not avarice that moved Spanish officials to arrange for the reconquest of New Mexico, but a desire to use it, like Texas, as a buffer province to guard the proved silver mines of Northern Mexico against the French.

Chapter Five

The Apaches
in the Reconquest
of New Mexico, 1692–1700

On 18 June 1688, the king appointed Don Diego de Vargas, descendant of one of Spain's noblest families, governor and captain general of New Mexico for five years. Vargas, who had proved his ability as soldier and administrator in Mexico, took over the government at El Paso on 22 February 1691, with the intention of reconquering New Mexico immediately and at his own expense. He planned a preliminary *entrada* to reconnoiter and to subdue the rebels, if necessary, before actually recolonizing the province (J. Espinosa 1940: 31–42), and on 16 August 1692, this expedition got under way (J. Espinosa 1940: 51–52). When Vargas arrived at Santa Fé and, on 13 September, offered the Pueblo Indians living there pardon, they replied that "when the Span-

iards formerly lived in this kingdom they offered peace to the
Apaches and then hunted them down and killed them, and that
I [Vargas] would treat them in like manner" (J. Espinosa 1940:
82). From this accusation, with which a Pueblo leader had also
faced one of Otermín's officers in 1681, it can be judged how
deeply the Spanish betrayal of friendly Apache groups in the
mid-1600s had disturbed the Pueblo people. And everywhere,
Vargas encountered evidence that many of the Pueblos were allied with one or another of the Apache tribes. When the Indians
living at Santa Fé finally surrendered, Don Luís, a Picurís and
one of the principal leaders of the rebels, sent word to Vargas
that he could not come to see him until the next day, because "he
had gone to see the Navajo Apaches, who had sent for him"
(J. Espinosa 1940: 98).

Don Luís, head of the Tewas, Tanos, and Picurís, asked Vargas to mediate between his people and their enemies, the Pecos,
Taos, and Faraon Apaches (J. Espinosa 1940: 106). Later, Don
Lorenzo, the brother of Don Luís and governor of Picurís
Pueblo, added Jémez and the Keres Indians of San Felipe, Santo
Domingo, and Cochití to this list of enemies (J. Espinosa 1940:
110). When Vargas went to Pecos, however, Indians of that
pueblo told his emissary that they did not want peace and the
friendship of the Spaniards—rather than surrender, some of them
would go to live with the Taos and others with the Apaches
(J. Espinosa 1940: 132).

On the eighth of October, the governor of Taos revealed to
Vargas that there had been a three-day meeting near Acoma of
the Zuñi, Moqui, Jémez, Keres, Pecos, Faraon Apaches, and the
Coninas of the Cerro Colorado, and they were plotting to am-
bush the Spaniards (J. Espinosa 1940: 155). Vargas arrived at
Jémez on 21 October and found the natives armed, and some
engaged in a war dance. He betrayed no fear and was not attacked but was invited to eat in an upper room of the pueblo.

> After this I went out, and various Apaches came out from the
> said house and rendered obedience, and in the corridor I spoke
> to them, telling them that I would return next year, if God, our
> Lord, gives me life, and that they should tell their tribe and

ranchería that if they are not Christians I do not want their friendship, and that what I said was to their interest, and they said that they were happy. I assumed, since they had the said Apaches separated in the said house and many others in those of the second plaza, that the report given by the Taos concerning the afore-mentioned council was true. (J. Espinosa 1940: 181)

At Acoma the Indians were reluctant to parley with the Spaniards, saying that "for the present they were very much afraid because they stood alone, having as friends only the Navajo Apaches," who would advise them (J. Espinosa 1940: 191). Later they admitted that two Manso Indians and some Apaches had warned them not to make peace because the Spaniards would have them all beheaded and hanged (J. Espinosa 1940: 192). The Acomas had, however, warned the Spaniards waiting near their mesa to beware of the Apaches, who intended to kill them (J. Espinosa 1940: 190).

The morning before Vargas arrived at Zuñi (11 November) Faraon Apaches drove off some cattle belonging to the expedition (J. Espinosa 1940: 200). The presence of Faraons in this area in 1692 is noteworthy because after 1700, Faraons are mentioned only in connection with localities farther east. While he was at Zuñi, Vargas heard of another attempt by Apaches to interfere with his plans. Navajos had warned the Hopi Indians that under the guise of peace the Spaniards would kill them and carry off their wives and children. (J. Espinosa 1940: 204).

Added to this evidence of communication between the Hopis and Navajos is another incident that casts light on Zuñi-Apache relations. Some "Salinero" Apaches arrived at Zuñi on November thirteenth and told Vargas through an interpreter that they were friends of the Zuñis and always entered there in peace. Moreover, they wished to be friends of the Spaniards. Vargas suggested that the Salineros could show their friendship for him by killing the Faraon Apaches, who had driven off some of his cattle. The Salinero captain, somewhat taken aback, said he had come to reassure Vargas that no Apaches would harm him on his way to the Hopi Pueblos (J. Espinosa 1940: 205). The Hopis had assembled in force, armed and ready, but Vargas was able to avoid battle. At the Pueblo of Walpi the Hopis had among them numerous warriors of other tribes, including Utes and Apaches, "their neighbors and allies" (J. Espinosa 1940: 220).

Back at Zuñi and ready to leave for the Río Grande, Vargas was warned that Apaches were lurking in wait for him. During the journey he acquired some information about the Apaches in the area when his guide pointed out a mountain called the Peña Larga, saying that the Apaches Colorados who lived there planted maize (J. Espinosa 1940: 238). On the way to El Paso, Vargas saw some fleeing Apaches and pursued them. In the resulting fight, one Apache was killed, and another was captured and executed but not before he had been baptized (J. Espinosa 1940: 250). Except for this incident, Vargas had committed no acts of violence on the entire trip, during which all the Pueblos of New Mexico had agreed to submit once again to Spanish rule.

In his report to the viceroy in Mexico City, Vargas said:

> The natives of the Zuñi tribe . . . have abandoned their five pueblos on account of the Apaches, their enemies, so that they might live in safety, slavishly reconciled to the repeated raids made by different rancherías, who eat their food supplies and upon leaving take with them the horses of their choice. (J. Espinosa 1940: 266)

He estimated that to hold New Mexico it would be necessary to place one hundred settlers at Taos *"where the Apaches continually make their entry* [italics mine], and fifty families at Pecos, also an Apache frontier" (J. Espinosa 1940: 285). Impatient to return to New Mexico with colonists, Vargas had to wait while men were recruited and the expedition was equipped. The government in Mexico City was slow to supply aid, but on 4 October 1693, a caravan finally started north from El Paso (J. Espinosa 1942: 128–31).

Although the Pueblos had agreed to a Spanish reoccupation in 1692 when Vargas visited them, they had used the time before his return in 1693 to form an alliance against him. But the Pecos and their friends the Faraon Apaches refused to join, possibly because they wished to resume trade relations with the Spaniards. The Keres Pueblos, except for Cochití and Santo Domingo, also decided on peace, probably because Zia and Santa Ana had been severely punished during previous Spanish attempts to reconquer New Mexico. All the other Pueblos and their Apache allies were determined to resist, however (Forbes 1960: 250), and although they did not immediately oppose Vargas with organized troops, the Spaniards were beset by major and minor intrigues and up-risings between 1693 and 1700 as a result of Pueblo hostility. As usual, the Pueblos were divided among themselves, but the alignments were not exactly the same as they had been when Vargas made his first trip north. For example, many of the Zuñis had joined the highly belligerent Jémez because the Zuñis were enemies of the Keres Pueblos of Zia, Santa Ana, and San Felipe which feared to resist the Spaniards. The Hopis, allied with Utes and Coninas Apaches as well as with other unspecified Apache groups, had attacked Zuñi (Bailey 1940: 133). Here old enmity may have flared up, for the Zuñis had been hostile toward the Hopis as early as the time of Coronado's *entrada*.

Having established a temporary camp near present Bernalillo, the returning colonists proceeded to reconnoiter. Near San Felipe Pueblo on 15 November 1693, Vargas was told that some Tanos and Tewas had succeeded in persuading the Indians in that vicinity to join the Taos, Picurís, Apaches of the Colorado River (present Red River north of Taos), and the Navajos in an attack on the Spaniards (J. Espinosa 1942: 137). The attack did not materialize, and the Picurís captains, Luís and Lorenzo, came with some of their followers to see the governor, "excusing their full armament with the statement that they had expected raiding Apaches" (Bailey 1940: 100). Don Luís explained his failure to come earlier by saying that he had been trading for deerskins with the Apaches, adding that his brother Lorenzo had been on the Buffalo Plains (J. Espinosa 1942: 138). The latter fact is of special interest because it was Don Lorenzo who, in 1696, took many of his own people, along with some Tewas, to the Buffalo Plains to live. The Cochití Indians, who had moved to a place in their vicinity called La Cieneguilla, received Vargas peacefully for the time being. They complained of Apache enemies against whom Vargas agreed to help them in the future (Forbes 1960: 251), suggesting that meanwhile at Cochití they replace their ramshackle habitations with wooden houses for protection against their enemies, apparently the Apaches who inhabited the hills near Socorro (Bailey 1940: 102).

On December seventeenth, the Spaniards reoccupied Santa Fé. The governor of the friendly Pecos Indians was in the town on 4 January 1694, at which time a Faraon Apache came to warn him that a large group of still rebellious Pueblo people with Apache allies were only two leagues from Pecos Pueblo. Vargas sent thirty soldiers to deal with this situation, but no battle took place (Forbes 1960: 253).

In February 1694, Spanish soldiers taking supplies from the abandoned Tewa Pueblo of Tesuque encountered a group of Apaches who had just stolen fourteen horses at Santa Fé. All but one were from the lower Río Grande area (Forbes 1960: 253). The other, whom the soldiers captured, was "from a group of those from the Río Colorado [Red River] who had five tents on the Chama River, from whence they had been making raids on the Spanish horses" (J. Espinosa 1942: 169). Thus these Apache allies of the Taos from the Red River were ranging west of the Río Grande in 1694.

In March, some Plains Apaches came to Pecos Pueblo and learned that the Spaniards had returned to New Mexico. On the twenty-seventh of that month the governor of Pecos, Juan de Ye, brought three of these Apaches to Santa Fé, where they told Vargas that their people had previously had friendly relations with the Spaniards and that they wanted to make arrangements for bartering the next October. Vargas, probably more than happy to renew the Plains trade that had been so important to the Spaniards before the Pueblo Rebellion, sent some of his men back to Pecos to convince the Apaches waiting there of his good will (J. Espinosa 1942: 177; Forbes 1960: 254). The rebellious Jémez had joined the Navajos and Apaches, and the Tewa rebels, too, had Apache allies, probably those also friendly to Taos and Picurís (e.g., Forbes 1960: 253). However, the Tewas of San Juan, at least, felt themselves to be menaced in the spring of 1694 by Apache enemies (Bailey 1940: 130–31). Apparently their leading part in the rebellion of 1680 and their continuing resistance to the Spaniards during the Reconquest did not exempt the Tewas from attacks by some of the Apaches, probably the Navajos who had been raiding them for nearly a century.

On 2 May, the governor of Pecos Pueblo brought in the chief of some Faraon Apaches from the Plains, who expressed his wish to become a Christian and insisted on being baptized. He told the Spaniards that his people wished to be civilized and that it would be best to destroy all the enemy rebels (Pueblos) (Bailey 1940: 140–42). Some details concerning Plains Apaches who may have been Faraons were recorded by Vargas on 2 May 1694, when

> Governor Ye of the Pecos and one of the principal chiefs of the Plains Apaches (Faraones), accompanied by eight warriors, arrived at Santa Fe. The Athapascan chief brought three very beautifully decorated buffalo skins and a fine tipi as a gift for Vargas, who was extremely pleased with them. The Apaches sought permission to hold another fair during the *"tiempo de elote"* ("when the corn begins to ripen") [parentheses in original]. The Governor of New Mexico took advantage of the opportunity to ply his visitor with questions about lands to the east. He learned that it was ten days to the buffalo and fourteen days to the chief's villages and that there was a small hill near by. The first settlements of the Kingdom of Texas were said to be seven days away from the chief's village, and the land in that area contained many buffalo. In reply to the question of whether or not there were any Spaniards in the Texas area, the chief declared that there had been some in past years but he did not know of any there now. The chief said that it was twenty-five or thirty days from his village to the first settlements of Quivira and that his people knew the distance well because they made wars there in order to capture children to sell for horses. The Apache chief spent two days in Santa Fe, and then he and Ye departed, because they each had to attend to the sowing of their fields, thus indicating that these particular Apaches were at least semiagricultural. Upon their departure, Vargas wrote that he was much impressed with the Athapascan leader, *"aunque gentil, y atheista sin Dios, sin Ley, y sin Rey, mostraba ser hombre de bien, de realidad, de ynteligenzia, y de razon."* (Forbes 1960: 255–56)

This episode affords the first specific reference to horticulture among the primarily buffalo-hunting Apaches of the Plains. It also indicates that the settlements of Quivira still existed in 1694 under the same name and that Plains Apaches were still capturing children in Quivira to trade for horses in New Mexico, as they had in Father Posada's time (1650s). Through all the turmoil in New Mexico the Apaches had remained masters of the Plains, although the acquisition of horses and horticulture must have caused numerous changes in their way of life.

Additional information on the mountain Apaches north of Taos was recorded when, early in July 1694, Vargas was forced to go to Taos to get food supplies. He found the pueblo deserted; however, there were crosses on the houses and in the maize fields, which he interpreted as signs that the Taos people wished to be friendly but were afraid because of their previous hostility. On the road the Spaniards met Apaches who gave up their weapons to indicate friendship. The Apache leader said his people were encamped nearby to trade with the Taos. These Apaches went with Vargas to parley with the Taos Indians, who were fortified near their pueblo, but the latter would not give in. It was said that the Taos had Apache allies among them and were expecting reinforcements from the Colorado River (probably Acho Apaches). Since the Indians would not make peace, the Spaniards took whatever food they wanted from the pueblo and departed (Bailey 1940: 149–52; J. Espinosa 1942: 190–93).

Because they were carrying heavy loads of Taos grain, they became highly vulnerable to surprise attack. They decided, after consultation, to return to Santa Fé by a roundabout way that would take them northward through Ute country, thus avoiding the difficult mountain passes on the Picurís route where they knew rebels were hiding (J. Espinosa 1936: 184). Moreover, older members of the expedition who had lived in New Mexico before the rebellion said the Utes had always been friends of the Spaniards and that it would be a good time to renew friendly trade relations (J. Espinosa 1942: 193–94). Leaving his camp near Taos, Vargas went ten leagues to the Río Colorado. An entry in his diary reads:

> On the eighth of the present month of July of this year, I, said governor and captain-general, called upon the interpreters of this expedition, and they informed me that the mountains that run along the edge of the Río Colorado are inhabited by the Apaches del Acho, and that the Ute nation, which we are looking for,

does not countenance them in their land, for which reason I should flee from this place, which is also the farthest point to which the rebel Taos Indians, who still have sentinels and spies watching us, come out on the trail of the buffalo, the dung of which has been found in different parts, as along the descents from the mountain to the river. (J. Espinosa 1936: 185 *n*25)

Nine long leagues north of the Río Colorado was the Culebra River, on which Vargas camped. Four long leagues to the west, the Culebra River emptied into the Río Grande (J. Espinosa 1936: 185).

From this record, then, we learn that the Acho Apaches, who had joined the Taos Indians in the rebellion of 1680 and presumably helped them kill the Spaniards in their vicinity, lived on the Red River north of Taos and that the Utes, who apparently lived across the Río Grande to the west of them, were their enemies, as stated by Father Posada in 1686. It is noteworthy also that the Acho shared their hunting territory with the Taos, who thus had access to buffalo without going out onto the Plains. Indeed, on their way home Vargas's party found approximately five hundred head of buffalo in the vicinity of San Antonio Mountain west of the Río Grande, and the Utes they finally met told them that since 1690, the Tewas, Tanos, Picurís, Jémez, and Keres Indians, had often come north dressed like Spaniards to hunt buffalo (Forbes 1960: 257). At this time, then, bison in significant numbers were ranging not only west of the Sangre de Cristos but west of the Río Grande.

It would appear that the Río Colorado Apaches mentioned in documents bearing on the Reconquest also lived on the Red River north of Taos. The vagueness of some Spanish references obscures the relationship of these two bands, if they were separate, allowing various possibilities. (1) The Río Colorado Apaches may have been a band that shared the Red River country with the Achos. (2) Río Colorado may have been an alternative name for the Achos that was sometimes used along with Acho to indicate geographical location (as in the case of the Carlana y Sierra Blanca Apaches). (3) The Río Colorado Apaches may have been a specific division of a larger group called Achos. In any case both names are associated with the same territory and designate Apaches who were friends and allies of the Taos Indians.

Three days after he returned from the Taos trip, Vargas began another campaign against the rebels. At Santo Domingo he learned that the Jémez, Cochití, and the Navajos had struck at Zía. At Jémez Vargas fought Pueblo rebels, and among the captives he ordered shot was an Apache (J. Espinosa 1942: 200). On 28 August 1694, the Pecos war captains made it known that Plains Apaches had again invited them to trade and suggested that the Spaniards go along (J. Espinosa 1942: 204).

In May 1695, some "Apaches de los Chipaynes," who were trading at Picurís, said that white men had defeated a tribe of Conejero Apaches who lived farther inland from them (J. Espinosa 1942: 227, 229). This news caused Spanish officials to suspect immediately that the French were moving toward New Mexico. When the band of Chipaynes, whose tribe was later said to be the same as the Faraon Apaches (Thomas 1935: 80–81), returned to Picurís in late September, they were questioned carefully by the *alcalde* or chief magistrate of the Pueblo to determine whether the white men to whom they had referred in May were French or Spanish. On 29 September the *alcalde* of Picurís, Captain Mathias Luján, reported the results of the interrogation to Luís Granillo in Santa Fé; Granillo, in turn, reported to Vargas who was away from Santa Fé at the time. "The news which the Apaches bring is that a large number of French are coming toward the plains of Cibola; That the Apaches are retreating to this neighborhood on account of the frequent attacks made on them by the French" (Hodge 1929: 73). However, in the same letter Granillo said, "I have already caused the said Captain Lujan to return to his alcaldia with orders to examine the said Apaches to ascertain whence come these people whom they describe as French or Spanish, and how many leagues or days' journey they may be from this town" (Hodge 1929: 73). On 4 October two Apaches gave information through interpreters who spoke their language, including two Spaniards, one of whom was the *alcalde* of Picurís himself.

They said that seven nations beyond the region where they live, very far from these parts, had informed them that certain white men came to the bank of the water and made war on the people of Quivira . . . and other parts, and presently they go away, and again return and make war and go away, and that it is very far off, and that they have not seen them, and that they have this report from other nations hostile to them, giving to understand that they who have given them the said information are their enemies and slaves. (Hodge 1929: 76)

In the end it appears that the New Mexico Spaniards were left uncertain as to the identity of the white men in question. However, the information given by the Apaches in both the spring and fall of 1695 was probably substantially true, for there were Conejero Apaches in eastern New Mexico by 1706 who may well have retreated to that area from the eastern plains in 1695. This withdrawal of the Conejeros to New Mexico may have marked the beginning of the convergence there of most of the Plains Apache tribes. Nor is it unlikely that the white men attacking both Quivira and Apaches of the eastern Buffalo Plains in 1695 were the French, since Canadian traders were among the Osages and Missouris by 1694 (Thomas 1935: 13). It may have been in alliance with the Osages, bitter enemies of the Caddoan tribes (Hodge 1907–1910 II: 157), that "Frenchmen" attacked the Wichitas of Quivira in 1695 and Jumanos (Wichitas) in 1700 (Escalante 1962: 413). The French, who were interested primarily in trade, apparently managed to advance across the Plains from one tribe to another by a series of alliances with former enemies. By 1706, individual Frenchmen were accompanying the Pawnees on raids against the principal village of the Cuartelejo Apaches in western Kansas and were probably also allied at this time with their former enemies the Jumanos (Wichitas), by then enemies of the Cuartelejos. But in 1724 Bourgmont made a treaty with "Padoucas" (Margry 1875–1886 VI: 398–449) who were probably Cuartelejo Apaches, and subsequently in 1727, Frenchmen were said to have accompanied these Apaches on an expedition in search of the Comanches (Thomas 1935: 256). In any case, fear of French encroachment aroused by the news the Chipayne Apaches brought to Picurís in 1695 caused the New

Mexicans to begin considering the defense of their eastern frontier. The close of this year also saw the Spanish colonists in want
from their inability to cope with the New Mexico environment,
and their problems were further increased when, in 1696, several
of the Pueblos revolted again. Once more the Apaches were said
to be involved, but if so, they remained in the background
(Bailey 1940: 228, 236, 237, 238, 239, 241), serving more as a
refuge for Pueblo rebels than as active fighters.

This time Pecos was divided into faction for and against the
Spaniards, and in July 1696 the priest was withdrawn from the
Pueblo because the Indians were acting strangely; it was said that
the people of Pecos could "retire and rise to the Piedra Blanca"
with their friends the Faraon Apaches (Forbes 1960: 267).

On 30 July 1696, Vargas reported to the viceroy that the
Pueblo rebels were going to the lands of "Apaches de Nabajo
Cassa Fuerte y Quartelejo" (Forbes 1960: 268). The Jémez did
flee to the Navajo country and stayed there for several years, establishing their present pueblo when they returned (Bailey 1940:
243). Moreover, on 27 August

> a Tewa of San Juan was questioned by Vargas at Santa Fe, and
> the Indian revealed that both the Picuris and the Taos were con-
> templating fleeing to the Apaches, although there were some
> among them who wished to make peace and remain in their
> pueblos. Concerning the "Apaches of the North," he declared
> that they had visited the Tewas twice—once with many people
> and clothing to trade but with no slaves to sell. The second time
> they brought many Ute women and children to sell and said that
> they wanted to see the Spaniards. The Picuris and the Taos told
> the Apaches that the soldiers would kill them, so the Athapas-
> cans did not come. (Forbes 1960: 269–70)

Finally on 13 October Vargas

> was notified by Antonio, a Picuris chief, that the Apaches had
> brought much clothing and other articles of trade and that some
> had passed on to the new *villa* of Santa Cruz in order to barter.
> These Apaches had declared that their only friends were the
> Taos, Picuris, Pecos, and the Spaniards. On October 18, Vargas
> received word from Santa Cruz that all of the Tewas of Santa
> Clara who had horses and all of the Picuris were going to live
> with these Apaches of the Plains and that the Puebloans had

taken all of their belongings with them. (Forbes 1960: 271; see also J. Espinosa 1942: 286–87)

Having organized a pursuit, Vargas arrived in Picurís on 22 October only to find the pueblo deserted. Pecos spies who had been reconnoitering the country captured a Tano Indian.

> Being questioned through Mattias Lujan where the people of Picuríes are, he [the Tano Indian] says that they are moving on the plains with the Tanos and Teguas, having set out three days ago. Asked how long since Don Lorenzo went, he maintains that he and his people left with the others, taking many loaded horses; that the Picuríes took more horses than the Teguas . . . and Thanos; that the Teguas are herding many ewes and goats, but no oxen or cattle at all. Examined concerning which way they are going, he specifies the river road. Asked if it is a good trail, he replied that it may be good on horseback up to the summit; that as far as that there are some hills, and afterwards it is a good road. It being inquired where he heard the Picuríes say they were going, he answers that they were headed toward the place where the bulls run. (Thomas 1935: 54)

The punitive expedition that ensued was apparently the first official journey across the Sangre de Cristos after the Reconquest, and Vargas's observations are of interest because they cast some light on the country east of Picurís. Vargas states:

> [I] followed the road which comes down the river of this pueblo to the east; the river on the right hand. I found the footpath between the two sierras like a canyon in some places, and wholly mountainous, and filled with stones which are in those hills. Having traveled apparently about five long leagues, I found the ranchería which the enemy had attacked first. (Thomas 1935: 54)

The next day Vargas "came upon the walls of a ruined farm which betokened a delay," the implication being that the fleeing Apaches had delayed their flight to destroy the farm. Since the trail had been lost because of rain, and Vargas could not decide whether to continue the pursuit because of the head start the enemy had, he "determined to spend all the day searching out the places where they had their huts." However, he found the trail and succeeded in recapturing part of the fugitives.

In his diary Vargas gives no clue as to the owners of the

ranchería and the ruined farm, both of which had apparently been damaged by the Apaches he was pursuing. These structures were too far from Picurís to have been either farming outposts of the Pueblo or the farms of Spanish settlers and were almost certainly the homes of mountain Apache farmers living along the tributaries of the Canadian River east of Picurís. Since these houses were on the main trail, certain to be used by the pursuing Spaniards, the Apaches may have destroyed them rather than allow the Spaniards the satisfaction. As for the "huts" that Vargas tried to find, probably in order to destroy them, the context indicates that they belonged to Apaches. Although the Plains Apaches "of the north" were probably the Cuartelejos of western Kansas, from whose villages some of the refugees were recovered in 1706, the mountain Apaches living in the vicinity of Picurís were apparently sympathetic to the Pueblo rebels in 1696 and hence were probably considered among the "enemy."

Having rediscovered their trail, Vargas resumed pursuit of the refugees. Soon a reconnoitering party brought in a Taos Indian who explained that he had been seeking a daughter who was among the fleeing Picurís but that since she did not want to give herself up, he was returning (Thomas 1935: 55–56). Continuing on the trail, Vargas overtook the refugees, killing some and capturing others. Counting those who straggled into his camp voluntarily, he brought back eighty-four persons along with forty horses and some goods belonging to the enemies. Most of the prisoners were apparently Apaches, who were later divided among the soldiers and settlers who had gone on the campaign (Thomas 1935: 53–59). Finding himself beset by adverse weather in strange country, Vargas returned to Santa Fé by way of Pecos Pueblo.

Back in the capital, the governor learned that some Tewas of Santa Clara had fled to "surrounding neighbors of the Apaches of Navajo, Embudo, and Sierra de los Pedernales" (Forbes 1960: 272). The Embudo mentioned may have been the site of the present town of that name north of San Juan Pueblo. If so, Apaches other than the Achos were living west of the Sangre de Cristos, at least seasonally, as early as the 1690s.

Vargas's first term expired in 1696, and Captain Pedro Rodrí-guez Cubero, having paid two thousand pesos for the appointment, was made governor of New Mexico before Vargas's application for a second term reached the king. Cubero took office on 2 July 1697. Vargas, who had become unpopular with the settlers for various reasons, was arrested and spent three years in jail in Santa Fé before being tried. He was not released until July 1700, whereupon he went to Mexico. There, after an investigation, he was fully pardoned and was given another appointment as governor of New Mexico, which took effect on 10 November 1703 (Bailey 1940: 246–55).

Vargas had been forced to give up his office before he could subdue all the rebellious Pueblos, and it was said in Governor Cubero's favor that he brought about the peace Vargas had failed to effect. In any case, the rivalry between Vargas and the Cubero faction apparently overshadowed Indian affairs between 1696 and 1700, and little information on the Apaches is to be found in documents of this period. However, one thing emerges clearly from the records of the Reconquest period as a whole—Apaches were deeply involved in intra-Pueblo factionalism when the Spaniards returned to New Mexico. After futile resistance to the latter-day *conquistadores,* many Pueblo people fled to the Apacheans as their ancestors had done in Oñate's time, creating a new wave of Pueblo influence on Apachean culture.

Chapter Six

The Apacheans
and the Buffalo

The reasons for the migration of proto-Apacheans from the north will probably never be known with certainty, but any attempt to explain the presence of Athabascans on the Southern Plains in the early 1500s should consider their culture at that time, its probable antecedents, and evidence for conditions on the Plains during late prehistoric times when their migration was probably taking place.

It would be easy to overemphasize the status of Apacheans as Plainsmen, for it was as Plainsmen that the Spaniards first observed them, and long after some Apache bands had taken up residence in the mountain ranges of the Southwest, it was the lifeway of the Plains buffalo hunters that continued to elicit the most graphic and detailed descriptions from Spanish writers. Nevertheless, the earliest Spanish accounts made it clear that the intrepid dog-nomads, however well adjusted to Plains life, spent only a part of their year in the short-grass country. If those no-madic bison hunters of whom Coronado's men acquired knowl-edge were wintering with sedentary village tribes on the eastern and western margins of the Plains, then it is a safe assumption that Apachean bands farther north, who, perhaps, were links in an unbroken southward extension of the Na Dene (Gunnerson and Gunnerson 1971; hereafter referred to as G & G), also took shelter near friendly villagers or in canyons and wooded river bottoms that provided fuel. In so doing, however, they may still have been following the bison, who also sought more sheltered locations in the winter.

This pattern of alternation between open Plains and wooded brakes and valleys probably also characterized the original pro-gress of the Apachean vanguard southward *if the open Plains held anything to attract these hunters at the time they were mi-grating*. It seems useless to argue the question of whether they clung to the mountains or took only seasonal shelter there until climatic sequences on the Plains are better known.

Whatever their subsequent history, it can be assumed that in the north the proto-Apacheans were once forest people, living, perhaps, like the historic Chipewyans. Concerning these North-ern Athabascans, Birket-Smith said:

> The life of the Chipewyan is dependent upon two factors, the caribou and the forest—the caribou, which provides them with food, clothing, etc., and the forest, which yields the fuel without which they cannot survive the winter. On the whole, life is therefore a continuous moving between the forest, in which they spend the winter, and the Barren Grounds, to which they follow the caribou in summer. (Birket-Smith 1930: 29)

How long this subsistence pattern had existed among the Chip-ewyans is not known, but if it was developed by the late prehis-toric, such a life-way could obviously have provided a model for proto-Apachean buffalo hunters, especially since the habits of the Barren Ground caribou were somewhat like those of the Plains bison (D. Gunnerson 1956). But whereas the northward move-ment of the Chipewyans out of their forests to hunt caribou is recorded fact, it remains to be demonstrated that the proximity of bison originally drew proto-Apacheans southward. The probability that bison motivated and sustained their migration is supported, perhaps, by their retention of the skin tipi. According to Wissler the occurrence of the tipi in North America seems to be related to caribou and bison hunting and "is everywhere definitely associated with a nomadic hunting life" (Wissler 1950: 111–12). However, the Apacheans have used a wide variety of shelters in historic times, all of which have parallels among the Northern Athabascans and/or Eskimos. This variety of structures may well reflect a long-continued exploitation of varied environments by the Apacheans.

It is also interesting that the Plains Apacheans, like the Chipewyans, used dogs as pack, rather than draught, animals. In addition, the Apachean practice of linking pack dogs in long single files has a parallel among the Chipewyans in whose country, according to Birket-Smith (1930: 40), single lines are most practical on narrow forest paths. Insofar as the dog harness of the Chipewyans (Birket-Smith 1930: 40–41) and that of the Plains Apaches described in Spanish accounts can be compared, they seem similar. But these points are only additional evidence bearing on the already generally conceded northern origin of the Apaches. Questions about the beginning and the nature of their migration can at present, perhaps, be most profitably answered in terms of the region they traversed.

Since the time when Early Man hunted the giant herbivores that fed there, the Plains of North America, with their sensitivity to the vagaries of climate, have sometimes offered feast and sometimes famine to their inhabitants. The chief climatic factor influencing the fate of both hunters and farmers in this vast region has been rainfall, and from north to south the High Plains are never entirely free from the threat of drought. For several decades evidence slowly accumulated by means of archeology, geology and studies of the growth patterns of tree rings has provided limited insights into climatic sequences on the Plains. These data have suggested that during some prehistoric droughts, as in those of the recent past, men have managed to hold on in the area by reducing their standard of living. Sometimes, however, severe desiccation seems to have led to large-scale withdrawals from sections of the Plains, and even to intervals of near depopulation. Unfortunately, the dating of these episodes has been far from precise. Moreover, in considering conditions adverse for human populations, emphasis has been on drought, with special reference to its effect on horticultural peoples but with the assumption that climatic conditions adverse for gardeners would also be adverse for native vegetation and hence for game animals. Actually, cool, moist, cloudy summers unfavorable for the development of corn can be favorable for grasses.

Recently Bryson, Baerreis and Wendland (Dort and Jones 1970: 53–72; hereafter referred to as D & J) have given new directions to the study of Plains culture history by presenting evidence to suggest that climatic changes and related ecological effects can occur with relative suddenness—in a few decades or less. Fortunately, they have discussed the Plains and Prairie regions as specific examples of situations in which sudden, or nonlinear changes in the atmosphere produced not only nonlinear ecological effects but also sudden accompanying cultural changes and/or movements of people. These authors have also pointed out that quite different climatic conditions could and did prevail on different parts of the Plains at the same time.

From about 900 A.D. to 1250 A.D., when the proto-Apacheans were probably still in Canada, the first sedentary horticulturalists appeared along the "Middle" Missouri River in North and South Dakota, opposite parts of the Northern Plains. According to Lehmer (D & J 1970: 117), "enormous" quantities of bison bones were found in these villages, and their presence has been interpreted as evidence of lush grass and large herds so close by that it was feasible to bring heavy bones as well as meat into the villages. An alternative possibility is that bison came regularly to the vicinity of the Middle Missouri villages alive, to seek water or the shelter of wooded bottom lands on which the villagers themselves depended for winter shelter and fuel, or that bison floated down the river dead in prehistoric as in historic times and were fished out as whole carcasses by the prehistoric villagers just as they were later by historic tribes living in the same general area. The idea that the presence of the Missouri River itself was an important factor in providing the Middle Missouri villagers with bison between ca. 900–1250 A.D. gains credence when one considers the very different situation on the Central Plains, where villagers of the Central Plains Tradition also appeared about 900 A.D. in Nebraska and Kansas. According to Wedel's recent estimates (D & J 1970: 138), the occupation of southwestern Nebraska by Upper Republican people centered between 1050 and 1250 A.D. Published reports on Upper Republican sites in general, however, give the impression that they did not contain nearly so much bison bone nor so many tools made of bison bone as either the contemporaneous Middle Missouri sites or the later and much larger villages of the protohistoric Pawnee in eastern Nebraska (D. Gunnerson 1972). Probably significant in this connection is the presence of numerous small Upper Republican sites extending into eastern Colorado and Wyoming ca. 1150–1250 A.D. that Wood (1971) has interpreted as hunting stations. It would appear that in the Central Plains, in the period under consideration, the main herds of bison were well west of the small "hamlets" of the sedentary Upper Republican people. Moreover, the people on the Middle Missouri, whose villages did contain large quantities of bison bone, had very few hunting stations to the west (Wood 1971). In brief, it may indeed have been a channeling effect of the Missouri River rather than an abundance of animals that led to the quantities of bison bone in Middle Missouri villages.

Whatever the explanation for the seeming difference in availability of bison between the Northern and Central Plains up to ca. 1250 A.D., about that time the Upper Republican hamlets in southwestern Nebraska, Upper Republican hunting stations in Colorado and Wyoming, and even the substantial villages on the Middle Missouri were apparently all abandoned, probably because of drought. If some of the bison on the adjacent plains moved north, this may have caused a concentration of animals that attracted some Athabascans out of the forests onto the Canadian Plains. Or such an occurrence may only have made bison hunting more attractive to tribes for which it already formed part of the subsistence pattern. Until more information on the climate and archeology of the Canadian Plains is brought to bear on the problem, one can only speculate. As for human refugees from the drought-stricken Central Plains, Lehmer (D & J 1970: 125) finds no evidence of the arrival of people representing the Central Plains Tradition on the Middle Missouri until about 1400 A.D., leaving their whereabouts in the meantime a mystery.

There is growing evidence, however, that some Central Plains people (and apparently bison) lost little time in moving south. As early as 1200 A.D., an oasis developed suddenly on the Southern Plains with a substantial increase of July and August rainfall in western Oklahoma and northwestern Texas. People representing a southern variant of the Central Plains Tradition were quick to move in and take advantage of it; that is, the sudden climatic change, according to Bryson, Baerreis and Wendland (D & J 1970: 67–69), was followed by a *rapid* immigration of sedentary peoples into the Texas Panhandle. According to Wedel (1968: 9) these newcomers may have been from the region south of the Smoky Hill River in Kansas. It may be significant in this context, also, that bison bones become very common at sites in central Texas after ca. 1200 A.D., following a long period during which they had been very scarce.[1]

The refugee farmers who moved to the Southern Plains ca. 1200 A.D. established villages in the Canadian River drainage of the Texas Panhandle, where their archeological remains have been termed the Antelope Creek Focus. These and other related villages in the region were apparently abandoned ca. 1450 A.D. because of still another drought, but until that time the inhabitants had easy access to buffalo, since the sites yield quantities of bison bone. Farther south still, arable sandy tracts of the Llano Estacado, or Staked Plain, were probably farmed by Pueblo peoples until some time in the Glaze III period (ca. 1425–1490 A.D.) and then abandoned (Krieger 1946: 47–49; 1947: 144).

1 Edward Jelks, personal communication, 7 December 1972.

Conveniently, at about the time the Southern Plains were abandoned by corn growers (ca. 1450 A.D.) climatic conditions improved markedly on the Middle Missouri, and that area, according to Lehmer (D & J 1970: 125) was reoccupied. Concurrently, Wedel concludes, villages of the Great Bend Aspect, or protohistoric Wichita, were established in central Kansas, and he speculates that these Wichitas may have been migrants from the abandoned Panhandle sites (D & J 1970: 138; Wedel 1968: 7). In any case the favorable climatic conditions that permitted a new influx of people on the Middle Missouri and in central Kansas seems to have lasted only about a century, or until ca. 1550 A.D. Sometime during this period the large villages of the protohistoric Pawnees were also established in eastern Nebraska, so that intermittent clusters of flourishing sedentary large-village tribes in the tall-grass prairies paralleled the High Plains Corridor where the Apacheans were probably already exploiting, on the Northern and Central Plains, increased numbers of bison made possible by the improved climate. At 1450 A.D. these Athabascans were probably still in the process of moving south, unhampered by any human barrier in the short-grass country, free of restrictions imposed by the practice of horticulture, and both aided and attracted onward by the abundance of a large game animal that could fill most of their needs.

By the time the Apacheans reached the Southern Plains, the drought that had caused corn growers to abandon the Texas and Oklahoma Panhandles and the Llano Estacado by ca. 1450 was probably long since over, for by 1541, at the dawn of history in the area, there were large herds of buffalo there, along with the bands of dog-nomads who exploited them and who were probably only the southernmost of Athabascan groups that extended all the way back to Canada. It has often been suggested that these pedestrian "enemy nomads" kept horticultural peoples from reoccupying the Plains. However, early Spanish explorers found Indian farmers near the margins of the Plains more afraid of the buffalo than of the buffalo hunters. This fear, and the fact that Plains farmers had been able to co-exist with bison on the Plains in prehistoric times suggests a marked change in the over-all situation, and other evidence warrants the speculation that there was such a large increase in the number of bison on the Plains in protohistoric and early historic times that gardeners simply could not cope with the great herds.

The threat that these herds posed to farmers was recognized explicitly by village people to both the east and the west of the main buffalo country. In the southeastern United States in 1541, a reconnaissance party from the de Soto expedition reached Indians in the "province" of Caluça (Lewis 1907: 212–13) an area north of the Arkansas River in north-central Arkansas (Swanton 1939: 229, map 10). These Indians of Caluça

> stated that thence towards the north [northwest?], the country, being very cold, was very thinly populated; that cattle were in such plenty, no maize-field could be protected from them, and the inhabitants lived upon the meat. (Lewis 1907: 213)

Likewise, in the Southwest in 1581, members of the Chamuscado-Rodríguez expedition talked to some eastern Pueblo people who said that they lived far away from the herds so that the buffalo would not eat their crops (H & R 1927: 29; 1966: 86–87).

The buffalo presented other problems, one of which was their tendency to rub against substantial objects. Roe (1951: 439) points out that they sometimes rubbed down entire trees (see also [Castañeda] Winship 1896: 542). More important in the present context, about 1770, they are said to have rubbed down a settler's cabin in Pennsylvania two years in succession. "Almost the last herd" in Pennsylvania is said to have "stumbled in its blind heedless fashion into a settler's cabin which stood in the way with its door open; and trampled the mother and children to death in the ruins of their home" (Roe 1951: 844). Roe points out that not even large numbers of bison would have been necessary to cause such a tragedy. Such instances are a reminder that earth or stone houses as well as fields belonging to the Indians would have been vulnerable to buffalo, especially on the barren plains. When great herds were moving, permanent settlement there could have been physically as well as economically precarious. Moreover, pedestrian hunters faced the possibility of being trampled by buffalo herds, and the fear that town-dwelling

Indians probably had of such an occurrence is made vividly explicit in a tradition that Dorsey collected from the Caddo.

How the Buffalo Ceased to Eat Human Beings

When the world was new there were many wild and fierce animals, and the buffalo were among the fiercest, for they ate human beings. In those days the buffalo were many-colored and roamed the plains in great herds, and were so numerous that men could not go out on the plains alone for fear of being caught by them. There was one great man who received power from the Father, and he had the power to go right into the midst of these terrible animals and kill them without being hurt. That man was Buzzard, and he was the only man who possessed such power. All the other people had to live in villages together that they might protect each other and hunt together. One time some men went out in the timber alone to hunt turkey and deer. They wandered far, and when they started home they found that they had to cross a long stretch of lonely prairie. While they were hurrying across the vast stretch of country they saw a black cloud arise in the west and come nearer and nearer, until at last they knew that a great herd of buffalo was sweeping down upon them. They threw the game from their backs, threw away their bows and arrows, and ran as fast as the wind. The buffalo, dangerous as they were, were not good runners, and so the men reached the timber before them and ran into the dense thicket.

After these men succeeded in escaping, the people took courage and ventured farther away from home. One time four men went out to hunt bear. They went into the timber that lay between two mountains and there they found the fresh tracks of a bear. They trailed it all through the timber and over the mountain, and found it at the edge of the timber at the foot of the mountain. The bear ran out to the open plain and the men pursued and killed it. While they were cutting it up to carry home they heard a great noise, like thunder, coming across the plains. They looked and saw that the buffalo were upon them. They tried to escape, but it was too late. The buffalo caught all but one man, who succeeded in gaining the timber and climbing a tall tree. All day the buffalo surrounded the tree and tried to butt it down, but could not. Night came on, then they returned to the plains and the man climbed down and ran to his home. He told all the people how the buffalo had surprised them and had killed his three companions. The people hastened to the place, but found nothing but a few bones scattered about. From that time on the buffalo ate many people, until Coyote came. Then the people left this dangerous country and went into another. They went through the gate to the new country, and Coyote went with them. He was the last to go through the gate, and as he went he shut the gate, so no dangerous animals could enter, and he let through only a few buffalo who had never tasted human flesh and so were not dangerous. (Dorsey 1905: 50–51)

This tradition could be interpreted as suggesting that the Caddo actually migrated to avoid large buffalo herds. It also lends significance to the fact that Pueblo peoples called the Plains nomads who followed the bison in the 1500s "brave" men (H & R 1940: 258; 1966: 87), especially since the Pueblo Indians themselves seem not to have ventured onto the Plains alone in historic times until much later. Even in the mid-1700s, long after the advent of the horse, reconnaissance on the Plains was considered very rare and risky for Pueblo Indians (Thomas 1940: 124). Although this was probably due in part to their lack of ability to cope with the plains environment, a fear of the bison herds may also have been involved. Father Marquette, who saw bison on or near the Mississippi, described their mode of attack.

They are very fierce; and not a year passes without their killing some savages. When attacked, they catch a man on their Horns, if they can, toss Him in the air, and then throw him on the ground, after which they trample him under foot, and kill him. (Roe 1951: 225)

Inexperienced horses fared little better. At first, all the horses of the Coronado expedition fled from the buffalo, who killed several of them and wounded many (H & R 1940: 187, 279, 289). When Vicente Zaldívar's men attempted to corral buffalo somewhere on the High Plains east of Pecos Pueblo in 1598, they found them unusually wild and fierce. On this occasion the buffalo killed three of the Spaniards' horses and wounded forty others badly (H & R 1953: 402). However, this episode illustrates the advantage enjoyed by the mounted hunter for it was the horses that suffered and not the riders.

The possibility that the bison population became especially dense on the High Plains in the early 1500s is supported by evidence for an apparently late overflow of modern bison into some peripheral areas. This evidence is best for the eastern, and especially the southeastern, United States. Álvar Núñez Cabeza de

Vaca, who survived Narváez's shipwreck to eventually wander across Texas, did not see bison until he reached the vicinity of what may have been present Austin. Of his location in 1532 or 1533 he said, "Cattle come as far as here. Three times I have seen them and eaten of their meat" (Smith 1871: 106). Cabeza de Vaca is more specific when he says,

> [the "cattle"] come as far as the sea-coast of Florida [probably the Gulf Coast of Texas], from a northerly direction, ranging through a tract of more than four hundred leagues; and throughout the whole region over which they run, the people who inhabit near, descend and live upon them, distributing a vast many hides into the interior country. (Smith 1871: 107)

Thus it would appear that the author had acquired, largely by hearsay, knowledge of the vast north-south extent of the Buffalo Plains, of the seasonal migrations of the buffalo, which apparently consisted of movements both up and down the Plains (Kinnaird 1958: 148) and movements from the center to the margins and back. Cabeza de Vaca's comments also suggest that Indians marginal to the Plains confined their exploitation of the buffalo to those animals that came nearest them. Since this Spaniard's journey westward across Texas took him far south of the route Coronado later followed eastward across the Plains, it is unfortunate that his comments do not reveal whether *large* herds such as those described by Coronado were reaching the coast ca. 1530. Since Cabeza de Vaca was much impressed by the bison as an animal, it is probable that he, like other explorers, would have described the great herds had he seen them. It is also noteworthy that none of the Indians he describes were like the nomads with pack dogs and skin tents found living farther north among the main herds by Coronado in 1541. In both Mexico and Spain Cabeza de Vaca's descriptions of the "cattle" intrigued all who heard them. Coronado sent out a preliminary scouting party to sight the buffalo, and there are indications that members of de Soto's army were, from the beginning, also eager to find these animals, of which they had previous knowledge (Bourne 1904 II: 162).

Although de Soto's party is thought to have penetrated Texas at least as far as the Trinity River and perhaps beyond (Swanton 1939: 288–89, map 10), no member of it ever actually saw live buffalo. According to various accounts of the expedition, however, these explorers began to see evidence of buffalo well east of the Plains in the form of objects probably obtained through trade. The first such evidence was apparently "breastplates like corselets and head-pieces made of rawhide, the hair stripped off; and also very good shields," said by Ranjel to have been present in the "mosque, or house of worship" in the town of Talimeco (Bourne 1904 II: 101) in eastern Georgia. And in his secondary account, avowedly based on information obtained from one of de Soto's men, Garcilaso de la Vega mentions that in a room in the "temple" at "Talomeco" "there was a great quantity of round shields made of wood and of cowhide *that had been brought from distant lands*" [italics mine] (V & V 1951: 314, 323; Garcilaso de la Vega 1605: 174v).

According to the account by the "Gentleman of Elvas" the first buffalo robe found was brought back by a scouting party from the "province" of Chisca in southeastern Tennessee (Lewis 1907: 182; Swanton 1939: map 10). In Pacaha, according to Elvas, they found shields of raw cowhide from which they made armor for their horses (Lewis 1907: 209), and Ranjel says that in Casqui in the principal cabin, "over the door, were many heads of very fierce bulls, just as in Spain, noblemen who are sportsmen mount the heads of wild boars or bears" (Bourne 1904 II: 138–39). Both Pacaha and Casqui were apparently in eastern or southeastern Arkansas near the Mississippi.

Biedma states that in the town of Coligua (in south-central Arkansas) the explorers found "a large quantity of dressed cow's tails, and others already cured"; while Ranjel says, "And from there, at midday, they went to kill some cows, of which there are very many wild ones" (Bourne 1904 II: 31, 146–47). This hunting trip must have been in vain, however, for (as stated previously) no member of the army ever saw a live buffalo, and Elvas, who discusses the fruits, birds and beasts of the country traversed, does not mention them (Lewis 1907: 271–72).

Two of the explorers noted the presence of buffalo robes at

Tula in western or southwestern Arkansas. According to Elvas the chief of Tula, after attacking de Soto, first sent emissaries bearing "cow-skins" and then came himself, bringing

> a present of many cow-skins, which were found very useful; the country being cold, they were taken for bed-covers, as they were very soft and the wool like that of sheep. Near by, to the northward, are many cattle. The Christians did not see them, nor go where they were, because it was a country thinly populated, having little maize. (Lewis 1907: 220)

Garcilaso de la Vega says of Tula:

> In the town (for we would give an account of its details) our men found serving as bed covers a great number of cowhides which had been softened and dressed without removing the hair; and there were in addition many others ready to be dressed. Moreover, there was beef; but no cows were to be seen in the fields, and it could never be learned from whence the hides had been brought. (V & V 1951: 457; see also Garcilaso de la Vega 1605: 247*v*)

After de Soto's death, his army started westward again and eventually arrived at a province called Hais by Biedma, who says that there

> in seasons, some cattle are wont to herd; and as the Indians saw us entering their country, they began to cry out: "Kill the cows—they are coming;" when they sallied and shot their arrows at us, doing us some injury. (Bourne 1904 II: 36–37)

The Hais or Aish Indians were Caddo and beyond them were a less settled group tentatively identified as Bidai or Tonkawa (Swanton 1939: 279–80, 288–89, map 10). Of the latter Garcilaso de la Vega says,

> These houses were constructed badly and arranged worse, and they appeared more like the huts of melon growers than dwelling places. Nevertheless, the Spaniards assuaged their hunger with great quantities of beef which they discovered within the houses along with recently skinned hides. But still they found no cows on the hoof, and the Indians would never say from whence they had brought these things. (V & V 1951: 516; Garcilaso de la Vega 1605: 279)

According to Garcilaso, and to him alone, de Soto's men called "that sterile and sparsely populated place" "the Province of the

Herdsmen [*La Provincia de los Vaqueros*]" because of the beef and cowhides they found there (V & V 1951: 516; Garcilaso de la Vega 1605: 279). Other Indians they questioned told them that the "cows" lived to the west in very flat and sandy lands and that there were also Indians ahead who did not live in houses but were roving hunters and gatherers (V & V 1951: 520–21). The army, discouraged, returned to the Mississippi River. They had apparently reached lands (among the Caddo and Tonkawa) to which the buffalo migrated seasonally but had not penetrated the heart of the buffalo country.

As for the eastern United States in general, Roe, who appears to have reviewed the evidence exhaustively, favors the hypothesis that the modern buffalo arrived compartively recently on the eastern side of the Mississippi, and in "relatively scanty numbers" (Roe 1951: 228).[2] He further generalizes: "The available evidence indicates a westward extension of the buffalo habitat in a manner which resembles the animal's progress eastwards from the Mississippi toward the Atlantic" (Roe 1951: 258). No Spanish explorers reported live bison in Arizona or in New Mexico west of the Río Grande in the 1500s. Buffalo drifted seasonally into eastern New Mexico south of the Sangre de Cristos by the late 1500s, if not earlier (H & R 1966: 87) and in dry years came to the salt lakes close to the Tompiro Pueblos in the early 1600s (Milich 1966: 88). Not until the late 1600s, however, were they reported in the upper Río Grande Valley, on the Red River, and west of the Río Grande near San Antonio Mountain (J. Espinosa 1936: 185–87).

In Chihuahua, as pointed out earlier, there were apparently some bison on the central plateau before 1565. Members of Ibarra's expedition, which reached Casas Grandes from the west in that year, found "hides of the cattle that had died and also bones and manure" in the vicinity. Indians they met told them that live "cattle" were to be found "four journeys toward the north" (H & R 1928: 202). If the remains seen by Ibarra's men were

2 According to Robert Neuman (personal communication), there has been no authenticated find of modern bison in a prehistoric archeological site in the southeastern United States.

those of buffalo and not of the wild domestic cattle which had proliferated unbelievably in New Spain in less than fifty years, then the bison inhabited the high plains of Chihuahua only seasonally, for the grass there disappeared completely in the dry season (Mecham 1968: 208).

In the north, in historic times, bison were extremely numerous on the plains of the Saskatchewan River, apparently thinning out through the woods to Great Slave Lake (Roe 1951: 286). Hence, they occurred in the territory occupied by the Northern Athabascan Sarsi and Chipewyan, overlapping the range of the barren ground caribou and especially the woodland caribou. In historic times the Sarsi were confirmed buffalo hunters, whereas the more northerly Chipewyans, to whom the term for caribou was the same as the term for meat, apparently did not value the buffalo. Even in this northern region the bison seemed to have moved westward quite late, for an Athabascan (Beaver) informant told MacKenzie in the late 1700s that within his lifetime the vegetation on Peace River west of Lesser Slave Lake had changed, and the buffalo had come in from the east (Curtis 1907–1930 XVIII: 3, 12, 18, 23, 91, 93). Of interest in this connection is the statement of Bryson, Baerris and Wendland that "the encroachment of vegetation into the formerly glaciated area of Canada took all of post-glacial time, so that dates of successional changes are dependent on when the terrain became available (D & J 1970: 56).

Roe considers the possibility that the late appearance of buffalo in areas peripheral to the Plains (especially the well-documented instance of the southeastern United States) was due to acute overcrowding on the High Plains after 1540 but discards this idea, in part because accepting it would involve postulating "an incredibly recent date for their appearance as the historic buffalo—in their historic habitat" (Roe 1951: 494). Actually, it is not at all necessary to assume the recent appearance on the Plains of the modern bison as such—only the recency of *large numbers*.

And there is another aspect of buffalo history that could help to explain the movement of the animal into peripheral areas, if over-population is not reason enough. Although eastern Indians marginal to the Plains were exploiting the buffalo in the 1530s, it is possible that the pressure exerted in the opposite direction by the more mobile Plains dog-nomads, the Apacheans, was even more intense. These people were commercial hunters—they killed not just for food and for hides to make their own tents and clothing but also for a surplus of meat and hides to carry in to such warehouse Pueblos as Pecos, from which products of the buffalo were "retailed" throughout other parts of the Southwest. Even the early Spanish colonists and the Pueblo Indians became dependent on these traders from the Plains for skins from which to make footwear, clothing, and numerous other necessary items (Ayer 1916: 55).

The Coronado narratives give excellent descriptions of the way in which the Plains nomads used their pack dogs, but it remained for Oñate's nephew, Vicente Zaldívar, to report in 1598 that the Vaquero Apaches had these pack dogs in large droves (H & R 1953: 401). This latter statement lends support to Benavides's comment in 1630 that the pack trains of the Vaquero Apaches customarily included as many as five hundred dogs (Ayer 1916: 56), giving some idea of the volume of Apache-Pueblo trade. Yet Benavides says,

> although each year so many cattle are killed, they not only do not diminish but are each day more, for they gorge the plains and appear interminable. (Ayer 1916: 55)[3]

Spanish accounts refer to the Plains Apaches as following the buffalo, but in following they were also, inevitably, pushing. In 1598, Zaldívar observed how buffalo moved away from a group of traveling Vaquero Apaches. His own party, having sighted a herd estimated at four thousand animals, started to build a corral to round them up, but before construction could be completed, the buffalo had moved some twenty miles away (H & R 1953: 400). It may be, then, that the activities of the early Plains

---

3 Benavides may have spoken accurately, for the Neo-Boreal Climatic episode, which according to Bryson, Baerris and Wendland began about 1550 A.D. and continued without a break until the first half of the 1700s, was a period of cool, moist, cloudy summers that were unfavorable for horticulture (D & J 1970: 117, 125, 138–39), but may well have been favorable for grass and hence for bison.

Apache hunters, along with overpopulation and the tendency of the buffalo to move seasonally, was a factor in the historic overflow of the animals from the Plains.

Some results of human pressure on the buffalo in later historic times, when their movement away from the High Plains was reversed, have been described as follows:

> The buffalo ranged to the eastern border of Kansas as recently as 1835. About that time the United States authorities removed the Delaware, Pottawattamie, Kaws, and other tribes of Indians to "Reservations" in the eastern part of what is now Kansas. These Indians soon *drove* [italics mine] the buffalo as far west as the Blue River (one hundred miles west of the Missouri River), which was as far as the reservations extended. The buffalo held that range till 1854, when Kansas was made a Territory and whites began to settle here. For fifteen years from that time the buffalo receded, on an average, about ten miles a year [Mudge]. (Wedel 1959: 18)

An obvious question arises. If farming Indians in the Southwest and Southeast felt that it was impossible or impractical to plant crops on the High Plains in the 1500s because of the buffalo and if they feared the large bison herds, as history and tradition suggest, how were the pedestrian Apaches able to live among the buffalo and hunt them with apparent impunity? Their success may have been due to previous experience in hunting large-herd animals such as caribou and/or northern bison, to devices and techniques such as the portable, sewn skin tent and dog packing acquired in the North, and to the mobility that such culture traits gave them. They undoubtedly had an intimate knowledge of the behavior patterns of the buffalo, singly and in groups, and/or were able to adjust to the animal's lack of predictability, for on foot and with primitive weapons, the early Apaches seemed perfectly at home among the herds. Actually, it would appear from Spanish accounts and the study by Roe (1951) that ordinarily bison were not dangerous. They would graze quite close to stationary tent camps and simply moved away from traveling groups, running only if pursued. However, they charged if hard pressed or attacked, and early Spanish colonists found it impossible to "round up," "drive," or "surround" buffalo, techniques successful with domestic cattle and other game animals (H & R 1953: 401–2; Ayer 1916: 38, 54), although mounted Plains Indians later became skillful at keeping herds of buffalo milling in a circle.

Moreover, in contrast with Spanish methods, Apache hunting techniques observed in the 1500s and early 1600s were covert rather than overt. Then, as later, the Apaches seem to have been masters of camouflage, hiding behind brush shelters at watering places or lying, covered with local mud, in the buffalo trails. Also, they were skillful bowmen who could kill an animal with the first shot so that the victim would never know it had been hit and the rest of the herd would not be greatly startled (H & R 1940: 239; 1953: 404; Ayer 1916: 55). (For a more recent appreciative account of Apache stalking techniques see Cremony 1868: 28–29, 290–93). Perhaps the early Plains Apaches lived among the buffalo and killed them so unobtrusively that they themselves were seldom in danger. (Compare the behavior of the rattlesnake in its relations with prairie dogs, described to Cremony [1868: 290–93] by an Apache.)

As for the danger presented by stampedes, the plainsmen might have been able to avoid or escape threatening situations. They could break camp and start moving with a speed that amazed the Spaniards and no wonder, if they matched or exceeded a group of Sioux timed by Catlin. Upon a prearranged signal the Sioux had their tents flat on the ground in two minutes, after which their beasts of burden were speedily loaded (McClintock 1910: 208–9).

Even if the Plains Apaches were able to survive among the buffalo herds so long as they remained mobile, how did their descendants dare to establish semi-permanent horticultural villages on the plains, as they did before 1700? First of all, corn was apparently a luxury rather than a staple for the Plains Apaches, who seem to have eaten or processed all or most of their crop green. Therefore they could afford to take a calculated risk in planting. Also, by long observation, they may have been able to choose as garden spots places where bison were not usually numerous in the season when crops were in the field. A

careful study of what is known of the movements of both the
buffalo and of those Indians most dependent upon them would
almost certainly reveal other ways by which the early Apaches
managed to coexist with the buffalo on the Plains. If the plainsmen lost a village of tents, brush shelters and/or small hogan-like
structures, they lost an investment of energy less than that involved in building a village of earth lodges such as those of the
Pawnee.

Possibly, then, it was an influx of bison *in large numbers* that
made the High Plains inhospitable to Caddoan farmers ca. 1500
and at the same time attractive to proto-Apacheans. However,
the advent of the Apacheans in the Central and Southern Plains
would have constituted a further deterrent to reoccupation by
the Caddoans. Although the Plains nomads traded and even wintered with village tribes on both sides of the High Plains, the
attitude of the sedentary peoples toward these buffalo hunters
was ambivalent, and the Pueblo people, from whom Chamuscado learned of the plainsmen, refused to accompany his expedition to the Plains for fear of the nomads (H & R 1940: 258;
1966: 87, 88, and see Kelley 1952). Whether Caddoans, for example the Pawnees who eventually overcame the Central Plains
Apaches only to be faced by other buffalo-hunting tribes, would
ever again have divided into small isolated communities like their
Upper Republican ancestors in order to reoccupy the High
Plains once they had lived in large communities is another question. The Anasazi of the Southwest, having formed large settlements, preferred to maintain them (Schoenwetter and Dittert:
1968).

Because no fifteenth- or sixteenth-century sites attributable to
the Plains Apaches themselves have been found, one can only
attempt to detect the presence of Apacheans by discovering evidence of their possible influence on sedentary groups. For
example, there was, in the large villages into which the protohistoric Pawnees gathered in the prairies, a marked increase in the
number of tools associated with the dressing of heavy hides, and
some of these tools seem to appear for the first time in the protohistoric period (Wedel 1940: 337–38). Such new items as elk

antler tine scraper handles and bison metapodial fleshers (often serrated) may well represent the adoption of heavier tools to do a heavier job.

The reason for this shift of emphasis in the artifact inventory has never been adequately explained. Wedel, whose several works are indispensable for the study of culture change on the Plains, early surmised that new items connected with heavy hide working were taken over by the protohistoric horticultural tribes from their "hunting contemporaries," but rightly pointed out that it was impossible to prove that such traits were actually earlier among the hunters (Wedel 1940: 338). He also speculated that if the hunters had not received horses and firearms from the Whites, horticultural prairie peoples "might again have extended their occupation westward beyond the 99th meridian" (Wedel 1941: 27–28).

These speculations aside, it seems possible that once the Pawnees became a large village tribe living east of the main herds, it was their need to hunt buffalo at longer range that led to some of the changes in their artifact inventory. Perhaps the marked increase in heavy hide working tools reflects the fact that, in hunting at long range, the large-village tribes had more need for skin tipis than they had had earlier. Long-range hunting would also have made a beast of burden desirable, if not necessary, and tribes, other than Apaches, that hunted on the Plains utilized the dog before as well as with, the horse. Since the increase in heavy hide working among the protohistoric Pawnee is apparently very close in time to the date previously suggested for the advent of the Apacheans on the Southern Plains (ca. 1525), perhaps the Athabascans introduced the sewn skin tent (see Wissler 1908: 202), dog packing, and possibly heavy hide working tools to the eastern Plains villagers with whom they traded and wintered.

Whether Central and Southern Plains bison moved to the Northern Plains because of drought and thrived there until they lured some Athabascans into becoming committed Plainsmen, then moved southward when climatic conditions permitted with the proto-Apacheans following (and pushing) is a question that merits further consideration in its own right. If some bison survived up and down the Plains in spite of drought, a return of lush grass and a temporary absence of predators may have permitted a phenomenal growth of huge herds comparable to that of domestic cattle in Mexico (Mecham 1968: 29–30, 208). It seems desirable to remain alert to the possibility that the advent of large bison herds, the advent of the Apacheans, and the appearance of some new traits in protohistoric, large-village culture, especially in the Central Plains, are related phenomena.

Part II

The Jicarilla Apaches

Chapter Seven

Rovers of Mountains and Plains

The Jicarilla Apaches were the last American Indian tribe to be permanently settled on a reservation. Not until 1887 (Hodge 1907–1910 I: 632) were they placed, starving and indigent, on the lands they now occupy in north-central New Mexico. This move, far from solving their problems, seemed to hasten their decline. American military and civil authorities had considered the condition of the Jicarillas desperate before 1887, but it was only after some thirty years of reservation life that tribal fortunes reached their lowest ebb.

At the root of their trouble were despair and the apathy born of despair. According to one Jicarilla myth, the tribe emerged into this world near its heart, somewhere in the vicinity of Taos Pueblo. Monster Slayer, their culture hero, made a country for them in northeastern New Mexico and southeastern Colorado and decreed that they live in it always. Otherwise, he prophesied, they would perish (Mooney 1898a: 200; Goddard 1911: 206).

The Jicarillas insisted on remaining in this area or returning to it, and their tenacity was a major source of friction with American officials. Placed once and for all on a reservation outside their own country, they were rendered helpless by the belief that they would all die—and they did begin to die. The Jicarillas had been healthy when they were put on the reservation, but by 1914 ninety percent of the tribe had tuberculosis, and the people were dying so fast that officials estimated they would be extinct by 1932 (Cornell 1929).[1]

The chief natural resource of the reservation in those days was timber. The agency superintendent, casting about for a means of helping the tribe toward its own salvation, obtained government permission to sell enough of the timber to buy sheep. He had to plead with the despondent Jicarillas to accept these animals, but most of those who took them cared for them conscientiously. This step marked the beginning of slow but steady progress toward economic recovery (Cornell 1929). Special measures were employed to check tuberculosis, and today, although the tribal council and agency officials are planning toward optimum use of tribal resources, it is clear that the reservation will not support the growing population.

The Jicarillas were not the only American Indians to deteriorate under conditions of reservation life. In general, their experiences were comparable to those of many other tribes. However, the Jicarillas are of special interest because by one means or another they survived nearly two centuries of precarious existence through their own efforts before they reached the verge of extinction as wards of the United States Government.

The Jicarillas and the other Apacheans, like all the Northern Athabascan tribes, call themselves by some form of the Athabascan term for person or people, variously rendered in the north as

---

1 Lois Cornell's work is of value mainly for the information it provides on the Jicarillas during their early years on the reservation and especially during the period ca. 1919–1929. Miss Cornell, the daughter of the doctor hired by the government to care for the Jicarillas when they were suffering from tuberculosis, spent ten summers on the reservation.

"Tinneh" or "Dene" (Hodge 1907–1910 I: 63, 108; Hoijer 1938: 77). The probability that the name Apache was not derived from Zuñi or Yavapai, as previous scholars have suggested (Hodge 1895: 233; 1907–1910 I: 63; Harrington 1940: 512–13), but that it came from Nahuatl "mapachtli" → Spanish "mapache" → (variant) "apache" meaning "raccoon" was pointed out earlier in this work. Also, whatever the origin of the name, the Spanish colonists that arrived in New Mexico in 1598 recognized a relationship between the various Southern Athabascan groups that encircled the Pueblos, and soon came to use Apache as a generic term for all of them. One of the clues to the interrelatedness of the Apacheans—probably the most important one—was that they spoke mutually intelligible, and thus obviously similar, dialects of the same language, a fact that Benavides stated explicitly in 1630 (Ayer 1916: 40).

Even while they were becoming aware of Apache linguistic unity, the Spanish settlers were beginning to use salient characteristics of local subgroups to distinguish them from one another. The earliest dichotomy was that between the Apaches of the Plains, called Vaquero Apaches because they lived off the "cattle" (buffalo), and the mountain Apaches, who were still undifferentiated by descriptive terms in 1600. Interestingly enough, this geographical split parallels roughly a basic linguistic division noted by early ethnologists.

As the Spanish colonists became better acquainted with individual Apache groups, however, they gave them names derived from a variety of languages and bestowed for a variety of reasons. All the Apacheans, like the southern groups known by Cremony "generally receive their distinctive appellations from some peculiar characteristic or from the place which they most inhabit" (Cremony 1868*b:* 203). Sometimes the reason for a particular name is made explicit in the documents and sometimes it can safely be deduced from circumstantial evidence. The name of the Mescalero Apaches exemplifies the latter situation. There seems to be no document contemporary with the first appearance of this name that says the Mescalero were so called because they gathered, roasted, and ate the crowns of the mescal plant, but history and ethnography record this habit and provide a reasonable explanation for the name (Cremony 1868*b*: 203; Harrington 1940: 519–20).

Observations made by interested travelers, military personnel and early ethnographers after the United States took over New Mexico in 1846 led to Turner's (1852) discovery that Apachean was related to Northern Athabascan. Interestingly enough, the limited Apachean vocabularies on which he based his conclusions were elicited from speakers of Jicarilla and Navajo. Ultimately Pliny Earl Goddard, in the introduction to his *Jicarilla Texts* voiced succinctly the same conclusion reached by Benavides in 1630, and in remarkably similar words: "While there is considerable diversity within the southern division [of Athabascan], the speaker of any one dialect seems to be understood by speakers of all the others" (Goddard 1911: 7–8).

More recent and intensive linguistic studies of Southern Athabascan by Hoijer (1938, 1956*a*, 1956*b*) have confirmed the extremely close relationship among Apachean dialects. At one time Hoijer (1956*a*: 226) suggested that the Apachean dialects did not begin to diverge until a little more than four hundred years ago. This dating agrees spectacularly well with the hypothesis, supported by various lines of evidence, that all the Apacheans reached the Southwest at about the same time (ca. 1525) and that some of them began to move west after Coronado's return to Mexico in 1542 (D. Gunnerson 1956, and supra).

Notwithstanding the similarities, there are certain differences among the Apachean dialects that permit us to describe the linguistic position of the Jicarillas more specifically. Two basic subdivisions of the Southern Athabascan speech communty are recognized—an Eastern group comprised of the Jicarillas, Lipans, and Kiowa Apaches and a Western group variously divided by scholars, but according to Hoijer's (1938: 75) classification composed of the Navajos, San Carlos, Chiricahuas, and Mescaleros. These subgroups are differentiated primarily by the fact that the Athabascan strongly aspirated "t" has been retained by the western tribes but has shifted to strongly aspirated "k" in the speech of the eastern tribes. This difference, discovered by Goddard

(Harrington 1940: 509), has been illustrated and discussed by Hoijer, who, after a comparison of consonantal schemes, concluded that within the eastern group, Jicarilla is most clearly related to Lipan (Hoijer 1938: 86). Without going into detailed cross-cultural comparisons here, it may be added that these linguistic data are compatible with the similarities between Jicarilla and Lipan mythology (Opler 1938: xviii; 1940: 2–6), and with the probability that the Kiowa Apaches have been geographically and politically more remote from the Jicarillas than have the Lipans, and for a longer time. Actually, it is possible that half of the Carlana or Sierra Blanca Apaches, friends and neighbors of the Jicarillas, joined the Lipans in 1718 (G & G 1971).

While sound shifts reveal a basic east-west split in the Southern Athabascan stock, subsequent intergroup contacts may have done much to lessen the sharpness of this cleavage. The percentage of vocabulary retained in common by all the Apache tribes is high, and when different pairs of Apache tribes were compared on this basis, the closest relationship was not always between tribes placed in the same subdivision on the basis of sound shifts. For example, both the Jicarillas and Lipans retain about as much vocabulary in common with the Chiricahuas as they do with each other (Hoijer 1956a). Nor do cultural similarities always follow linguistic lines; the close cultural similarities of the Jicarilla (Eastern group) to the Navajo (Western group) have been recognized for a long time (Curtis 1907–1930 I: 53; Opler 1936: 202). The reasons can be found in early geographical contiguity and in the continuing interaction mentioned in Spanish documents to be cited later (and see Hoijer 1938: 85–86).

Mooney says of the Jicarillas, "They call themselves *Dǐně*, the generic term used by so many tribes of cognate stock" (Mooney 1898a: 197). Goddard (1911: 137) records *dīn de* as a word used by a Jicarilla informant to refer to an Apache of his own tribe. The Jicarilla word for person given by Hoijer (1938: 77) is *dì-ndé*, while Curtis (1907–1930 I: 135) indicates that the Jicarilla name for themselves was more elaborate: "*Haisndayin* (People Who Came from Below)."

Unfortunately, the reason that the Spaniards applied the term

Jicarilla to these Apaches is far from clear. The word *jicarilla* is a diminutive formed by suppressing the final vowel of the word *jícara* and adding the Spanish suffix *-illa*. *Jícara*, in turn, is a Hispanicized version of the Aztec word *xicalli*. Santamaria (1942 II: 147–48) gives the background of the word *jícara* in some detail. In Mexico, a *jícara* was the spherical fruit of a particular variety of the gourd tree called a *jícaro*. The word *jícara* was also used to designate a hemispherical vessel (*vasija*) with a wide mouth made from the rind of a *jícara*. Such a vessel was used to hold food or liquids. By extension, *jícara* came to mean any kind of vessel used for such purposes, although it was used principally to refer to a chocolate cup—its original use. When *jícara* means chocolate cup it also carries the connotation of a hemispherical shape or of a small vessel with a rounded bottom.

It was undoubtedly through the word's general connotations of hemispherical shape and/or use as a container for food or liquids that *jícara* took on the meaning of basket in New Mexico (Hill 1940: passim; Kiddle 1944: 133, 137–38), a connotation that has apparently misled scholars who have undertaken to explain the derivation of the tribal name Jicarilla, since their statements are in some respects mutually contradictory or at odds with ethnographic fact. It is therefore possible that their statements were simply educated guesses by persons who were more or less acquainted with the etymology of the word *jícara* and knew that the Jicarilla Apaches made pots and baskets. John C. Cremony, an American Army officer whose personal experience with Southern Athabascans was mainly with the southern Apaches, stated: "The Jicarillas are so called on account of their manufacture of a small water-tight basket, resembling a gourd, and named *jicara* in Spanish" (Cremony 1868b: 203). Cremony's is a reasonable statement because the basketry water bottle of the Jicarillas, to which he is almost certainly referring, does resemble a gourd in shape. However, such water bottles are not unique to the Jicarillas, and whether or not they can be considered small depends on the standard for comparison.

James Mooney, one of the first ethnologists to publish on the Jicarillas says: "They are expert basket-makers, whence the name

Jicarilla, meaning, in Spanish, 'little basket' " (Mooney 1898*a*: 197). Frederick Webb Hodge, in the *Handbook of American Indians* (1907–1910 I: 631), also states that *jicarilla* in Mexican Spanish means "little basket," and that these Indians were first so called by Spaniards because of their skill in making vessels of basketry.

Edward S. Curtis, whose work was edited by Hodge, says of the Jicarillas:

> They exhibit fair skill in basketry, this being their chief industry and source of barter with neighboring tribes; indeed it was through this custom of making "little baskets" that the Spaniards applied to them the name by which they are popularly known. The Pueblos of the Rio Grande use many baskets, which they obtain chiefly from the Jicarillas in exchange for corn. During late years many of these *jicarillas* have been disposed of to traders. Like the Navaho they make but little pottery and that only for utilitarian purposes. . . . The Jicarillas make a great many baskets of fair quality, from which industry the tribe gained its popular Spanish name. The most typical of their baskets is tray-shaped; this not only enters largely into their domestic life, but was formerly the principal article of barter with their Pueblo neighbors and Navaho kindred. Some pottery is made, practically all of which is in the form of small cooking utensils. The large clay water jar was not used, their wandering life necessitating a water carrier of greater stability. (Curtis 1907–1930 I: 54, 135)

In 1916 Hodge stated that the name of the Jicarillas was "derived from the small cup-shaped baskets (*jicaras*) [parentheses in original] which they manufacture" (Ayer 1916: 264 *n*43*b*). But John P. Harrington says that "the Spaniards always called these people Apaches de Jicarilla, literally 'shallow-bowl-shaped-basket Apaches,' referring to their manufacture of certain large coiled baskets" (Harrington 1940: 511).

Not only are there discrepancies among the statements cited above, especially as to the size and shape of the baskets for which the Jicarillas were supposed to be named, but ethnographic collections of Jicarilla baskets exhibit a wide variety of shapes and sizes. Complicating the problem still further is the fact that the Jicarillas were also well-known in the past for their pottery, perhaps even more than for their baskets.

The first official American report on the Indians of New

Mexico was made by Charles Bent. General Kearny appointed
Bent civil governor of New Mexico on 22 September 1846, little
more than a month after United States forces marched into Santa
Fé (Bancroft 1889; 416, 426 *n*21). As governor of the Territory
of New Mexico, Bent was also *ex-officio* Superintendent of
Indian Affairs, and on 10 November 1846, he submitted a
summary of the condition of the New Mexico Indians to the
Commissioner of Indian Affairs at Washington. Since he was a
resident of Taos, it is not surprising that his report began with
the Jicarilla Apaches, of whom he said,

> Their only attempt at manufacture is a species of potter ware,
> capable of tolerable resistance to fire, and much used by them
> and the Mexicans for culinary purposes. This, they barter with
> the Mexicans for the necessaries of life, but in such small quan-
> tities as scarcely to deserve the name of traffic. (Abel 1915: 6)

In 1852 John Greiner, then acting superintendent of Indian
Affairs in New Mexico, reported that nearly a hundred Jicarillas
under Chief Chacon intended to "settle down and manufacture
tenajos[2] and baskets to trade with" (Abel 1915: 530). Domenech
(1860 II: 8) mentioned that the Jicarillas manufactured "a sort
of pottery which resists the action of fire." Moreover, in the
Report of Indian Affairs for 1863, Levi Keithly, an agent for the
Jicarillas while they still had an agency on the Maxwell Grant,
stated that the Jicarilla Apaches manufactured "a species of
coarse earthenware, which they exchanged for corn and wheat."

Father Antonio José Martínez, resident priest at Taos for many
years, said of the Jicarillas in 1865, they "always lived between
the villages and the intermediate mountains, working and selling
earthenware to our people" (Keleher 1964: 48–49). Such statements may have furnished the basis for Bancroft's assertion that
the Jicarilla Apaches were "so named in early times from the pottery made in small quantities by their women" (Bancroft 1889:
665). Goddard, who did field work among the Apacheans before 1913, said that the Jicarillas still made pottery for household
purposes and that "the Jicarillas were rather noted for the excel-

2 *Tinajos* are large earthenware jars.

lent cooking pots which they made" (Goddard 1913: 143). Yet neither documented Jicarilla pots in collections (e.g., those in the Peabody Museum at Harvard) nor what has been recorded concerning Jicarilla pottery-making seems to warrant the idea that the vessels were "little." The account of pottery making obtained by Opler (1946: 94–95) indicates that the Jicarillas made vessels of various shapes and sizes, including "tall" *ollas* and large water jars, and more than one document of the American Period in New Mexico refers to their making large water jars.

No Spanish writer seems to have commented on the origin of the tribal name Jicarilla until the lawyer José Pichardo, in compliance with a royal order of 1805, prepared a defense of Spanish claims with regard to the Louisiana boundary. Among the documents he consulted was the diary of Juan Ulibarri, who traversed Jicarilla territory in northeastern New Mexico in 1706. Northeast of the Jicarilla villages, Ulibarri crossed that spur of the Rocky Mountains lying along the present New Mexico-Colorado border. Pichardo pointed out that in crossing this spur Ulibarri "left the cerro de la Xicarilla on the right" and goes on to say:

> It appears that the Cerro de la Xicarilla is a *cerro* that has the appearance of a little *xícara* (chocolate cup),[3] and therefore it was given this name. It appears also that some Apache Indians live in its vicinity, to whom, for the same reasons, the Spaniards also gave the name of Apaches Xicarillas, that is to say, the Apache Indians who live in the valley in which is the Cerro de la Xicarilla. (Hackett 1931–1946 III: 249)

It may be that Pichardo's explanation of how the Jicarillas got their name was pure conjecture, but the Spanish version of Ulibarri's diary does indicate that he passed a landmark or physical feature which he referred to as the "serro de la Xicarilla." In other New Mexico documents of the early 1700s, *cerro* often means an individual or isolated hill or mountain, so that the *cerro* mentioned by Ulibarri could have been shaped like a *jicarilla*, whether the word meant little basket, little pot, or chocolate cup.

---

3 The interpretation of *xícara* as "chocolate cup" here is that of the editor, Charles W. Hackett.

Actually, the identification of this peak depends on the accurate determination of Ulibarri's route. Thomas (1935: 17–18) seems to have thought that Ulibarri crossed from New Mexico into Colorado by or near what is now Ratón Pass, since he thought Ulibarri reached the Purgatoire River near present Trinidad. However, Albert H. Schroeder, in a mimeographed study of the Jicarilla Apaches issued in 1959,[4] suggests that Ulibarri struck out to the northeast after leaving the mountains near present Rayado, New Mexico, and crossed the low mountains along the New Mexico-Colorado border by using first a pass between Tinaja and Laughlin Peaks and then Emery Pass (Schroeder 1959: 20–24). A personal survey of the country between Rayado and Emery Pass has led the present author to agree in general with Schroeder and in addition, to suggest an identification of Ulibarri's "cerro de la Jicarilla" with a local landmark.

Thomas apparently transliterated the phonetically spelled *serro* as "sierra." In any case he translated it as ridge and thought that Ulibarri was calling the entire east-west mountain spur or ridge the "sierra de la Jicarilla" (Thomas 1935: 17, 64, 263 *n*15, 268 *n*61). In this interpretation Schroeder (1959: 23) has followed him. However, a lone peak representing the cerro de la Xicarilla is shown in roughly the location suggested by Ulibarri's diary on various copies of Miera's maps of 1778, not only on the one reproduced by Wheat (1957: map 176), which shows the "Cerro de la Xi," but also on two described as having "Cerro de la Xicarilla" written out (Wheat 1957: 111–13, maps 177, 178). Map 177 is reproduced in Bolton (1950). The original of this map is in the Archivo General in Mexico City. A section of the original is reproduced here as figure 3. As for the identity of the cerro de la Xicarilla, a prime candidate presents itself. About thirty miles east-southeast of Ratón, New Mexico, and within view of the pass that Ulibarri probably used to cross the moun-

4 Schroeder's report was prepared for the United States Government in connection with Jicarilla land claims. It is based almost entirely on published materials which I had already read and cited in preliminary drafts of this work before Mr. Schroeder presented me with a copy of his report late in the summer of 1959 while I was working with the Spanish, Mexican, and United States Territorial Archives in Santa Fé.

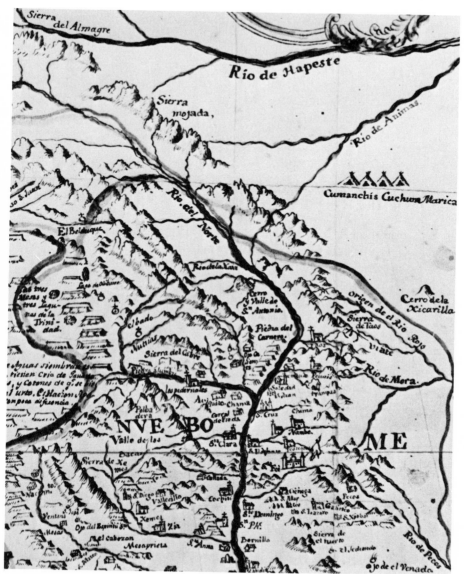

*Figure 3. Section of Miera's map of 1778 showing location of
"Cerro de la Xicarilla." Reproduced from a copy of original map
in the Archivo General in Mexico City.*

tains on the New Mexico-Colorado border is Mount Capulín, which has been described as the most nearly symmetrical volcanic cone in North America (Miller 1962: 269). In outline, Mount Capulín resembles the traditional chocolate cup of New Spain, inverted, or its crater might have suggested a chocolate cup to the settlers of New Mexico. In any case, Mount Capulín, now a national monument, is a striking landmark. If it was the cerro de la Xicarilla of the 1700s, those New Mexico settlers who named it might well have extended its name to the area between it and the Sangre de Cristo Mountains and to the Apaches who lived there.

Another bit of philological evidence constitutes an analogous situation and fortifies the belief that *jicarilla* did not denote a diminutive basket or pot, but rather a different item—the chocolate cup. A Spanish manuscript of 1716 indicates that *frixolillo*, which literally translated means "little bean," meant instead "peyote" (button) ([Hidalgo] Swanton 1942: 267).

When the Americans occupied New Mexico in 1846, the Jicarillas were divided into two bands that habitually lived apart. Contemporary government documents give no indication that American officials were aware of this dual band division as such, but ethnologists who worked with the Jicarillas in the late 1800s and early 1900s learned of it, and the two bands exist today. The origin of the two divisions, as well as the derivation of one of the band names, has been obscure.

Curtis, who apparently was among the Jicarillas sometime between 1898 and 1907, stated:

> The tribe is divided into two bands—commonly called by their Spanish names, *Olleros* (Potters) and *Llaneros* (Plainsmen)— within which marriage is not prohibited. In the days of the buffalo a part of the tribe, preferring the prairie country, remained there for a short time and received the name Kolhkahin, People of the Plains. The others returned to the mountains and from the pottery they there made were called Sait Ndĕ, Sand People, sand being used in mixing the clay. (Curtis 1907–1930 I: 54)

Elsewhere in the same work he says "the two bands into which the tribe is divided had their origin when a part of the tribe remained for a period on the plains after an annual buffalo hunt"

(Curtis 1907–1930 I: 54, 135). Curtis is the only author who gives an explanation for the original division of the Jicarilla into bands. Although he does not state the source of his information, it sounds as if he obtained it from the Jicarillas themselves.

Harrington refers to what must have been another early statement concerning the Jicarilla bands. It is unfortunate that he does not specify his source, for it apparently differs from Curtis in the interpretation of the band name "Ollero."

> It was long ago stated that the Jicarilla Lipanans were divided into two geographical divisions known, among other spellings, as the Olleros and the Ollaneros. Olleros was translated "mountaineers," referring to habitation of this division in the Taos mountains. Ollaneros was translated "plains people," referring to their location in the southwestern [southeastern] corner of Colorado and northeastern New Mexico. These two names should be Hoyero and Llanero. Hoyero is derived from Spanish hoya, "dell," "cove," or "corner in the mountains," being equivalent to rincon or rinconada. . . . Llanero is derived from llano, "plain." Hoyero thus means the same as serrano, "mountaineer," from sierra, "mountain." Hoyero is better however, since it refers to the division living in mountain dells instead of on the crests, which serrano, taken in its most literal sense, would indicate. . . . The Hoyero division ranged seasonally through the Taos Mountains. Apache Pass, east of Taos, still bears the name of these Apaches. . . . The old misrendition of Ollero as "pot person," from Spanish olla, "pot," . . . is of course absurd. (Harrington 1940: 511)

Harrington's opinion that Ollero should have been spelled Hoyero (the "h" being silent) makes good sense, because the chief difference between the two bands seems to have been one of environment. Although Hoyero cannot be found in a Spanish dictionary, recent questioning of Spanish speakers in a village in northeastern New Mexico revealed that there were still local traditions of "Hoyeros," so called "because they worked in the mountains" and "Llaneros," so called "because they worked on the plains." The band name "Ollero" is far less indicative of what was, historically, a real dichotomy between Jicarilla bands because both bands made pottery. The Ollero, however, were apparently more active in trading their ware in the New Mexican villages (Gifford 1940: 50, 141) and may therefore have come to be especially well-known as potters. The word Ollero does exist in modern Spanish with the meanings of potter and dealer in earthenware.

Meanwhile, there are reasons for doubting the statement of Curtis that the Olleros' Athabascan name, Sait Ndĕ (sand people) was derived from the fact that they mixed sand with their pottery clay. Gifford was told by both his Ollero and his Llanero informants that sand was not mixed with pottery clay, rather the tempering material was already in the clay (Gifford 1940: 50). This information is in agreement with the fact that modern Jicarilla pottery was made from heavily micaceous clay that needs no additional temper (J. Gunnerson 1959: 8; 1969).

Also, if one allows for known Apache dialectical differences and differences in the perceptions of those who recorded the words, the name of the Sait Ndĕ Band of the Jicarilla seems directly comparable to that of the Sejine Band of the Faraon Apaches mentioned in 1715 (Thomas 1935: 80) and to that of the Sejen-ne Apaches (Mescaleros) known to the Spaniards in the 1790s (Matson and Schroeder 1957: 336; hereafter referred to as M & S). These and other indications that the term may be pan-Southern Athabascan need to be considered before its meaning is defined in terms of one group. In this connection, the modern Mescaleros, like the Jicarillas, had a subdivision of "Plains People" known by their version of the Southern Athabascan term with this meaning (Gifford 1940: 188).

In March 1850, James S. Calhoun, United States Indian Agent at Santa Fé, submitted a map to the commissioner of Indian affairs showing the location of Indian tribes. He commented:

> The apparent dividing line between the Apaches and Utahs, commences on the Rio del Norte, about latitude 37°. The lands N.E. & E. from this point . . . to the Arkansas, is accorded to the Jicarillas, a band of Apaches well mixed with Utah blood— Occasionally, every tribe of Indians are to be found in this region—. (Abel 1915: 173–74)

On 18 November 1850 Calhoun said that the Jicarillas "for years past, have infested the vicinity of San Fernando de Taos, the country between it and Bent's fort, and that part of the Santa Fe Road which crosses the Rio Colerado [*sic*]." (Abel 1915: 269). It is noteworthy that in general the area indicated by Calhoun was that occupied by the Jicarillas and neighboring bands in the early 1700s.

Goddard, who worked among the Jicarillas in 1909, said that at the time of American occupation the Llanero Band made its home in the mountains between the Río Grande and the Plains and that the Ollero lived west of the Río Grande along the Chama River (Goddard 1911: 7). Gifford was told in 1935 that the Llaneros were formerly buffalo hunters who ranged from Trinidad, Colorado, to Las Vegas, New Mexico, and visited the Mora and Ratón areas (cf. figure 8). He, as well as Goddard, was told that the Olleros had lived west of the Río Grande, mainly along the Chama River (Gifford 1940: 188). In keeping with the information gathered by these ethnologists is the fact that the Jicarillas considered the Río Grande, Arkansas, Canadian, and Pecos Rivers sacred (Opler 1938: 44). The Jicarilla traditions and personal experiences recorded by Goddard (1911) document the fact that the Jicarillas camped in all parts of the area attributed to them. Moreover, living informants remembered when the Olleros and Llaneros had lived separately and on different sides of the Río Grande. One instance of a fight between the Olleros and Llaneros is recounted (Goddard 1911: 153). After all the Jicarillas were put on the same reservation, band affiliation seems to have become less significant, but only gradually. Opler, who studied the Jicarillas in 1934–1935, was told by informants that there were no cultural or linguistic differences between the Llaneros and Olleros. At that time the band difference served to provide opposing sides for the tribal relay race, held each year on 15 September (Opler 1936: 203, 216). In a Jicarilla myth collected then it is even stated that the bands were formed as a result of choosing up sides for the original ceremonial relay (Opler 1938: 86).

On the other hand, there seems to have been a tendency for the bands to live separately even on the reservation. An informant who lived among the Jicarillas before 1915 and remained for many years said that the Llaneros stayed mainly in flat country in the Horse Lake Region while the Olleros tended to cluster on the opposite side of the reservation. Moreover, while Opler was told that there were no cultural differences between the two bands, Gifford, who used a separate informant for each, found what Kroeber considered "an unexplained but consistent difference of coefficients between the Ollero and Llanero divisions," which he thinks may be attributed to the stronger plains relations of the Llanero remembered by native informants (Gifford 1940: 203). Wilson (1964: 315) mentions that the Olleros and Llaneros settled on different parts of their reservation and states that today the Olleros appear to be "progressives" and the Llaneros "conservatives" with regard to programs for change (see also Goddard 1913: 163, 169).

There is much in the historical record to suggest that the Jicarilla bands had an even more diverse origin than has been realized and that their association in recent times was the result of gradual coalition. The Olleros (Hoyeros?) were without doubt the descendants of the Jicarillas proper and possibly other Apache bands who early established themselves in the eastern foothills of the Sangre de Cristo Mountains, where they lived in flat-roofed adobe houses and irrigated their fields of maize, beans, and squash. The Llaneros are very probably the descendants of part of the Carlana or Sierra Blanca Apaches who once lived in the mountains of Colorado, augmented by Paloma and Cuartelejo Apaches from the plains of Colorado, Kansas, and Nebraska, where they had established seasonal or semi-sedentary farming villages after the Plains pattern with heavy reliance on buffalo hunting for subsistence.

Enemy aggressions brought these Apaches of the Plains and the foothills into closer proximity before the middle of the 1700s. Attacks by Utes and Comanches forced some of the Jicarillas proper to move at least occasionally into the western canyons of the Sangre de Cristos and the Taos Valley, and finally west of the Río Grande, while the Cuartelejos and Palomas of the Plains, suffering not only from Ute-Comanche forays but from pressures exerted by Caddoan and Siouan tribes in league with the French, finally moved into the eastern foothills of the Sangre de Cristos, once occupied by the Olleros.

Whatever the individual history of the Jicarilla bands, however, they are alike in that the core of their culture has remained Southern Athabascan (Opler 1936: 202). Indeed, Jicarilla history illustrates the Southern Athabascan talent for adapting to changed circumstances without losing the hard core of their cultural integrity; in fact, it is probably to this talent that the Jicarillas owe their survival.

Chapter Eight

The End and the Beginning: The Jicarillas from 1700 to 1760

The Jicarilla Apaches as such do not emerge into history until midway in the term of Governor Cubero (1697–1703). The name Jicarilla appears in the records without explanation, as if well-known, and the documents in which these Apaches are mentioned indicate that they were indeed already known, directly or indirectly, to Spaniards of various classes. The acquaintance was apparently based not only on visits of Apaches to Spanish-controlled territory but also on visits of Spanish subjects to the country of the Apaches.

Although the earliest documents from the 1700s do not reveal the exact location of the Jicarillas, they show that these Indians were a force with which the Spaniards had to reckon. At Santa

Fé on 28 June 1700, Governor Cubero ordered that one Miguel Gutiérrez, a condemned criminal, be executed, and his head stuck upon a pole in the Pueblo of Taos as a warning to the "apaches de la xicarilla" and other nations not to shelter fugitive Spaniards (Spanish Archives of New Mexico 77; hereafter referred to as SANM[1]). This order implies that it was Apaches de la Xicarilla who had harbored Miguel Gutiérrez. It also suggests that these Apaches frequented Taos and that the Spaniards knew it. The head upon the pole, distasteful as it would have been to Southern Athabascans, who fear the dead and things associated with death, apparently did not accomplish its purpose. Later in that same year some Pecos Indian ringleaders of a plot to kill the pro-Spanish governor of Pecos Pueblo escaped from prison in Santa Fé and fled to the "apaches de la Jicarilla" (Escalante 1962: 413–14).

In 1700, also, came another of the rumors concerning the French that were eventually to give the Jicarillas a prominent place in Spanish plans for the defense of their northeastern frontier. In this year the *alcalde mayor* of Taos relayed to Santa Fé the statement of a Plains Apache that the French had destroyed the village of the Jumanos (Wichitas), and the Spaniards, aware of the increasing activity of the French in both the northern and southern portions of the Mississippi Valley, feared that they might take over New Mexico, or at least make an unexpected attack (Escalante 1962: 413). Thus, although Spanish rule had been effectively re-established in New Mexico before 1700, the peace was an uneasy one. There was not only fear of French encroachment but, periodically, alarm caused by rumors of fresh Pueblo insurrections and Apache conspiracies as well as the very real annoyance of depredations by the Navajos and Faraon Apaches.

Bancroft, citing a New Mexico document now in the Pinart collection, says:

---

1 See SANM in *Bibliography*. Since these archives have already been listed and briefly described by Twitchell (1914) I have used his numbers. In 1968 these archives were made available on microfilm, along with a published *Calendar*, which also uses Twitchell's numbers, by the New Mexico State Records Center, Sante Fé.

In the spring of 1702 there were alarming rumors from various quarters, resting largely on statements of Apaches, who seem in these times to have been willing witnesses against the town Indians. Cubero made a tour among the pueblos to investigate and administer warnings, but he found slight ground for alarm. (Bancroft 1889: 225)

Another document corroborates the good behavior of the Apaches in the early part of this year and provides an additional reference to the Jicarillas. The *cabildo* (municipal government) of Santa Fé had supported Cubero in his bitter dispute with Vargas over the governorship. In 1702 the *cabildo*, attempting to enhance Cubero's standing with the viceroy of New Spain, stated (as a point in his favor) that "the Apaches del Acho, —de Jicarilla, —de Trementina, —de los Llanos, Faraones, and Chilmos, and the Janos, Utes and Navahos were now all at peace" (J. Espinosa 1942: 337 *n*76). But in spite of the efforts of the *cabildo*, the king reappointed Vargas governor.

During Vargas's second term, cut short by his death, the *cabildo* signed a complaint stating that Spanish settlers had been entering the country of the "Apaches de la Xicarilla" to trade, giving two and three horses for one boy or girl. The boys and girls sold by the Apaches were captives taken from other tribes and sold to the Spaniards for use as slaves or servants. The *cabildo* said that this custom, followed throughout New Mexico, was bad because most of the settlers were poor and had no breeding stock by means of which to maintain such prices. Moreover, failure to pay the price that the Indians had come to expect was said to be risky, leading even to loss of life. This complaint of the *cabildo*, dated 26 November 1703, concluded with a petition that the *alcalde* of Taos should not permit any person whatever to pass through in order to trade with any Apache tribe (SANM 91). From this document it appears that the settlers were dealing with the Jicarillas regularly somewhere beyond Taos and that Taos was the gateway not only to the Jicarillas but to other Apache groups.

The New Mexico that Vargas had taken over from Governor Cubero was not only poverty-stricken but was still vulnerable to attack from within and without. The settlers did not trust the Utes and Apaches; one of Vargas's chief complaints was that the town of Santa Cruz, which he considered essential for security against these tribes, had been abandoned during Cubero's administration and was in ruins (J. Espinosa 1942: 354). Early in 1704 there were fresh rumors of a revolt, and Vargas made a personal tour of investigation, finding no real cause for alarm. The "Reconquistador" died while on a campaign against the Faraon Apaches in April 1704, after designating his friend and lieutenant, Juan Páez Hurtado, as acting governor (J. Espinosa 1942: 356–58).

Late in December 1704 the Navajos and Utes, who had always been enemies of one another, were reportedly forming an alliance, together with some of the Apaches. Fearing another widespread rebellion, Hurtado held a general investigation that lasted into 1705. On 23 December 1704, a Tewa Indian named Philipe, formerly a governor of Santa Clara, declared that his own Pueblo was quiet. When he learned of the confederation of the "Yutas, Apache Navajoes, apaches de la Xicarillas, Yndios Xemes, y otras naciones" he was in the Pueblo of San Juan. "Los Naciones de apaches Navajoes, y Yutas, y Apaches de la Xicarilla" seem to have been considered the nucleus of the rumored alliance, but at a later point in the investigation, the cooperating groups are listed as Apaches "de Navajo, Xicarilla, Acho, trementina, Limitas, y Xilas." Other testimony stated that all "la apacheria de Navajo" had congregated with all the rest of the Apache nations "como son los de la Xicarilla, trementina, Acho, faraones, y Xilas" (SANM 104). Whether or not the alliance had taken place, it did not result in hostilities.

Since documents of the late 1600s and early 1700s show that Apaches, including some who lived in northeastern New Mexico, frequented the Pueblos, a statement of Father Fray Juan Alvarez made in January 1706 comes as no surprise.

> In the pueblo of Los Pecos, ten leagues distant from the villa of Santa Fé over a rough and mountainous road which is . . . always in danger from the hostile Apaches . . . Fray Joseph de Arranegui, is stationed. . . . In the mission of the Taos Indians . . . fifteen [leagues] from the nearest mission—the road

and posts along it infested with Apaches . . . is father preacher,
Fray Francisco Ximénez. (Hackett 1923–1937 III: 373–74)

Considering the time and energy expended by the Spanish
officials and military forces in political controversy, keeping
order within the province, and chastising enemies on its immediate borders, it is not surprising that little was accomplished
in the way of exploration beyond before 1706. In that year,
however, official attention was directed far to the northeast of
New Mexico. In the "unknown" land beyond Taos were the
apostate Christian Picurís who had fled to the Plains in 1696.
Many of these had already returned to their pueblo, for Father
Alvarez, in the document cited above, said of Picurís, "There are
about three hundred Christian persons, and others keep coming
in who have been among the Apaches" (Hackett 1923–1937 III:
374). Francisco Cuervo y Valdez, governor of New Mexico in
1706, said that the Picurís refugees had "sent several times to
ask my predecessors, the governors, to send squadrons of soldiers
to take them away and restore them to their old pueblo. Being
unsuccessful on those occasions, they repeated their request to
me" (Hackett 1923–1937 III: 383). This information had come
from three new emissaries who arrived at Taos on 22 June 1706,
with "ten tents" of Apache traders. These Picurís Indians said
there were about one hundred people, including both children
and adults, still among the Apaches, as well as many other
women whom the Apaches had captured (*cogidas*) and married
(Archivo General de la Nacion, provincias internas 36: 371–73*v*;
hereafter referred to as AGN. Prov. Inter.[2]).

Cuervo lost no time in acceding to the request of the Picurís.
Captain Juan de Ulibarri, *alcalde* of Pecos, was put in charge
of the party that left Sante Fé on 13 July to rescue the fugitives,
who were said to be "in captivity and oppressed by the barbarous
heathen Apache tribes of the plains and Cuartelejo" (Thomas
1935: 60–61) (see figure 4). Ulibarri's force included twenty-

2 For a guide to the collections in this repository, see Herbert E. Bolton, *Guide
to Materials for the History of the United States in the Principal Archives of
Mexico* (Carnegie Institution of Washington Publications 163, 1913). The copy
of Ulibarri's diary used for this study was a photocopy supplied by the Zim-
merman Library, University of New Mexico, Albuquerque.

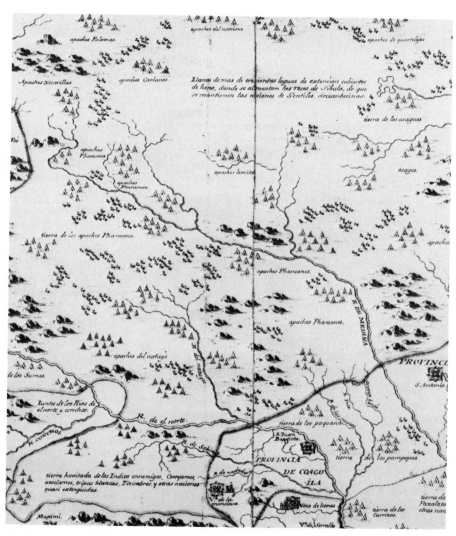

Figure 4. Section of Barriero's map of ca. 1728 showing locations
of various Apache bands east and north of Santa Fé. Reproduced
by permission of the trustees of the British Museum.

eight soldiers, twelve settlers who belonged to the militia, and one hundred Indians from the Pueblos and missions. An important member of the party was Captain José Naranjo, aptly called Kit Carson of the New Mexico frontier (Hallenbeck 1950: 209). This man, who spoke Tewa, Tiwa, Apache, and Spanish, had served as chief scout under Vargas in the pursuit of the Picurís in 1696, in the 1704 campaign against the Faraons, and was to later serve other important Spanish expeditions into the Plains in the early eighteenth century.

At Picurís, two "well-known" interpreters joined the group and also a guide—the Indian sent by the captives to carry their petition to the Spanish governor. The Indians still living at Picurís Pueblo furnished supplies for their kinsmen to use on the journey home, including cotton and woolen blankets and as many horses as they could collect. Ulibarri proceeded to Taos, where he heard that the Utes, so recently suspected of collusion with the Navajos and Apaches, were about to attack that Pueblo in league with the Comanches, a tribe never before mentioned in known New Mexico documents. The captain delayed his journey in order to provide defense, but the attack did not materialize. Having been relieved by Captain Felix Martínez, *alcalde mayor* of Taos and its jurisdiction, Ulibarri resumed his march. He followed Don Fernando creek, which still bears this name, for its entire length and crossed the first part of the mountains (figure 5). Once over the pass, he "descended to a very delightful valley which they call La Cieneguilla, eight leagues distant from the pueblo" (Thomas 1935: 62). Thus, Ulibarri was not the first to name this valley (the Moreno Valley), part of which is still known as La Cieneguilla.

Beyond La Cieneguilla, Ulibarri crossed a succession of ridges and valleys to which he himself gave names that have not survived. From the last summit he could make out the plains and "the unknown land with its trails." When he had "quite descended" the mountains he found a pleasant river of which he said: "To this I gave the name of Río de San Francisco Xabier (for him) under whose protection I was marching across unknown land, barbarously inhabited by innumerable heathens"

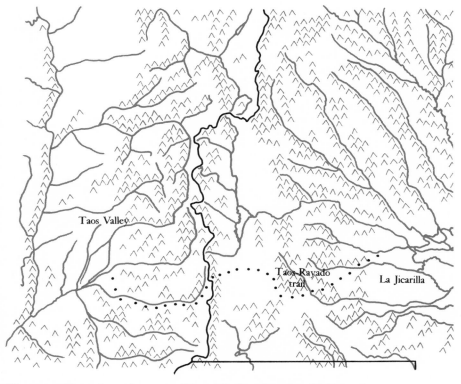

*Figure 5. Map of northeastern New Mexico showing Valley of
La Jicarilla and Taos Valley. East end of Taos-Rayado trail (dotted
line) is after William A. Keleher,* Maxwell Land Grant *(NY:
Argosy-Antiquarian Ltd., 1964), and is one variant. One inch equals
approximately ten miles. Based on 1968 USGS topographic map of
New Mexico.*

(Thomas 1935: 62). Clearly, then, even if Ulibarri was not familiar with the country, he knew very well that it was heavily populated. East of the San Francisco Xabier was another larger river to which Ulibarri gave the name Río de Santa María Magdalena.

> To this region the first heathen Indians of the Conexeros, Acho, and Río Colorado came down. They had been previously with some of those in the pueblo of Taos and had told me then in that pueblo, as they did now in this spot, that all the tribes were very happy that we Spaniards were coming into their lands and among their rancherías without doing them any injury. But that it would be well to guard ourselves from other nations who were on the road in the distance, particularly from those called the Penxayes, Flecha de Palo, Lemitas, and Nementina [*sic*, Trementina]. These had always been very bad thieves and had even injured them. I answered them that I esteemed very highly their information and advice, but that I was trusting in our God who was the creator of everything and who was to keep us free from the greatest dangers. After presenting them with much tobacco, knives, pinole, corn, biscuits, and having given them suitable presents, I said goodbye to them and they went away satisfied. (Thomas 1935: 63; AGN. Prov. Int. 36: 361)

Thus, even before he crossed the mountains Ulibarri knew that the Indians living on the other side were Apaches. Moreover, he had met some of these Apaches and knew the names of some of the bands.

Leaving the Santa María Magdalena, Ulibarri went on northward, crossing a series of streams. It is interesting that although he does not mention seeing Apaches or their villages on these streams on his outward journey, he visited Apache *rancherías* located between the San Blas and the Santa Cruz on his way back. Since he had both scouts and guides, it seems doubtful that he missed the Apache villages accidentally. He may have been in a hurry—he had already been delayed at Taos—yet the route he took involved him in boggy and treacherous terrain for three days. It is therefore possible that he deliberately avoided the Apache villages. Earlier documents already cited show that the Spaniards considered all Apaches a potential threat, and Ulibarri's mission in Apache country, the rescue of Pueblo Indians presumably being held by force, was not one which he could be sure would be welcomed. On the other hand, he may simply have changed his route after leaving the Santa María Magdalena because he had been warned of the Penxayes, Flecha de Palo, Lemitas, and Trementinas.

At any rate, Ulibarri apparently traveled for sixteen miry and difficult leagues to the north between the place where he met the Conexeros, Achos, and Río Colorados, and the spring of Naranjo, where he met the next delegation of Apaches.

> Other heathen Indians of La Xicarilla, Flechas de Palo, and Carlanas tribes came down to this place from the Sierra Blanca, under the leadership of different chiefs. The head chief was a lame man whom they called Ysdalnisdael. They showed a great deal of friendship toward us, saying that in the name of all the Indians of their tribe and of Chief Ucase [Ucate], they were coming to give me many manifestations of gratitude for having entered their land without doing them any injury; that they were all very happy; and that on my return I would find them together in the rancherías of the Jicarillas. There they would extend friendship that they had always maintained very consistently toward the Spaniards,[3] and not only they maintained it but also all the tribes that were living along the banks of all the streams I had seen and others that I had failed to cross, and others that I will meet further on; that they were very good people; they had not stolen anything from anyone, but occupied themselves with their maize and corn fields which they harvest, because they are busy with the sowing of corn, frijoles, and pumpkins. I, making use of this confidence, left with them some worn-out horses to keep for me, and having presented them with tobacco, knives, and biscuits, they went away very happy, carrying away the good presents which I gave them. (Thomas 1935: 63–64)

Although some writers, in interpreting the translation, have concluded that Ulibarri met Apaches who were not themselves Jicarillas in a region called La Jicarilla, the Spanish reads:

> aparar a el ojo de Naranjo, a este paraxe bajaron otros Yndios Ynfieldes, de las naciones Xicarillas, flechas de palo, y Carlanas, de la Sierra Blanca suxetos a distintos capitanes, y el muy principal un coxo a quien llaman Ysdalnisdael.

and the Apaches promise to await Ulibarri's return "en la Rancheria de la Xicarilla" (AGN. Prov. Int. 36: 361*v*). Thus

---

3 The Spanish reads "y alli que darian las paces que siempre avian guardado a los Espanoles mas firmes." (AGN. Prov. Int. 36: 361*v*)

Ulibarri met Apaches named Jicarillas, and their *ranchería*, or village, bore the name Jicarilla. In this passage, too, is evidence that the Jicarillas were already the principal band in the area, for the most important of the chiefs met by Ulibarri, later to be called "El Cojo," or "the Lame One," by the Spaniards, is identified as a Jicarilla in 1719 in the diary of Valverde (Thomas 1935: 115). Also the name of "Chief Ucase" reads "Ucate" in the Spanish diary (AGN. Prov. Int. 36: 361v). The existence of an Apache chief with such a name in 1706 is of interest because the remains of a seven-room adobe house attributed to Apaches and dated in the early 1700s has been found near the Ocate River, which appears with the variant spelling Ucate on a Spanish map made later in that century (J. Gunnerson 1969: 36). This word, which is actually Nahuatl *Ocóte* may have been a synonym for the Spanish tribal name Acho, which should have been spelled Hacho.

Leaving the spring of Naranjo, Ulibarri "marched ten leagues to the north and went over the stream of San Gil. We ascended to the pass of Buena Vista, crossed the ponds of San Pedro, passed on our right, the ridge of La Jicarilla" (Thomas 1935: 64). The Spanish actually reads "serro de la Xicarilla." The word *serro*, often spelled *cerro* in eighteenth-century New Mexico documents and now standardized in this form, refers to a hill or peak more often than to a ridge, therefore it was probably an isolated hill or small mountain that Ulibarri mentions (figure 3). In any case, with this passage the term "Jicarilla" is applied to a topographical feature in a manner suggesting that Ulibarri was not the first to name it.

Continuing on his way, Ulibarri reached the canyon of what was later to be called the Río de las Animas (figure 3) and is now called the Purgatoire River. On the flats bordering this stream, or one of its southern tributaries, the Penxayes Apaches had much land planted to corn, *frijoles*, and pumpkins. These Apaches showed fear of the Spaniards but came down from their mesa to talk. Ulibarri did not permit his party to injure their fields, which pleased and reassured them (Thomas 1935: 64). Shortly after leaving the fields of the Penxayes, Ulibarri climbed out of the canyon and started northward across the country. On their line of march the Spaniards intercepted an Apache of the Penxayes tribe who had with him two women and three little boys. "He [the Apache] said . . . that he was going to join all the rest who live along those rivers and streams in order to defend themselves together from the Utes and Comanches, who were coming to attack them according to the information of the rest of his tribe" (Thomas 1935: 65). Ulibarri gave them *pinole*, tobacco, and biscuits, and wished them a good journey, after which they were reassured and happy. The next day Ulibarri's party discovered a Penxaye Apache woman and a little girl picking cherries. The woman confirmed the threat of a Ute-Comanche attack and apparently also needed reassurances concerning the intentions of the Spaniards, for Ulibarri says, "Assured that we would do her no injury, given some pinole and biscuits, she was very happy" (Thomas 1935: 65).

When he crossed the large river called Napestle (Arkansas) by the Indians (figure 3), Ulibarri left behind him the allied Apache tribes who lived along the rivers and streams of the mountain canyons and foothills. On his return trip, he apparently did not see members of these tribes until he had arrived at or crossed the river he had named the Río de San Blas. The day after arriving at this river he says:

> We were among the rancherías of El Coxo and the rest of the chiefs who were awaiting us, and who entertained us a great deal. They gave us the news that the Utes and Comanches had attacked two rancherías; one of the Carlana and Sierra Blanca tribe, the other of the Penxayes tribe. They delivered to us the beasts we left with them to look after. We crossed the Río de Santa Cruz. (Thomas 1935: 76)

By sheer chance, Ulibarri's journey coincided with what seems to have been the first blow struck by the combined force of the Utes and Comanches against the Jicarilla Apaches and their neighbors (figure 4). Unfortunately, his expedition diary gives us only a brief glimpse of these Apaches before the decline of their peace and prosperity. And Ulibarri's diary contains puzzling contradictions. He calls the lands he traversed beyond the crest of the Sangre de Cristos "unknown," and yet the Apache bands in the area, and some of the landmarks, already bore Spanish or Nahuatl names. Some knowledge of the Jicarilla country was probably brought back to New Mexico by former settlers who had returned with Vargas. In 1694, for example, some of these men had been able to give Vargas information not only on the Utes but on the country of the Acho Apaches north of Taos.

In 1706 the Jicarilla country may have been officially unknown in that it had not been explored and described by persons of rank and authority, but documents attest that in 1700 it was a haven for fugitives from Spanish justice, and it seems reasonable that minor expeditions had entered Apache lands to bring these fugitives out. Also, the Santa Fé *cabildo* had stated explicitly in 1703 that private citizens were going to trade in the country of the "Apaches de la Xicarilla." The fact that such trade was subsequently prohibited probably accounts in part for the silence concerning the region beyond Taos.

Much in the statements of the Apaches met in 1706, too, suggests that Spaniards had been in their lands before. Their repeated expressions of gratitude for Ulibarri's kind treatment suggests that Spaniards did not always come into their lands in peace and friendship. Their protestation that they were very good people and had stolen nothing suggests that they were sometimes accused of stealing and thus reveals a possible source of trouble between them and the Spanish. However, their assertion that they and all the other Apaches along the streams in that area were always friendly with the Spaniards shows that all the foothills Apaches had contact with the latter. The fact that these groups had received little or no attention in official documents is not surprising; it was nearly always, in those days, the hostile groups who warranted the use of the scarce "stamped paper" used for official reports.

Although Ulibarri did not mention seeing Apache fields south of the Sierra Blanca, the people there said that they raised corn, beans, and pumpkins, and the Spaniards observed fields of these crops among the Penxayes to the north. In brief, the canyons and foothills of the Sangre de Cristos in 1706 were indeed inhabited by "innumerable heathens," as Ulibarri knew before he started out. He may have failed to visit their villages because they were not directly on his route, but he may have avoided them deliberately because of his mission to recover Picurís "captives."

While Ulibarri was on the Plains in 1706, Governor Cuervo, reporting on affairs in New Mexico, indicated that the Navajos bordered on the "Yutas, Carlanas, and Comanches" (Hackett 1923–1937 III: 381), suggesting that the Navajos were still more or less contiguous to the Apaches of northeastern New Mexico.

The Santa Fé Archives yield nothing concerning the Jicarillas for the next several years, perhaps because Governor Peñuela, who took office in 1707, was more interested in the Hopis and Zuñis and had to campaign against the Navajos (Bancroft 1889: 229–31). On the other hand, according to Cristóbal de la Serna (Thomas 1935: 105), the Utes and Comanches asked for and were granted peace in Peñuela's term (1707–1712), and no trouble with these tribes seems to have been reported during that time.

In 1714 during the regime of the elderly Governor Mogollón (1712–1715), trouble broke out again on several fronts. In March the Navajos violated the peace, and *Maestre de Campo* Roque Madrid attacked them at various rocky heights (*peñoles*) and towers (Escalante 1962: 453–54).

In September the Carlana Apaches reported that some Frenchmen from Louisiana, in the company of the "Jumanes" (Wichitas) had arrived at El Cuartelejo the month before and attacked an Apache *ranchería*. They had killed thirty Apaches and taken twenty-eight prisoners. At first the chief of the Cuartelejos had thought that the French were Spaniards from New Mexico but had later changed his mind (Escalante 1962: 454).

The Utes in 1714 were living at peace on the banks of the Río Grande among the Tewa Pueblos. In that year, however, they took offense at the Taos Indians and stole twenty-six horses from them. The Taos retaliated by killing three Utes and stealing forty horses. Outright war was averted by the Spanish governor, who forced both groups to give back what they had stolen (Escalante 1962: 447).

The Faraon Apaches had been harassing not only the Spaniards and some of the eastern Pueblos, but the Jicarillas as well. In a council of war held between 30 June and 6 July 1714, the Jicarillas are mentioned frequently as enemies of the Faraons (SANM 206).

Probably as a result of the rumor that Frenchmen had participated in an attack on El Cuartelejo in August 1714, it was supposed that the French were established in or near that area. Governor Mogollón of New Mexico tried to organize an expedition to reconnoiter and carry a letter to these Frenchmen (or whatever literate nation might be there). Captain José Naranjo had volunteered to carry the letter, but when, in keeping with standard procedure, the governor had asked the vice-custodian of the Franciscans to designate a chaplain for the expedition, the latter had refused because it was too dangerous. Thereupon, in April 1715, Mogollón submitted the matter to the viceroy of New Spain, the Duke de Linares, sending him a statement by José Naranjo that he would be willing to go to El Cuartelejo or beyond if necessary, taking only Indian volunteers. The objections of the vice-custodian were also forwarded. In June the *fiscal* (attorney general) of New Spain decided that the vice-custodian should be commanded to assign a chaplain to go with Naranjo. The viceroy finally decreed, on 11 July 1715, that if no Franciscan could be found who would go willingly, Captain Naranjo should go with a volunteer escort of Indians and soldiers (SANM 226).

No account of Naranjo's journey has been brought to light, but it seems highly probable that he made the expedition, for later, in 1719 he claimed he had been to El Cuartelejo four times. And Antonio Valverde, governor of New Mexico in 1719, said that Naranjo had reached and named the River Jesús María (Platte River), on which the Pawnees were settled. Moreover, by 1719, the Duke of Linares himself had conferred directly upon Naranjo the special title of "Captain Major of War of

New Mexico" (Thomas 1935: 101, 156), possibly as a reward
for undertaking the special mission to El Cuartelejo in 1715.

While authorities in Mexico City were considering the ad-
visability of sending José Naranjo to El Cuartelejo to contact
the French, the Spaniards in New Mexico were again discussing
campaigns against enemy Apaches (SANM 224), and during a
later council of war held on 20 July 1715, it was recorded that
the Jicarilla Apaches were numerous and powerful and inclined
to help the Spaniards against their congeners the Faraons. Testify-
ing during this council, Don Gerónimo, the lieutenant governor
of Taos Pueblo, identified the Apaches Chipaynes with the
Limitas, both of whom had been mentioned in earlier Spanish
documents of the post-Reconquest period. This witness clarified
Apache synonymy further by stating that the Chipaynes or
Limitas were Faraons and said in their own language they were
known as Sejines. These Faraons traded peacefully in Pecos at
the time of the ransoming, or fairs, but when they left they
stole animals from the jurisdictions of Santa Fé and Cañada
(Santa Cruz) and among the Indians of Jicarilla, "who enter in
peace in the pueblo of Taos and who have always kept it."
In spite of the depredations committed among them by the
Faraons, the Jicarillas apparently visited the latter in their
rancherías. Don Gerónimo stated, "The Jicarillas said that
always when one goes to their [the Faraons'] land, there are
many mules and horses in their possession which they have
stolen from here" (Thomas 1935: 80, 81).

The testimony of this Taos Indian indicates that there was
a specific place called La Jicarilla, for he comments that there
was no road from La Jicarilla to the territory of the Faraons that
had enough water for the Spanish herd. Moreover, he advised
that no Pecos Indians should be used against the Faraons, for
the two groups were so intimate as to be almost the same, and the
Pecos would warn the Apaches. He suggested that only the
Tegua (Tewa), Picurís, and Taos Indians should go, along with
"all the Jicarillas, who are many." Apparently he had authority
to speak for the Jicarillas, for he said that they offered both to

attack the Faraon *rancherías* and to serve as spies (Thomas 1935: 80–81).

Judging from the documents concerning the expedition that finally went out (Thomas 1935: 82–98), the Spanish did not use the Jicarillas as auxiliaries against the Faraons in 1715, but the governor may have been referring to the Jicarillas when he ordered General Juan Paez Hurtado to "take every precaution so that the heathen Indian allies who may be met on the route shall not be maltreated in any respect by the soldiers, the settlers, and the Indians of the pueblos" (Thomas 1935: 87).

Hurtado failed to locate the Faraons and assumed that they had learned of his campaign at Pecos and left their *rancherías* on the Colorado (Canadian) River. Hurtado's diary seems to be the first document in which the river is given this name, which he indicated was the Spanish equivalent of an Indian name identified later by Valverde as Apachean (Thomas 1935: 95, 116).

Two other observations in Hurtado's diary are of special interest. He went to the Plains through "the valley which is called Mora," where he saw an old house with adobe walls that may have been the one noted by Governor Vargas in 1696. Five and a half leagues farther he halted in another valley of which he said, "I called it the Valley of Corncobs because of the great quantities there are in it; it is a land famous for grain and herds" (Thomas 1935: 94). Since there is no evidence that Spanish settlers penetrated the Mora Valley until much later, in 1715 it was probably the territory of Apache farmers, the heathen Indian allies whom Hurtado might be expected to meet on this route, and the herds were probably buffalo.

Although the Comanches seem not to be mentioned in the decade between 1706 and 1716 and the Utes were more or less at peace, the hostility between these groups and the Jicarilla Apaches did not diminish. In 1716, while Governor Felix Martínez was away on an expedition, the Utes and Comanches, who were then living together, became hostile and committed many depredations at the Tewa Pueblos, at Taos, and at some of the Spanish settlements. The usual council of war was held between 20 August and 14 October 1716, and it was decided that Captain Cristóbal de la Serna should attack the enemy where they were settled at the Cerro de San Antonio, thirty leagues north of Santa Fé. It was also suggested that the "apaches de la Xicarilla y Sierra Blanca" should be asked to go on the campaign because they were known certainly to be good friends of the Spaniards and declared enemies of the Comanches and Utes (SANM 279). Fifty friendly Indians did go on the campaign, but their tribal affiliation is not specified. The battle was decisive—the Spaniards and their allies killed some of the Utes, put others to flight, and returned to Santa Fé with the greater part of the Utes as prisoners. This victory caused the Utes to seek peace the next January in 1717 and to ask for the return of their people captured by the Spaniards. But the interim governor, Felix Martínez, had sold the Ute prisoners into slavery in Nueva Vizcaya, although he told the Utes that some had died of small-pox and others had been baptized[4] (Escalante 1962: 456–58). It may have been this behavior of Martínez that caused the Utes, again allied with Comanches, to carry out in 1718 the depredations on Spanish settlements and Apache villages that are documented in records of 1719.

From Madrid, under date of 30 January 1719, came news of an international intrigue that was to influence Spanish relations with the Jicarillas for years to come. The Marquez de Valero, viceroy of New Spain, received notice that the duke of Orleans, regent of France, had allied himself with the king of England to declare war on Spain and that the "ports, plazas and presidios" of New Spain were to be guarded with all care (Thomas 1935: 139–40). Valero had these orders by 13 July 1719 (Thomas 1935: 140–41); at about the same time he received an undated letter from a Franciscan missionary stationed at Taos that may have suggested to him a means of strengthening the Spanish border defense. The missionary, Fray Juan de la Cruz, had been asked by a tribe of heathen Apaches to give them holy baptism, and he apparently had begun their con-

---

4 Once baptized, Indians could no longer live among "heathens."

version, meanwhile writing to the viceroy for advice on the matter (Thomas 1935: 137–38).

Valero responded by directing that a dispatch (dated 1 August 1719) be sent to Governor Valverde of New Mexico

> ordering him to employ with the greatest efficiency all his care to allure and entertain them [the Apaches] extensively, as all that is spent in this will be compensated as soon as he advises its import. Warn him that it is necessary to hold this nation because of the hostilities which the French have launched among the Tejas [Texas or Caddos], because the Duke of Orleans has threatened to declare war on our crown, in which France is not participating. As the Apache nation aided by ourselves could inflict considerable damage on the French and block their evil designs, the governor must assist with all the people that he can and on such occasions which offer themselves which await his zeal. Having recommended this to the governor, this father will be advised that the governor himself concurs in subjugating and entertaining the Apache Indians, taking advantage of the occasions which they have given, concerning which he wrote. (Thomas 1935: 138–39)

The evidence in later documents makes it certain that the Apaches referred to by Father de la Cruz were Jicarillas and possibly allied bands, who by September 1719 had already been suffering attacks from the Utes and Comanches for at least a year (Thomas 1935: 115). Their request for baptism was apparently the first move in a series of negotiations through which they hoped to obtain Spanish protection by becoming (or promising to become) Christians and subjects of the Spanish king.

The attacks on the Carlanas and Jicarillas in 1718–1719 seem to have been part of a general Ute-Comanche outbreak, for the Spanish settlements and Christian Pueblos had also experienced increasingly bold attacks from these tribes for about a year when Governor Valverde, on 13 August 1719, called a council of war to consider marching against them.

This council revealed that the Utes had been committing a growing number of depredations in New Mexico, especially in the valley of Taos. Statements of veterans of his Majesty's service indicate that under the guise of peace and friendship, the Utes had been stealing horses in the province for several years. The thefts had been tolerated by the settlers in order to preserve peace, but by 1719 the Utes were committing murder, and it was felt that the time had come to take action. Most of the soldier-citizens believed that the Utes were carrying out their current depredations in alliance with the Comanches and that this alliance had existed since the Utes began their misdeeds. It was recognized that the Comanches and Utes went about together, spoke the same language, and cooperated in all the robberies. One settler said that the Utes and Comanches interfered with "the little barter which this kingdom has with the nations which come in to ransom. They prevent their entrance and communication with us" (Thomas 1935: 105). (These "nations" were undoubtedly Apaches of various bands.) Juan de Archeveque, a prominent trader and frontiersman, was more specific. He stated that for more than seven or eight years the Utes and Comanches had come "to steal horses and rob herds and run away with the goods in the trade which this kingdom has with the Apaches of El Cuartelejo" (Thomas 1935: 107).

Because of the length of time required for dispatches to travel between Mexico City and Santa Fé, Valverde had probably not received the viceroy's injunction to "allure and entertain" the Apaches before he held this council of war at which a decision to chastise the Utes and Comanches was reached. He had received it, however, before the punitive expedition left Santa Fé on 15 September 1719, for the keeper of the expedition diary refers specifically to the viceroy's command (Thomas 1935: 131). Moreover, the diary makes many allusions to Valverde's kindness, generosity, and diplomacy in dealing with the Apaches, perhaps in order to impress the viceroy.

Valverde, like Ulibarri, went out to the Plains by way of Taos and the Valley of La Cieneguilla (the Moreno Valley), east of which the Spaniards found some stone landmarks placed by Apaches "so that they may not lose themselves" (Thomas 1935: 111). Seven leagues from La Cieneguilla, at the foot of a slope, was a stream that Valverde called San Joseph. In the vicinity was a small lake and a league from the lake were red hills with outcroppings of ore. About half a league from the spot where Valverde reached the San Joseph, members of his party found "a small adobe house where there were some pagan Apaches, who had sown and reaped their maize fields" (Thomas 1935: 112). These Apaches came to see Valverde and told him that "the Comanches were persecuting and killing their kinsmen and others of their nation." They declared this through interpreters—captain of war José Naranjo and an Indian of the Taos tribe, Don Gerónimo, both of whom were well-versed in the Apache tongue. When Valverde told them that he had come to punish their enemies, they were extremely pleased (Thomas 1935: 112). It appears, however, that these particular Apaches had not suffered *directly* from Comanche attacks.

Later the same day, a group of Apaches arrived from the *ranchería* of La Jicarilla. An old Indian woman on horseback said the Apaches' kinsmen had given them word that the governor had come, and they were coming to put themselves at his service. These Apache visitors carried a cross, at the foot of which was a parchment engraved with an image of the Virgin Mary adoring the rosary. They said they customarily wrapped up and guarded the image, which they also carried in battle. Their village, apparently called La Jicarilla, had been repeatedly attacked by the Utes and Comanches who had killed and captured so many of their people that they "no longer knew where to go to live in safety." When Valverde assured them that he was going to punish their enemies, the Apaches called him their father and said that they loved him a great deal "since he spoke courteously to them and was going to defend them." Then they offered to be baptized (Thomas 1935: 112–13).

On this occasion, Governor Valverde gave everybody—Indians and settlers—chocolate, and distributed tobacco to the Indians. "He commanded that if they had need of anything, they should let it be known so that they could be helped immediately. They answered that they needed nothing." Moreover, before leaving, these Apaches offered to accompany Valverde on the campaign (Thomas 1935: 113). At this time, then, in spite of what they had suffered, the morale of the Jicarilla Apaches seems to have been fairly high.

The next day, 22 September, the Spaniards left the vicinity of the San Joseph River. Three leagues away they found another river which the Apaches called La Flecha. There were Apache fields of maize, beans, and squash by the river, and a short distance up the stream was an adobe house with a cross on top. Eight more Apache houses were found farther up the river. The Spaniards stopped on the river of La Flecha, Valverde forbidding his soldiers to loot the fields. While the governor was eating, the Apache chief Carlana, some of whose people had been met by Ulibarri at the foot of the Sierra Blanca in 1706, arrived with three other Indians. Carlana greeted the governor with "Ave María," and Valverde, handed him the plate of boiled meat and vegetables from which he himself was eating. To the surprise of the Spaniards, Carlana ate the mutton that was on the plate but left the chicken, an action that may have reflected a general Apachean dislike for fowl (Schwatka 1887: 46; Goddard 1913: 139; Cornell 1929: 41). After Carlana had eaten, the governor asked him what he was doing and why he had come.

> To this he answered that he had come fleeing from his country, the Sierra Blanca, with half of his people to get the help of the Apaches of La Jicarilla. The rest of his people, he said, had gone for protection farther into a land of Apaches whom Chief Flaco governed, because of the continual war that the Ute and Comanche enemy made upon them. (Thomas 1935: 114)

When Carlana learned that the Spaniards were going out to fight the Utes and Comanches, he said that all his people would go with them to serve as guides. Then the Carlanas left, apparently pleased with the reception Valverde had given them.

On the twenty-third, the Spaniards left the La Flecha River and camped two leagues away

> on a small river where the Apache ranchers of La Jicarilla were living. Their chief is the one whom they call El Coxo (who) on this occasion was absent because he had gone to the Navajo province. This news his two sons gave, who, as soon as they had tidings of the arrival of the governor, came out with the rest of their people to see him. He received them with his accustomed kindness, entertained, fed them and gave them tobacco. These

said that on the very site and spot where the camp was placed, the Comanche and Ute enemies had attacked a ranchería of their nation, causing sixty deaths, carrying off sixty-four women and children, burning and destroying a little house in the shape of a tower which was there, and even the heaps of maize. There were none of their possessions that were not destroyed. For this reason, they had deserted that locality a year ago and had gone up the river to live. Since that had happened, they were sad and filled with misgivings and fear that the enemy might return and finish them entirely. (Thomas 1935: 115)

They were exultant when they heard that Valverde was going to campaign against the common enemy. This entry in the diary indicates that the lame chief, "El Cojo," who had been the most important in the area in 1706, was still alive. It is also the first of several suggestions that the Jicarillas were on good terms with the Navajos.

The governor took some of his men and rode up the river a league and a half to "seven terraced houses where some Apaches lodged." Many women and children, frightened by his arrival, fled to the hills, but others welcomed him.

It was seen that they had already gathered their crops of corn because they had placed it in the shape of a wall about a half a yard high. Many rows of the same (torn out) [parentheses in original] abundance, from which it was evident that the land is very fertile. On it they have many ditches and canals in order to irrigate their fields. Some had not finished harvesting and there was much corn in heaps not yet husked [on 23 September]. In this spot and region where the chief, Carlana, was domiciled there were counted twenty-seven tipis. The Indians showed great hospitality because they gave the soldiers many ears of green corn. On this occasion, Chief Carlana himself offered to go with all his people on the campaign, repeating the proposal which he had made previously; the Apaches of La Jicarilla did the same. (Thomas 1935: 115–16)

The governor left El Cojo's village and, after marching for eight leagues, came to "an arroyo which the Apaches called the Rio Colorado" (Thomas 1935: 116). Shortly after the Spaniards reached this river, which has been identified as the Canadian, twenty Apaches from the La Flecha River appeared and joined the expedition. They brought the news that the

Comanches had attacked two houses on the La Flecha and burned the inhabitants (Thomas 1935: 116).

Additional reinforcements were soon to appear. On 27 September, while Valverde was waiting out bad weather on the Rió de las Animas,

> Chief Carlana, the Apache chief of the Sierra Blanca, arrived in camp with sixty-nine Apaches of his ranchería and tribe. They circled the camp on their horses, jubilantly singing and shouting. In the evening these same messengers danced according to their custom, some covered with red and others with white paint. (Thomas 1935: 117)

They danced for a good part of the night, after which they feasted at the expense and request of the governor.

The next day they caught many deer, "so that the Indians were sufficiently provisioned with good, fat meat." On this day, Chief Carlana, after consulting the governor, sent out spies armed with arrows, *machetes*, and oval leather shields (Thomas 1935: 117).

They moved on again and made camp on another river. "In the woods some deer were caught by the Indians who, surrounding them, drove them into the camp, at which there was great glee and shouting." The river, named the San Miguel by the Spaniards, was in Apache territory, for the diary commented that many deer abounded there. Although these were good hunting grounds, the Apaches were fleeing from fear of the Utes (Thomas 1935: 117–18).

On 30 September, the governor ordered a count made of the horses which the Apaches had brought on the expedition with them. There were one hundred and three Apache horses, presumably belonging not only to Carlana and his sixty-nine Sierra Blancas but also to the twenty Apaches from La Flecha River who had joined Valverde first. Thus there were one hundred and three horses for eighty-nine Apaches.

On this day, Valverde's party must not have been far from the *ranchería* that Carlana and his people had once occupied in the Sierra Blancas. Apache spies sent out the night before had found and followed the trail of some Comanches who had gone to that abandoned *ranchería*. The spies were back with the main body of the expedition by ten o'clock the next morning. And at four o'clock the same afternoon more Apache spies returned with news that the enemy was very close. The Apaches who had remained in camp crowded around the spies, and "the Christian Indians tried to go where the latter were, but the governor would not allow it, but kept them alone." When the spies had reported, "considerable tobacco was given to the Apaches and the interpreters, for this is the best gift that can be made to them" (Thomas 1935: 119).

By the tenth of October, the expedition had seen several signs of the Utes and Comanches but had not yet encountered them. At sunset on that day, Valverde asked Chief Carlana to send out more spies.

> Chief Carlana agreed to this. It was decided that in order better to bolster up the fidelity of the Apaches two of his nation should go with four outside Indians, two of the pueblo of Taos and two of those from the Picuríes. All these were quite experienced because of the long time that they wandered among the heathens, for as apostates they fled during the rebellion they had. (Thomas 1935: 126)

Although they had found buffalo, and both the Indians and Spaniards had hunted successfully,

> Chief Carlana had not gone out to get meat on account of the great irritation he felt in not having found the enemy whom he desired punished if a good opportunity should present itself. He wanted the enemy restrained from the attacks they were making each day on his rancherías, killing many and capturing their women and children. The señor governor consoled him with gentle words designed for that purpose and presented him with a quantity of meat, tobacco and pinole, with which he went off very pleased. (Thomas 1935: 126)

Four days later the Spaniards came upon the tracks of a large number of the enemy. There were signs of "a multitude of horses, as well as the tent poles they carried, dragging along behind." However, because bad weather might lead to the loss of valuable horses, and for other reasons, Valverde decided to turn back.

On the same day, ten Apaches arrived from the region of El Cuartelejo. These messengers said that all of the Cuartelejos, more than two hundred tents, were on the Napestle (Arkansas) River. Word had reached them that the governor was in the area to punish the Comanches, and the Cuartelejos moved from their land in search of him.

On 18 October, Valverde sent two Taos Indians to the Cuartelejo camp. They returned with the information that the Cuartelejos were on the way and were bringing with them "another nation or *rancheria* of the same Apaches whom they called the Calchufines" (Thomas 1935: 130). The viceroy of New Spain had been

> pleased to command Valverde to solicit by all means possible the reciprocal friendship of the Apaches of El Cuartelejo, both for the good purpose and Catholic zeal of his excellency to convert them to our faith, and to be able, by means of them, to attain a knowledge of the location, designs, and movements of the French. (Thomas 1935: 131)

Therefore, Valverde received a Cuartelejo chief who arrived two days later with much friendship, and from this chief he apparently obtained information about the French.

On the twenty-first about a thousand Apaches, including three hundred warriors, reached the Arkansas River where they encamped across from the Spaniards "in the form according to their custom and military arrangement." Visiting the Cuartelejo camp, Spanish officers saw "the dogs, on which were loaded the poles for tents and other utensils they used." Valverde questioned an Apache chief who appeared to have a gunshot wound. This chief and his people had lived "farther in from El Cuartelejo, on the most remote borderlands of the Apaches." The French, allied with the Pawnees and the Jumanos, had ambushed them while they were planting corn. These Apaches had escaped, "protected by a walled ditch," the night after the encounter (Thomas 1935: 132, 232). The Apaches who had suffered this attack were apparently called Palomas, and their lands were now held by their attackers. Since the French and their Indian allies were coming closer every day, the Apaches had moved to the lower part of the Napestle River where they could live in relative safety from their enemies.

Still other Apaches of the same *ranchería* were on their way to join those camped near Valverde, but he could not wait to meet them because his supplies were exhausted. Having returned to Santa Fé, Valverde wrote to the viceroy on 30 November 1719 giving a brief account of his expedition. In it he gave details on the culture of the Jicarilla Apaches. It is significant that in a statement made in Santa Fé before Visitor General Pedro de Rivera, Valverde spoke of all his Apache allies on this expedition as Jicarillas (Thomas 1935: 232). The Jicarilla settlement pattern was reported to be flat-roofed houses "at some distance from one another." Valverde's diary mentioned single, isolated houses but also small clusters of seven or eight. Of the Jicarillas he said: "They work hard, gather much Indian corn, squashes and kidney beans, lay out ditches to irrigate their crops," and of Spanish relations with the Jicarillas, they "have always maintained and at present maintain friendship with us" (Thomas 1935: 141–42).

The statement that the Sierra Blanca Apaches of Chief Carlana were living in tipis at La Jicarilla should not be taken to mean that this was their normal mode of existence. They were farmers as much as the Jicarillas but had been driven from their original *rancherías*, and in their land Valverde passed by many abandoned and ruined *rancherías*. He apparently attributed these *rancherías* to Carlana's Apaches, and if there were actually "ruins," then they must have been some sort of structure other than tipis. Again, Valverde mentions the "enclosures" that exist in the *rancherías* of the Apaches (Thomas 1935: 142). Valverde's account of how El Cojo's Jicarillas had moved their village a few miles upstream after a Ute-Comanche attack does not make sense strategically, since they had not moved far enough to avoid the enemy, but it is meaningful in terms of the Apache custom of abandoning a place where people have died.

The governor's letter added a few details to previous knowledge of the Cuartelejos, most of which comes from Ulibarri's diary of 1706. First, some Cuartelejos had been in Taos trading while Valverde was there and had carried the news of his coming through all "Apachería." In the letter, moreover, Valverde states that Paloma Apaches, among others, were with the Cuartelejos. Although the chief of the Cuartelejos had a horse in 1706 and a Spanish soldier had at that time traded two more horses to Cuartelejo Apaches for two guns captured from the French (Thomas 1935: 173), Valverde says these Apaches were carrying their tents on dogs. Moreover, he calls their tents war-tents, perhaps implying that they had other types of structures. In Valverde's diary, it is stated that the Palomas had abandoned their own country to flee from the French, Pawnees, and Jumanos (Wichitas). The governor's letter adds that although the Palomas had begun to settle in El Cuartelejo, they were now deserting that spot because they were molested by the Utes (Thomas 1935: 144). When the Apaches said they were establishing themselves on the lower part of the Napestle, they may have meant as far south as they could get on the "great bend" of the Arkansas, rather than farther downstream.

On the date he wrote the letter summarized above, Valverde, probably in consequence of an order from Valero, was already planning a reconnaissance to locate the French who were supposed to be northeast of New Mexico. "I am prepared for the time being, as I mentioned in my former letter, to attend to the matter personally, or my lieutenant-general will do it until the enemy is seen, so that I can report to your Excellency in regard to everything with more certain knowledge, if in the interim I have no new superior order" (Thomas 1935: 145). Back in Mexico the auditor of war, Revolledo, interpreted this to mean that in the following year (1720) Valverde would attempt to penetrate as far as the French settlements (Thomas 1935: 14), and it was apparently in a letter by Revolledo written on 29 December 1719 that the idea of a *presidio* and mission in El Cuartelejo was first advanced (probably because the auditor confused Valverde's accounts of the Cuartelejo Apaches with his accounts of the Jicarillas).

That which has suggested itself to the auditor general is that in El Cuartelejo, to the vicinity of which the governor of New

Mexico penetrated, and where he intends to go in the coming year, a presidio be placed with twenty or twenty-five soldiers and two or three missionary fathers who should instruct the Apaches and establish a perpetual alliance with those who are in their nation very numerous. By this means and that of military forces, the boundaries of the kingdom may be safeguarded, and the ingress of the French impeded. . . . He [Valverde] should persuade the Apaches that for their safety they congregate about the presidio, and at the same time take advantage of their alliance and work in the fields, for sowing and other necessary things. The light of the Gospel and the royal protection will be given them. It should also follow that, being so scattered they extend to the Tejas and the Mississippi River, we shall use them as an auxiliary in those parts for defense. (Thomas 1935: 150)

Apparently the "lords of the council of the treasury" held a meeting late in 1719, at which it was agreed that Valverde or his lieutenant-general should reconnoiter the French and that the *presidio* should be placed at El Cuartelejo as suggested by Revolledo. A dispatch informing Valverde of the decisions was sent on 10 January 1720; Valverde, who was in El Paso, received it on 4 March. By 27 May he was back in Santa Fé where, on that date, he formally set out in writing his objection to the establishment of a *presidio* in El Cuartelejo "which is at so great a distance, in the center of Apachería, that they could not be assisted with military forces" and suggested that La Jicarilla must have been meant instead. With his opinions he included those of settlers who had knowledge of Apachería, and from them can be gleaned additional information on both El Cuartelejo and La Jicarilla.

Captain Major of War José Naranjo, who had been to El Cuartelejo four times and opposed a *presidio* there, describes La Jicarilla thus: "the spot promises great resources since its valley have [*sic*] a great abundance of water and timber, twenty-five men were not even sufficient for the post of La Jicarilla, because it is forty leagues distant from this villa, is very rough, and the number of Apaches is great and . . . these have great readiness in assembling" (Thomas 1935: 157).

Captain Miguel Tenorio . . . alcalde mayor of the valley of Taos and Picuríes . . . has seen the valley of La Jicarilla [figure

5] many times. . . . He is informed that between the valley of Taos and that of La Jicarilla, there are veins of minerals in the range which divides the two valleys, so that this valley developed and settled, some wealth could be hoped for, and *it is the key of the frontier of the northeast* [italics mine]. (Thomas 1935: 157–58)

The opinions of Valverde's officers, given in council on 2 June 1720, were summarized by Valverde in an additional letter in which he states that he wishes to establish the proposed *presidio* in La Jicarilla if the viceroy has no better thought. In this letter, likewise, he announced that his lieutenant-general, Pedro de Villasur, would set out on the reconnaissance of the French settlements.

The details of Villasur's defeat by the Pawnees and the French have been examined at length by historians. Several points should be reiterated here. The Spanish were massacred on a river said to be the boundary between the Cuartelejo Apaches and the Pawnees (Thomas 1935: 163). Among those killed were José Naranjo and Juan de Archeveque, who knew Apachería from previous expeditions. Naranjo, moreover, knew the Apache language and had served as an interpreter. Phelipe Tamaris, a survivor of the expedition, testified in 1724 that Villasur took along

half a load of tobacco, a little baize, some sombreros, and some short swords and knives, in order to satisfy with them the chiefs of the Carlanas, Jicarillas, and El Cuartelejos, who might serve as guides. This was done among the Carlana tribes, where they opened what they carried and gave baize, knives, sombreros, and tobacco to those who were guides on their route. (Thomas 1935: 251)

Other, less detailed testimonies corroborate most of Tamaris's statements, but it is still not clear whether any Jicarillas actually went with Villasur.

The survivors of the Villasur expedition

on their return had the good fortune of finding refuge among the Indians of the Apache tribe who came out to meet them with great tenderness, giving signs of much sympathy on account of the misfortune of those who were left dead. It must be wondered at that they, being heathen and seeing our men so

weakened in health and strength, did not attempt to take away
the horses they had with them; otherwise more than those who
perished in the encounter would have been lost. They not only
did not do this, but kept them in their company with much
kindness for two days, supporting and succoring them with their
poor provisions. Their excellent conduct did not stop here, but
they all offered to take revenge, manifesting a great desire that
the Spaniards return to those frontiers in order that, allied together, they could make war effectively on the French and
Pawnees [Valverde]. (Thomas 1935: 165–66)

If it was not the Jicarillas themselves who sheltered Villasur's
men, the behavior of these helpful Apaches was at least consistent
with what we know of the relations between the Jicarillas and
Spaniards at the time.

After the Villasur affair had been investigated in Mexico
City, the auditor Revolledo, in a letter to Viceroy Valero dated
9 December 1720, stated that the much-discussed *presidio* originally intended for El Cuartelejo should be placed in "the region
of La Jicarilla . . . to aid the assembled Apaches in this very
area of La Jicarilla, and to serve as a bulwark for that realm
because it is on the road which goes directly to the settlements
of the Pawnees and French" (Thomas 1935: 176).

What, if anything, was done concerning the Jicarillas and
their *presidio* during the next three years is not revealed in the
documents available. On 8 November 1723, however, three
"captains" of the Apache nation (Thomas 1935: 201) appeared
in Santa Fé before Valverde's replacement, Governor Bustamante, and reported a new and especially devastating attack
by the Comanches. These captains were Carlana, chief of the
Carlana or Sierra Blanca Apaches (who were apparently living
still or again as refugees in the valley of La Jicarilla), and two
others of the "heathen" Apache nation (Thomas 1935: 194).
Whether the other two of these were Churlique, whose name
first appears in Bustamante's diary, and Cojo (or Coxo) "the
lame one," met not only by Bustamante in 1723 but by Ulibarri
in 1706 and Valverde in 1719, is not entirely clear. In any case,
these seemed to be the most important leaders living in the
valley of La Jicarilla in 1723, for no others are noted by name.
Their story was pathetic.

[The Comanches] had attacked them with a large number in their rancherías in such a manner that they could not make use of weapons for their defense. They launched themselves with such daring and resolution that they killed many men, carrying off their women and children as captives. . . . Because they recognized that they are not safe from their enemies any place, they are asking me [the governor] to protect and shield them with the arms of his majesty. Concerning this, they have conferred and communicated with the rest of the captains and people of the rancherías of their nation, because they have the same fears. In order to get away from them [the Comanches], they are seeking more pleasant living in entire peace and tranquility under the security of the arms of his majesty, giving him henceforth the required obedience. For this reason, they are praying that I administer to them the sacrament of holy baptism, and their entire nation, having received it with all their heart, will settle in their pueblos in the same form and economy with which the Christian Indians of this kingdom live; that priests be assigned them to teach and instruct them in the mysteries of our holy faith, and that an alcalde mayor govern them. They will submit themselves to everything with punctual obedience commanded them, since they realize that the ruin they have suffered and which their enemies have inflicted on their rancherías has been because they have been remiss in coming to the fold of our Catholic and true religion. For the success of their good desires they have asked me, the governor, to go to the valley of La Jicarilla to survey the place and situation which offers the most advantages for the foundation and establishments of said pueblos with their lands so that they may reap their crops. (Thomas 1935: 194)

A council of war (9 November 1723) at which the Apache captains were present decided that Bustamante should give up plans for a campaign against the still troublesome Faraon Apaches and instead aid the Jicarillas and their allies. It was hoped that if these peaceful Apaches became settled, other tribes of the Apache nation, which was still so dispersed that it bordered on the Pawnees, Cadodachos (Caddos), and Canzeres (Kansas), would follow their example and thus provide a bulwark against the French. Moreover, the valley of La Jicarilla (figure 5) was apparently especially important, for it was a passageway for the French (Thomas 1935: 196). The decisions of the council were explained to the Apache captains through Gerónimo Ylo, Indian chief of the Pueblo of Taos, and Juan Luján, a soldier, who acted as interpreters.

Bustamante set out from Santa Fé on 17 November 1723 and eight days later arrived at the "chief river" of La Jicarilla, the Río de Guadalupe, at the spot "where the valley of La Jicarilla begins." The Río Guadalupe, said in Bustamante's diary to be the principal stream of La Jicarilla, must have been named otherwise by Valverde, who presumably went through the same territory. Where the valley began, Bustamante was met by Carlana and six other captains. Again the interpreters were the Taos chief and Juan Luján the soldier. But when Bustamante told Carlana's Apaches that he had come to select a site for their pueblo, where they would have to live like Christians, the Apaches said that they would confer with other captains at *rancherías* "further in" concerning the matter. The next day, after traveling five leagues farther, Bustamante arrived at the *ranchería* of Captain Churlique, who had an engraving of the Virgin Mary wrapped in buckskin.[5] Churlique wanted the Spanish to join with various *rancherías* of Apaches to make war on the Comanches, but Bustamante insisted that first the Apaches must be baptized and settled in pueblos. Churlique, like Carlana, wanted to postpone a decision until he had conferred with the chief of a *ranchería* nearby, which may have been that of Cojo, only four leagues down the "valley." Cojo wanted to be baptized also but apparently had been baptized before, for it was explained to him that since he was already a Christian he could only be absolved of apostasy. He told Bustamante that the Apaches, who were dispersed among various *rancherías*, would write and inform the Spaniards about bringing them missionaries and an *alcalde mayor* the next spring. Bustamante gave each captain a horse and some flour and took possession of the land with a three-gun salute. "I received and admitted under the royal protection all those vassals who were present and all the rest who were absent and were natives of those rancherías" (Thomas 1935: 200–201). Thus, *the Jicarillas and the followers*

5 The chief who possessed such an engraving in 1719 was not named by Valverde.

*of Carlana became Spanish subjects, legally entitled to the
protection of Spanish military forces.*

It is difficult to compare Valverde's diary of 1719 with that
of Bustamante because of the differences in terminology. Both
Spaniards encountered Carlana and El Cojo; both encountered
a chief who carried an engraving of the Virgin wrapped in
buckskin. Both noted *rancherías* a few leagues apart along their
way. La Jicarilla and its population in 1723 was apparently
much as it had been in 1719. However, in the earlier year, the
Jicarillas and Carlanas, in spite of their problems with the Utes
and Comanches, had declared themselves in want of nothing,
whereas 1723 found them almost willing to trade their freedom
for peace and safety under Spanish domination.

As a result of his journey to La Jicarilla, Bustamante urged
upon the new viceroy, Casa Fuerte, the desirability of a *presidio*
in that area (Thomas 1935: 202–3), and the *fiscal* asked that the
laws which required "special care and vigilance in the conversion
and voluntary submission of the Apaches" be fulfilled (Thomas
1935: 204–5). The auditor Revolledo, too, recommended missionaries and soldiers for the Apaches of the valley of La Jicarilla,
"who, with those of El Cuartelejo, and Sierra Blanca of *the
same nation of Apaches* [italics mine], esteem the Spaniards of
New Mexico either because of the preference which they have
for our people or because of the hatred they have for that of the
Comanche" (Thomas 1935: 205). Here the Jicarillas, Cuartelejos, and Sierra Blancas are lumped in the same subdivision of
the much larger Apachean population, and the idea that these
tribes (plus the Palomas)were all Jicarillas seems to have persisted, though it was not always made explicit.

While the matter of a *presidio* in La Jicarilla was being considered in Mexico City, the Utes and Comanches attacked the
Jicarillas still another time, apparently early in 1724. The
governor called the usual council of war, and it may have been
then that the priests, Fathers Mirabal and Irazábal, gave the
opinion that since the Jicarillas were Christians, and the Comanches had been notified of it, retaliation against the Comanches
was justified by the scriptures (Bancroft 1889: 239). An expedi-

tion was sent out, and Bustamante was able to recover sixty-four Jicarillas. Even so, the Jicarillas had decided that since they had no protection in their own land, they would go to the Navajo country (Thomas 1935: 208). The *fiscal*, however, urged that the Jicarillas not be suffered to "escape" to the region of the Navajos and suggested that they be settled close to the Pueblos already under Spanish control (Thomas 1935: 209).

Then, by order of 21 October 1724, Viceroy Casa Fuerte had the pertinent documents given to Brigadier Don Pedro de Rivera, who was about to begin a tour of inspection of frontier posts (Thomas 1935: 209, 281). Rivera did not reach Santa Fé until late June (Thomas 1935: 281 *n*177). In his *Diario y Derrotero* he says almost nothing of the Jicarillas, and what he says is in error, for he identifies the Jicarillas, Cuartelejos, and Palomas with the Gilas, Faraons, and others as enemies of the Spaniards (Porras 1945: 78), a statement that is controverted by the historical record.

However, in a letter to Casa Fuerte several months later, Rivera, having been asked to review the Jicarilla situation and give advice, shrewdly suggested that the desire of the Jicarillas to become Catholics and subjects of the king was prompted only by a desire for protection from the Comanches. He said that La Jicarilla was too far from secure Spanish territory to be effectively defended and suggested instead that the Jicarillas be settled near Taos Pueblo.

> The larger part of this nation fled to the said pueblo of Taos in order that it might serve them as a refuge, because of news which they had that the Comanches were coming. I, having had word that they were in the said pueblo, requested the reverend father missionary of the cited pueblo to advise, induce, and persuade them to remain in the vicinity of that pueblo, as the lord fiscal suggested in his last cited opinion of October 20, 1722. (*Marginal note:* It was a mistake of the señor brigadier, as may be seen in number 78; it is of 1724.) On no other occasion and in no better place could the settlement of the said nation be confirmed, even though it were larger because in the neighborhood of the said pueblo of Taos, the best of that kingdom, there are valleys as rich and abounding with water as there are in that of La Jicarilla. With the cost alone of what the tools and the corn which they could consume in a year would amount to, they

could be settled in the cited spot at the greatest security for them and without the increased expenditure which would ensue with the erection of a presidio. For in crossing from the pueblo of Taos to that of La Jicarilla a ridge of mountains intervening makes traveling less easy in case of succoring them. (Thomas 1935: 212)

The *fiscal*, the auditor, and the viceroy accepted Rivera's recommendation, and the file on the *presidio* for La Jicarilla was closed on 1 April 1727 (Thomas 1935: 219). Undoubtedly, a dispatch was sent to the governor of New Mexico ordering him to carry out Rivera's recommendation, but at the end of April, before Bustamante could have received such a dispatch, he sent the viceroy news that shed additional light on the Jicarillas and Cuartelejos and suggested strongly that the French were ingratiating themselves among the outlying Apache tribes. There were in Taos a number of Jicarillas. These were probably still living in La Jicarilla, since he said their territory adjoined the jurisdiction of Taos. Also six Frenchmen were in El Cuartelejo. Five had gone with the Apaches in search of the Comanches. This information was corroborated by another source.

> During the month of September of the year of '26 an Indian chief of the pueblo of this government went out, among others of his nation, to hunt meat and it happened that, having arrived at the land of the above mentioned Jicarilla nation, many Indians of this tribe told him, because he was supposed to be one of themselves, that if he wanted to see a Frenchman, they would take him inside of three days where one was. The latter, either because of his shyness or because he had sufficient affairs to occupy himself, did not wish to comply with that which they asked of him. They indicated to him that the Frenchman was stopping in the vicinity of El Cuartelejo, and that other Frenchmen who came with him had left him there. Those went with a great force of Apaches of the nations Palomas, Cuartelejos, and Sierra Blancas to look for the Comanches (a people widely scattered because of the numerousness of their nation) [parentheses in original] to see if they could force them to leave these regions. The information which I am giving according to the Jicarilla Indians from the context of their tale is that the French have conquered and won to their devotion the greater part of the infidel Indians who were living on the plains, which they call the buffalo (plains). (Thomas 1935: 257–58)

In the same letter Bustamante mentioned that Escalchufines and Palomas had brought Comanche prisoners to Santa Fé during Rivera's visit in 1726. These Comanches told the Spaniards that there were white men among the Apaches who captured them. Since the Pueblo Indian referred to by Bustamante found Jicarillas still occupying their lands in September 1726 and since there is no indication that those Jicarillas who were in Taos in April 1727 were refugees, it seems that some Jicarillas were still living in La Jicarilla as late as 1727. Also, Apaches still held El Cuartelejo, but Frenchmen were among them and attempting to help them deal with the Comanches. It is noteworthy that Pichardo (Hackett 1931–1946 III: 244) gives a different version of Bustamante's letter, previously cited. Pichardo indicates that the Frenchmen with the Cuartelejo Apaches were trying to get the Comanches to settle down.

By this time, however, officials in Mexico City were no longer excited by rumors of Frenchmen in the vicinity of New Mexico. It was Revolledo's opinion that the French were in El Cuartelejo only to trade with the Indians and that they had no intention of attacking the Spanish. This relaxed point of view probably arose from direct experience with French traders who had penetrated as far as Mexico City via Texas (Folmer 1941: 249–60). Nevertheless, it was considered desirable for the governor of New Mexico to continue to investigate, through the Indians, rumors concerning the French and keep the viceroy informed of their activities (Thomas 1935: 260).

As the Spanish fear of French encroachment from the northeast abated, so did the desire to extend permanent Spanish settlements beyond the Sangre de Cristos. The poverty of New Mexico virtually forbade such expansion. Moreover, since the brunt of Comanche attacks had fallen on the peaceful Apache tribes, the Spaniards were not yet fully aroused against the marauders on their own behalf. This made it easier for them to feel that they were satisfying any obligations they might have to the Jicarillas, nominally Spanish subjects, by settling them west of the Sangre de Cristos near Taos.

As late as 26 August 1727, Governor Bustamante had not

himself taken action in this matter, as is shown by his letter of that date to the viceroy.

> Most excellent señor. Señor: I received your Excellency's superior despatch on the occasion when I was ready to march with the forces of this presidio to make a campaign, the motives for which the nations of the Faraones Apaches supply me every day. For this reason, and because the Apaches of La Xicarilla are scattered, fearful of the Cumanche nation, their chief enemies, some of them having taken refuge in the province of Navajo (whose heathen inhabitants are their friends) [all parentheses appear in original] and others on the extensive plains of Los Cíbolos, in order to comply with the superior despatch, as soon as I return from the said campaign and learn that the said Xicarillas are restored to their country, I shall go to them in person (when the winter is partly over) to execute that which is provided in the said despatch. I shall give a detailed report to your Excellency of everything I do, and of the result. May God keep you many years, as you merit and as I desire. Villa of Santa Fé, in New Mexico, August 26, 1727. Most excellent señor, at your Excellency's feet. Juan Domingo de Bustamante. To the most excellent señor viceroy, the Marquis of Casafuerte. (Hackett 1931–1946 III: 246)

When Bustamante finally did go to see the Jicarillas, they did not want to settle in the Taos Valley because their own lands were very fertile, and they could get good harvests with very little effort (SANM 347). This statement would suggest that they were still farming in 1727.

Actually, however, there are some indications that Jicarillas had already begun to settle in the Taos Valley, either through their own initiative or through the efforts of Father Mirabal of Taos. Entries in the records of the Taos mission indicate that Fray Juan José Pérez de Mirabal served there between 26 October 1722 and 29 July 1727 and that during this period Apaches who settled on the Río de las Trampas (the stream that flows through the present village of Ranchos de Taos) in Taos Valley asked for him as missionary. The request was granted, and it seems likely that he departed from Taos in 1727 to work among the Jicarillas, not only before the date of Bustamante's letter but well before the time at which the governor intended to carry out the viceroy's instructions. It may have been Father Mirabal who initiated construction of the Jicarilla mission church, at which he was apparently serving in 1733 (Adams and Chávez 1956: 337; hereafter referred to as A & C).

In 1727, the Apaches of the Sangre de Cristos were drawing near the end of an era. There are several indications that the Jicarillas proper and Carlanas went different ways at about this time. Bustamante's letter of 30 April 1727 had said that the Frenchmen reported to be in El Cuartelejo had gone with Palomas, Cuartelejos, and Carlanas to look for the Comanches. His statement suggests that the Carlanas who had sought safety with the Jicarillas and had not found it had decided instead to join the Plains Apaches (with whom they were still associated at mid-century).

When Bustamante said, in August 1727, that some of the Jicarillas had taken refuge on the Plains, he was apparently referring to the Carlanas and lumping them with the Jicarillas, as Valverde did in more than one instance in 1719. In any case, it is clear that the several groups of Apaches found in La Jicarilla by Valverde in 1719 and by Bustamante in 1724 had indeed begun to disperse by 1727. Some were in Taos Valley on the Río de las Trampas, some were on the Plains, apparently in El Cuartelejo, some were living with the Navajos, but others apparently continued to hold out in La Jicarilla.

It is difficult to trace the Jicarillas through the 1730s and 1740s, in part, no doubt, because many of the original New Mexico documents from these decades disappeared long ago from the Santa Fé Archives (Twitchell 1914 II: 208, 213–14, 248). Before launching into this critical and confusing period in Jicarilla history, therefore, it is desirable to review the status of the Jicarillas proper at this time and the probable limits of the region they inhabited, as well as the status of important allied tribes mentioned along with them in the documents.

From the Spanish version of Ulibarri's diary of 1706 it appears the Jicarillas were only one of several Apache *naciones* or bands living on tributaries of what is now called the Canadian River. The chief of the Jicarillas, El Cojo, was the most important of the Apache leaders in the area, and his village was called the "ranchería de la Jicarilla," although this phrase may also have been used to describe the entire settled area in later records. Here it may be desirable to repeat that in crossing the mountain spur separating the drainages of the Canadian and the Purgatoire, probably via or near Emery Pass, Ulibarri saw to his right (i.e., to the south) the *serro de la Jicarilla* (figure 3). This name may have been the equivalent of "Chocolate Cup Peak," and the peak itself may well have been the symmetrical volcanic cinder cone now called Capulín Mountain. The Jicarilla Apaches, as well as the region in which they and their Apache neighbors lived, may have been named for the landmark noted by Ulibarri, no matter which peak it was.

In his diary of 1719 Valverde still distinguishes the followers of El Cojo from other bands in the same region, but in this and later documents the geographical application of the term Jicarilla varies. Captain Miguel Tenorio, a soldier of the Santa Fé *presidio* and *alcalde mayor* of the valley of Taos and Picurís, testified in a council of war on 2 June 1720 that he had seen the "valley" of La Jicarilla many times and speaks of the range that divides the valleys of Taos and La Jicarilla (Thomas 1935: 158). Captain Major of War José Naranjo testified that La Jicarilla was forty leagues from Santa Fé (Thomas 1935: 157), and Governor Valverde refers to the "spot and valley of La Jicarilla," the "valley of La Jicarilla" and the "region of La Jicarilla" (Thomas 1935: 160, 161).

On 13 November 1720, Captain Don Felix Martínez, a former captain of the *presidio* of New Mexico, gave a deposition in Mexico City wherein he testified that "he, the witness, had traveled from the capital to the pueblo of Taos, which is thirty leagues to the north, from there northeast to the pueblo of La Jicarilla, fifteen leagues, where is a nation of the Apache" (Thomas 1935: 170–71). Note that this witness calls La Jicarilla a "pueblo," a word that can refer to any settled place. While the distance from Santa Fé to Taos given by Martínez is excessive in terms of the present route, the fifteen leagues (thirty-nine miles) he gives as the distance between Taos and La Jicarilla is almost exactly that between Taos and present Cimarrón.

From these statements and other evidence that will be discussed shortly, the implication is that the "valley" or "region" of La Jicarilla was not the valley of a single river but rather all the low canyons and plains drained by those tributaries of the Canadian River between the Mesa de Mayo and Rayado Mesa, the latter being a southeastward projection of the Sangre de Cristos that separates the Rayado and Ocate Rivers and the settlements named for them. Today, as it probably did in the past, Rayado Mesa marks a sort of division in the population of the area in that Rayado has its principal ties with towns to the north, Cimarrón and Ratón, while Ocate has ties in the opposite direction with Mora and Las Vegas. In brief, if this interpretation of the evidence is correct, the "valley" of La Jicarilla was roughly the region between Rayado and Ratón and thus very comparable to the Taos Valley, which is basically a plain crossed by streams (figure 5).

In the early 1700s the route eastward from the present Moreno Valley seems to have descended the mountains near Rayado, following essentially the Taos-Rayado trail of the 1800s (Thomas 1935: 63, 163 *n*11; Schroeder 1959: 20), although travelers probably varied the last part of their descent according to whether they were continuing eastward or turning north. Ulibarri, for example, probably did not come down by the route shown in figure 5. Regardless, the records strongly suggest that the Rayado River and the settlement of Rayado both got their names because of their association with the trail. The trail, in turn, seems to have been so named because it was the best way to reach the crest of the mountains between Taos and La Jicarilla. For a time in the early 1800s, at least, the crest of that portion of the Sangre de Cristos known as the Taos Range seems to have been called "the Rayado."[6] This information can be found in documents occasioned by the fact that in 1818, Spanish officials already on guard against Anglo-American encroachment were greatly disquieted by discovery of an anonymous description

6 I surmise that in this case *rayado* meant line and that the term was used because the eastern boundary of the Alcaldia that included the Taos Valley followed the mountain crest for a way. The Rayado, then, was a kind of "county line." (See figure 3.)

of New Mexico that revealed its military weaknesses and enumerated the passes by which the province could be entered from the east. The unknown author stated that one could reach Taos Pass (El Cañon de San Fernando) from the east "by going up a little branch of the Red [Canadian] River . . . and following a footpath made by the savages" (Thomas 1929: 63). In his own description of the passes into New Mexico, Melgares, governor of the province in 1818, makes it clear that the crest of the Taos Mountains was then called "the Rayado" (usually spelled "Rallado"). Melgares stated:

> The Cañon de San Fernando begins along the crest of the rallado, and in order to take it one travels an entire day over the sierra [from the east]. The crest road [road to the crest from the east] is troublesome on account of the large rocks and undergrowth (palizada) [parentheses in original], but clearing it somewhat extensively would make it satisfactory to transport cannons, etc. It has its origin at the very foot of the sierra; opposite there are plains, and at about twenty-five leagues a mesa which they call Sicorica or El Mayo and various little scattered hills. (Thomas 1929: 68)

> From the *slopes of the Rallado* [italics mine] to Taos there are fifteen or eighteen leagues through the Canyon of San Fernando, which is the best entrance. (Thomas 1929: 71)

Hence, it seems the present Rayado River was so named because it was that little branch of the Canadian near which one began to ascend up to the "Rayado" in order to reach the Moreno Valley and the eastern end of Taos Pass itself. On his way to the Plains in 1706 Ulibarri descended a long slope, probably Melgares's "slope of the Rallado," before reaching the foot of the mountains on the east side. Moreover, the distance across the mountains by this route as given by Melgares—fifteen to eighteen leagues—agrees with the distance from Taos to La Jicarilla as reckoned in the early 1700s. From high points near the present settlement of Rayado, too, one sees some of the "scattered little hills" between that settlement and the Mesa de Mayo (spelled "Maya" on modern maps).

The strategic importance of the Taos-Rayado Pass, stressed in the early 1700s, was still recognized in the early 1800s, since in 1818 the Spaniards were guarding it with two cannons placed somewhere on the crest of the mountains (Thomas 1929: 69). As early as 1808 there was apparently a Spanish structure, probably a military outpost, on the Rayado River, for on 20 June of that year, interim governor Maynez ordered the commander of the military detachment at Taos to send out a company every eight days to reconnoiter the frontier via the "casa del Rayado" as far as the Río de las Animas, or Purgatoire River (SANM 2122).

About 1844 Carlos Beaubien, one of the original holders of the Maxwell Grant (which included all of La Jicarilla), stated that it was one and a half days' journey from Taos to Rayado, indicating that Rayado was indeed a known point at the eastern end of the trail. Lucien Maxwell began building at Rayado "as early as 1847" (Keleher 1964: 18, 29). The Apaches (Jicarillas) and Utes (Moaches) were first issued United States Government rations at Rayado, where Kit Carson became purchasing agent for these tribes. In the spring of 1849, both Kit Carson and Lucien Maxwell moved to the Rayado settlement which, in the winter of 1849–1850, became an outpost of United States Dragoons. The dragoons remained at Rayado until Fort Union was established (Sabin 1935 II: 616–17, 618, 631–32). Part of the reason for stationing the dragoons at Rayado was the easy access to the Taos area from that point.

The use actually made of the area around the mouth of Rayado Canyon supports the probability that the Rayado River was "the Jicarilla River" by means of which the Comanches, in the 1740s, habitually entered New Mexico through a pass (Twitchell 1914 I: 148–50). However, it does not seem that the Rayado was called the Jicarilla River because El Cojo's band of Jicarillas proper lived there earlier in the 1700s, because this particular band of Apaches probably lived on another stream farther north. Rather, it was probably sometimes called the Jicarilla River because it was the route most used for going from the settled portion of New Mexico to the valley of La Jicarilla.

Archeological work done on the tributaries of the Canadian River suggests a long period of Apachean occupation in the area, beginning perhaps as early as the mid-1500s. And the earliest

Apache pottery from the region, a highly micaceous culinary ware, shows that the Apaches of La Jicarilla already had close associations with Taos at the time it was made (J. Gunnerson 1969; G & G 1971).

In Part I of this study it was suggested that the Cuartelejo Apaches were already semi-sedentary when the Taos Indians fled to El Cuartelejo ca. 1640. However, members of Ulibarri's 1706 expedition (Thomas 1935: passim, esp. 59–80) provided the first direct historical evidence that the Cuartelejo Apaches lived in "huts or little houses" and raised crops, abandoning their several villages in winter because of lack of fuel. These Spaniards also brought back information that the Cuartelejos were carrying on warfare against the Pawnees and also against some Jumanos. The geographical context suggests that the latter name was being applied in this instance to the Wichitas, and in 1750 Governor Vélez Cachupín of New Mexico specifically identified the Jumanos as "Panipiquees" (Bolton 1917: 399; Folmer 1939: 162–63), or Wichitas (Hodge 1907–1910 II: 947).

Although the Cuartelejos continued to trade in New Mexico in the years that followed Ulibarri's visit, the next record that sheds any light on their condition is the diary of Valverde, who in 1719 went into southeastern Colorado to chastise Utes and Comanches for raids on settlements in New Mexico. On his way he found part of the Sierra Blanca Apaches under Chief Carlana living with the Jicarillas (Thomas 1935: 114–16). The Utes and Comanches had chased the Carlanas out of their own country, perhaps permanently, and they seem to have lived among the Jicarillas for the next several years. Valverde did not penetrate far into Cuartelejo territory, if at all, and did not visit any of the Cuartelejo villages. However, the Cuartelejos, having heard of his expedition, came by the hundreds to visit him at a place where he encamped to wait for them on the Arkansas River. From them he learned that their settlements (figures 4 and 6) in what is now western Kansas were being attacked from two directions. The Pawnees and Jumanos, aided by Frenchmen, were striking from the east, and the Utes (probably allied with Comanches) from the west. The Cuartelejos

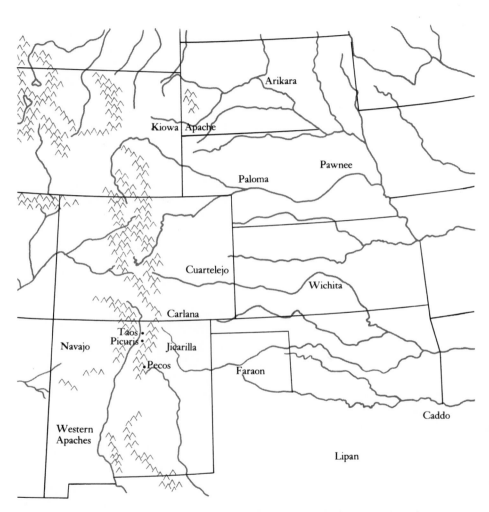

Figure 6. Map showing locations of various tribes ca. 1720. After James H. Gunnerson and Dolores A. Gunnerson, Apachean Culture History and Ethnology, *ed. by Keith H. Basso and Morris Opler (Tucson: University of Arizona Press, 1971).*

themselves had not yet abandoned their lands, but they had with them part of another Apache group who were already refugees. These were variously called Calchufines (Thomas 1935: 130), Escalchufines (Thomas 1935: 257) and (most often) Palomas (Thomas 1935: 132, 142, 229, 257). The name Paloma, which generally means dove in Castilian Spanish but may have had a different meaning in New Mexico, was the one that survived longest. It is possible that no Spaniard had ever really reached the territory of the Paloma Apaches (Thomas 1935: 143). By their own account, their original lands had been "farther in from El Cuartelejo, on the most remote borderlands of the Apaches" (Thomas 1935: 132). They had been driven out of their territory, where they raised corn, by Pawnees who had French allies (Thomas 1935: 132, 144, 229, 232). In 1719, the refugee Palomas were in the process of settling in El Cuartelejo, but some had already left that area and dispersed themselves among other, unidentified, Apache *rancherías* because of the attacks being made by the Utes (Thomas 1935: 144).

The account given by the Palomas, and the evidence bearing on the subsequent expedition of Pedro Villasur to reconnoiter the Frenchmen they described, strongly suggest that the Palomas originally lived west of the Pawnees and north of the Platte River. The Platte, called the Río de Jesús María by the Spaniards (Thomas 1935: 134, 144, 163, 229) and called the River of the "Panis" (Pawnees) by the French (e.g., Vermale's map of 1717 *in* Wheat 1957: map 98) apparently divided the lands of the Cuartelejo Apaches from those of the Pawnees (Thomas 1935: 163).

For several years after 1719, the activities of the Paloma Apaches are obscure. El Cuartelejo was still occupied by the Cuartelejos and Palomas in 1726, and by then the Palomas themselves were coming into New Mexico to trade. By that year, also, the Carlanas, who had earlier sought refuge in the Sangre de Cristos with the Jicarillas, had apparently decided to cast their lot instead with the Cuartelejos and Palomas. These three groups had banded together and, reinforced by some Frenchmen then living in El Cuartelejo, were making what may have been a last-ditch effort to either drive out the Comanches (Thomas 1935: 257) or make peace with them (Hackett 1931–1946 III: 244). According to information given by an Apache from the "interior," El Cuartelejo was still occupied in 1727, and Jicarillas visiting in Taos led Governor Bustamante to conclude in that year that the French had won over the Plains Apaches (Thomas 1935: 256, 258). These seem to be the last contemporary references to El Cuartelejo as Apache territory.

In and after 1730 there occur in the records promising statements suggesting that the allied Carlanas, Cuartelejos, and Palomas began to live part of the time in the Sangre de Cristos and to develop closer ties with the Jicarillas, perhaps sometimes even being identified as Jicarillas. In 1730, for example, Bishop Crespo of Durango, after visiting New Mexico, stated that the priest at Taos could "if he is zealous, . . . make expeditions to Jicarilla and Cuartelejo, fifteen or twenty leagues away, where there are many pagan Indians who have formed settlements and sown land" (Adams 1953: 223–24). Although Crespo's information may have been garbled, it is possible that the Central Plains Apaches had by this time taken refuge with the Jicarillas, as the Carlanas alone had done ca. 1719. There is some further evidence to strengthen this idea. Not long after a mission was founded near Taos for the "Jicarillas" in 1733, some of the Apaches there "returned to their place of origin, that was more than one hundred leagues to the north," while others, those customarily allied with the Taos Indians, remained (Villaseñor 1748 II: 240). It may be that the mission had attempted to incorporate all the friendly Apaches but that the Cuartelejos, Palomas, and Carlanas returned at least temporarily to the Central Plains, while the Jicarillas of the Sangre de Cristo mountains remained. By 1748, with the sedentary villages of the original foothills Apache tribes abandoned under Comanche pressure, there seem to have been groups called Jicarillas living a less settled life in northeastern New Mexico, and they were differentiated according to whether their primary affiliation was with Taos or Pecos (Twitchell 1914 I: 148–50; Lummis 1898: 74–78).

In 1752 some Apaches called Jicarillas *and* Carlanas by the governor of New Mexico were on the Gallinas River fifteen leagues from Pecos (Thomas 1940: 102, 108), but these same Apaches were identified only as Carlanas by the parish priest at Pecos (Thomas 1935: 90). In 1752 and 1754 it was specifically the Carlanas, Cuartelejos, and Palomas who were living in or near Pecos Pueblo, except in the latter year the Palomas are not mentioned at all. Also, in 1754, after referring to the Cuartelejos as a "subordinate" group of the Carlanas, Governor Vélez Cachupín continues, in the same document, to refer to the Carlanas alone and to emphasize the fact that they should be encouraged to maintain their independence (Thomas 1940: 124, 135–36). This they did, for various later archival materials show that the Carlanas (probably still including the Cuartelejos and Palomas) kept their identity, apparently to some extent even into the 1800s (e.g., [Pino] Carroll and Haggard 1942: 128, 246).

The post-1730 archeology of the Cuartelejos and Palomas, formerly Dismal River peoples of the Central Plains, is not yet known. Dismal River pottery has not yet been found in eastern New Mexico, although the surveys have been far from exhaustive. It is possible, however, that baking pits and certain stone and bone artifacts of Dismal River types found in a late historic context at Pecos (Kidder 1932; 1958: 119–20) represent some of these displaced Dismal River people (J. Gunnerson 1960: 241–44; G & G 1970).

As for the Carlanas, or Sierra Blanca Apaches, who apparently absorbed the Cuartelejos and Palomas after all three tribes had become refugees, their archeology is not yet defined on any time level. The "Sierra Blanca" in which they lived until ca. 1719 probably included the main range of the Sangre de Cristos between Ratón, New Mexico, and Trinidad, Colorado and also the Mesa de Mayo which projects eastward from the main range along the present New Mexico-Colorado state line. In 1720 they supposedly had their *rancherías* on "shoulders" of this mesa which face south (Thomas 1935: 142, 170, 171, 174). If the Carlanas, Cuartelejos, and Palomas eventually became the Plains

Band of the modern Jicarillas, they began at some point to make pottery like that of the original Mountain Band, for both divisions apparently made the same kind of micaceous pottery in recent times (e.g., Gifford 1940: 50–51).

The fact that those Apaches still in La Jicarilla in the winter of 1727 had flatly refused to move to Taos Valley as Bustamante urged and their implied intention of continuing to farm their own lands lend credence to Crespo's statement that there were still Apache farming communities in La Jicarilla in 1730. Since there is no reason to believe that more than two of the several hamlets in La Jicarilla had been destroyed by Utes and Comanches in 1723–1724, the Jicarillas proper, at least, were probably still living in their adobe houses in 1730.

Actually, continued occupation of La Jicarilla may have been made possible by a cessation of Ute-Comanche attacks. The popular interpretation is that the Comanches were a relentless foe who never eased the pressure they began to exert on the Apaches in 1706. The records, however, do not bear out this supposition. In the early part of the eighteenth century, major attacks by Utes and Comanches seem to have been made only at widely spaced intervals. It has already been pointed out that there is no record of their attacking the foothills Apaches between 1706 and 1718, and during that time, with one or two exceptions, the Utes and Comanches committed no major depredations against the Spaniards and Pueblo Indians. Perhaps they had simply transferred their attention largely to the Navajos. The diary of Valverde's expedition testifies to the severity of the attacks made on the Jicarillas and their Apache neighbors in 1718 and 1719, but the records pertaining to the term of Governor Bustamante give evidence of only two actual attacks on La Jicarilla—one in 1723 and another in 1724. After the latter, Bustamante campaigned against the Utes and Comanches, as has been noted, and rescued sixty-four Jicarillas. How decisive a defeat he inflicted on the aggressors is not clear, but there are no more references to specific Comanche attacks on the Jicarillas. On the other hand, it is clear that after 1724 many of these

Apaches were badly shaken. Those Rivera reported seeing in Taos in 1726 had fled there not because of an actual attack, but because they had heard that the Comanches were coming. All or part of these were probably the Jicarillas who settled on the Río de las Trampas (now called Río Grande de Ranchos), since Rivera had at the time asked Father Mirabal to induce them to settle near Taos, and it was Father Mirabal whom the Jicarillas of the Trampas River obtained as a missionary in 1727.

It seems reasonable to suppose that improved relations between the Spaniards and the Utes and Comanches benefited the Jicarillas. Rivera's diary reveals that people of New Mexico, probably including Spaniards, were trading with Comanches at regular intervals as early as 1726 in Comanche camps (Porras 1945: 78–79). From his description it appears that Rivera had personally observed the Comanches and the trading.

This barter was still going on in 1735, for in April of that year a Spanish official of the Chama district was charged with having attempted to barter with the Comanche Indians before the time set for the regular trades. The buffalo hides which he had purchased from the Indians were confiscated (SANM 402).

Apparently the Utes were also generally quiet at this time, for on 14 April 1736, some settlers of the Paraje del Río del Oso in the Chama district made a complaint against the Utes for having killed their livestock in times of peace (SANM 409). Bancroft comments on the absence of Indian troubles during the period 1731–1739. No serious eruption that affected the Jicarillas seems to have occurred until the Comanches broke the peace in June 1746 with a raid on Pecos, and Governor Codallos y Rabal caught and punished the offenders (Bancroft 1889: 242–43, 249). Not until 1748 was it definitely stated that the Jicarillas were no longer in La Jicarilla and that they had been forced out by the Comanches (Twitchell 1914 I: 150). The records suggest, however, that it was only their adobe houses that the Jicarillas abandoned. In spite of their enemies, they continued to hunt and camp in their own country, even raising crops wherever and whenever possible. In 1752, certainly, they were

somewhere between Taos and La Jicarilla, for they were considered a threat to Comanches traveling between these two
places (Thomas 1940: 121).

In 1731, the Jicarillas are mentioned in a complaint made by
Taos Indians against settlers in their vicinity. The livestock of
the settlers was damaging Taos crops, and the Indians added that
some of the settlers were branding Taos stock with their own
brand. They said the Baltazar Romero, for example, had kept
among his own mares a young filly belonging to a Taos Indian
and had finally sold it to the Jicarillas, among whom the Taos
Indians found it. The same Baltazar Romero had killed an animal
belonging to Diego Romero, "el collote" (the coyote, or half-
blood), who had reported the incident to the *alcalde mayor* of
Taos (SANM 361). This Diego Romero may well have been the
one who owned Ranchos de Taos on the river then called las
Trampas, south of Taos Pueblo (cf. Chávez 1959: 272), and the
Jicarillas mentioned may have been those apparently already
settled near the same stream—perhaps then as later south of the
Río de las Trampas on the slopes at the foot of the mountains
and along the road to Picurís.

Another bishop of Durango visited New Mexico in 1737, and
in 1738 Bishop Crespo wrote a revised memorial incorporating
the results of this and his own earlier visitation (Bancroft 1889:
240–41, 242). He stated that a settlement of "tame" Apaches
had been attempted at Ranchos or Trampas de Taos in Father
Mirabal's time (A & C 1956: 112). Father Juan Menchero, who
had been in New Mexico during the period referred to, said
(in 1744):

> At a distance of five leagues to the north [of Taos] there is a
> nation called Xicarillas. When the reverend father custodian,
> José Ortís de Velasco, founded a mission for them in the year
> 1733 and began to assemble and instruct them, the governor who
> was in office at that time, instead of treating them kindly and
> joining with the said father in a work so pleasing to God, for
> unknown reasons ordered the soldiers of the presidio to put
> them out, and they have feared to return, although some of them
> come to seek the fathers at the said mission. (Hackett 1923–
> 1937 III: 403)

Menchero's statement that the Jicarillas were living five leagues north of Taos has no support from other contemporary sources, but he does not, like other sources that apparently draw on him, state that the Jicarilla mission was itself located five leagues north of Taos. Villaseñor, in his secondary work, keeps this point straight.

> At a distance of five leagues in the same direction [north of Taos] is a nation of Indians that are called Xicarillas, having founded a mission for them in the year 1733, of short duration, because they returned to their place of origin, that was more than 100 leagues to the north, and only some rancherias of these pagans have remained in this area, those who were accustomed to join Taos when they felt the attack of the Comanches. (Villaseñor 1748 II: 240)

Villaseñor obviously had more information than was available from Menchero's statement. The "Jicarillas" who returned to their point of origin may have been the Cuartelejos, along with the Palomas and Carlanas. If these groups were in La Jicarilla in 1730, as Crespo indicates, they may have been included in the Jicarilla mission in 1733. The last part of Villaseñor's statement accords well with the general configuration of evidence which suggests that the Jicarillas proper, those who originally inhabited La Jicarilla and had the closest ties with Taos, were those who continued to live near that Pueblo, at least seasonally.

Father Morfi, in his geographical description of New Mexico dated 1782, was the first to say that the Jicarilla mission itself had been located north of Taos.

> Five leagues to the north of Taos there was founded a mission with the Indians of the Xicarilla nation in 1733 by the Father Custodian Fray Josef Orter de Velasco but the governor cut off from their trade in hides, the simple living of these new colonists; this unexpectedly the whole garrison put into effect, which filling them with forboding, drove them back to the hills. Although for some time the hope of reassembling them in Taos was held, it was frustrated unhappily because fear swayed them. They dispersed themselves among the Utes and Comanches. (Thomas 1932: 96–97)

Morfi's statement on the location of the Jicarilla mission probably represents an oversimplification of earlier comments. Since

Menchero and Villaseñor had said that the Jicarillas lived north of Taos and had not stated specifically where the mission was built, Morfi may have assumed that it was built at the Jicarilla settlement. However, the whole object of resettling the Jicarillas was to get them into a defensible location, and while all of New Mexico was vulnerable to the attacks of hostile Indians in those days, the area north of Taos, near Ute and Comanche country, would have been especially so.

It is interesting that each of the three statements on the Jicarilla mission gives details not included in the others. One would suspect that each was drawing on some common and more detailed source, except that Menchero, whose knowledge could have been firsthand, states that the governor drove the Jicarillas away from their mission for some unknown reason. Morfi's account which, because of its secondary nature and much later date, might be thought less accurate suggests an occurrence more in keeping with Spanish policy. It indicates that the soldiers were trying to confine the Jicarillas to their mission rather than drive them away, undoubtedly on the premise that sedentary Indians could be more easily Christianized and rendered docile. Moreover, driving the Jicarillas away would have been a direct violation of earlier orders from the superior government in Mexico City. Morfi's statement that the governor tried to eliminate the Jicarilla trade in hides gives a possible clue. By this time the Jicarillas may have been dependent on trade with Plains Apache tribes, some of them hostile to the Spanish, for supplies of buffalo meat and hides; and the governor, fearing the bad influence of such enemy Apaches on the Jicarillas, may have attempted to prevent the latter from going to the Plains. This was precisely the case in the early 1750s when Governor Vélez Cachupín, by his own account, was trying to minimize contacts between the friendly Carlanas, Palomas, and Cuartelejos and the less trustworthy Natagé Apaches (Thomas 1940: 135–36). Morfi's statement that the Jicarillas who fled the mission dispersed themselves among the Utes and Comanches can have no validity so far as the Comanches are concerned, for Jicarilla-Comanche enmity remained strong. Since Morfi's account was written long after the events he refers to took place, his comment may reflect cognizance of the Jicarilla-Ute alliance made soon after the Utes broke with the Comanches ca. 1747. Menchero's statement suggests that the Jicarillas left their mission almost as soon as it was founded, but he indicates that some of the Apaches were still coming to seek the mission fathers at the time he wrote. Thus the mission was still in existence in 1744 and apparently being served by more than one missionary. Bancroft, who cites both Crespo's 1738 memorial and Villaseñor (1748), says that there were one hundred-thirty Indians at the mission in 1734, but few or none were left in 1748 (Bancroft 1889: 242).

In spite of the confusion in eighteenth-century sources concerning the location of the Jicarilla mission, the mission has become associated with the church at Ranchos de Taos, a farming community near the foothills of the Sangre de Cristo Mountains, seven miles south of Taos Pueblo. The stream on which this village is located was known as the Río de las Trampas in the eighteenth century, and the community itself was sometimes referred to by that name. Because the connection of the Jicarillas with Ranchos de Taos is not clear from the records, it becomes desirable to consider the nature and origin of that settlement in some detail.

The volume on New Mexico issued as part of the American Guide Series demonstrates the vague nature of the data.

> According to Indian tradition, Ranchos de Taos was founded by members of Taos Pueblo who sought better fields for their crops. With the coming of the Spaniards, the settlement became known as Las Trampas (the traps) [all parentheses appear in original]. As with other frontier towns of New Mexico, it was raided by Apache and Comanche. In the center of the village is the SAINT FRANCIS OF ASSISI MISSION, built c. 1730 (but not registered at Diocesan headquarters, Durango, Mexico, till 1772) by the Franciscans. It fell into disuse and was rebuilt about 1772, but there is a dispute as to the date of its founding. This fortress-like adobe building, famous for its exceptionally thick walls supported by great abutments and its white stucco exterior, is 120 feet long and is surrounded by a six-foot wall. (Miller 1962: 287)

Tradition persistently calls the Taos Indians the first settlers of Las Trampas. Years after, the family of Romero seems to have owned practically the whole place. A series of wills go back to a Diego Romero of 1724. This Don Diego and his sons probably helped build the first mission about 1733. Forty years later its walls fell into decay and the present edifice slowly rose on the old foundations. (Grant 1934: 18)

The second wife of the Diego Romero who owned Ranchos de Taos was Barbara Montoya. Several papers concerning her estate are listed by Twitchell (1914 I: 82–84) under SANM 240. Among these is Diego Romero's petition to register a brand, dated 1714, 1715. Also among these papers is a document in which heirs of Cristóbal de la Serna conveyed a *rancho* in the valley of Taos to Diego Romero on 5 August 1724. On 24 November 1724, Diego Romero's title to the *rancho* was validated. At this time Romero was referred to as an inhabitant of a pueblo, probably Taos, since some of the documents in this group are dated there. It has already been mentioned that in a document of 1731 containing references to settlers living near Taos (SANM 361) a Diego Romero is mentioned as a coyote (half Spanish, half Indian). However, he was not a Taos Indian (Chávez 1954: 272; Twitchell 1914 I: 43–44). The will of Diego Romero was dated 1742, and his lands were apparently called Los Ranchos de Taos. In 1743, at Taos Pueblo, his heirs petitioned for the division of his ranch, which in this document was called Río de Las Trampas (Twitchell 1914 I: 207).

Father Menchero, writing in 1744, says:

> The ranches of Taos, four in number, are situated in a beautiful spacious plain, which is crossed from south to north by the Río Grande del Norte. In a craggy mountain range rise three rivers, which run from east to west and at a distance of three leagues unite in the said plain; one league farther on they come to an end, having precipitated their waters into the current of the Río del Norte. These ranches have ten Spanish families, who live thirty leagues from the capital and are employed in planting and cattle raising. They are administered by the father of the mission of Taos, five leagues away. (Hackett 1923–1937 III: 400)

Like the Jicarilla mission and settlement these "Ranches of Taos" are said to be five leagues from Taos Pueblo; however, the direction is not specified. The ranches mentioned by Father Menchero may not have been on the Trampas River, since there is evidence that the settlement pattern in the Taos Valley changed during the 1700s.

Bishop Tamarón, who visited Taos in 1760, made a "midday halt" on the Trampas River at "the large house of a wealthy Taos Indian, very civilized and well-to-do. The said house is well walled in, with arms and towers for defense" (Adams 1953–1954: 215). This statement suggests that the population of Las Trampas consisted of both Taos Indians and Spaniards, unless Tamarón thought the Romero *hacienda* was that of a Taos Indian.

In 1762, the name Romero emerges again in connection with this settlement. In that year one Miguel Romero, "alias El Chayo, coyote," was charged with adultery, and one of the women involved was an Apache. In one place Romero is referred to as a "vecino [inhabitant] of Taos" and in another as a "vecino del Rio de las Trampas" (Bancroft Library New Mexico Originals[7]; hereafter referred to as BLNMO).

The report of Fray Francísco Atanasio Dominguez, made in 1776, clarifies the situation to some extent. Apparently both the Taos Indians who had outlying ranches and the Spanish settlers in the valley maintained two residences. When at Taos Pueblo the Spaniards lived, at first, in a kind of hostel area near the Pueblo and then, as Comanche attacks increased, moved inside with the permission of the Taos Indians. In 1760, as a result of an especially violent Comanche attack that took place shortly after Tamarón's visit, the Spanish ranches in Taos Valley were apparently abandoned. The Spanish settlers were living in Taos Pueblo itself in 1776, while what seemed to be an entirely new settlement—a plaza surrounded by houses for defense and containing a church—was under construction (Adams 1953–1954: 217; A & C 1956: 112–13, 251). According to observations made by Father Morfi in 1782, this settlement was apparently the present Ranchos de Taos.

At three leagues (south) from the pueblo [Taos] is a ranch with abundance of arable lands even more fertile than those of

[7] These items were searched out, identified, and listed by Father Angélico Chávez (1950).

the pueblo. The largest of four rivers which water the valley irrigates them. There is a free-flowing spring of hot water. The settlement frames a square plaza, very capacious. Its houses were almost finished in 1779 with towers at proportionate distances for their defense. All the lands of this ranch belong by right of possession to the Indians of the pueblo. But those contented with such as they can cultivate close to their dwelling-places cede the rest to the Spanish settlers freely without demanding the smallest rent. (Thomas 1932: 97)

From the evidence, then, there were several "Ranches of Taos," and the name alone has little value as a point of reference. Unless further historical and archeological work clarifies the matter, the location of both the Jicarilla settlement and the Jicarilla mission said to have existed in 1733 will remain problematical. The known statements suggest that the facts became confused a long time ago. The inclination is to believe that any Jicarilla settlement formed in or near the Taos Valley in 1733 would have been south of Taos and probably connected with already existing ranches on the Río de las Trampas. These ranches, vulnerable to enemy Indians, would certainly have welcomed the additional protection afforded by friendly Apache allies. It has already been pointed out that some Jicarillas were actually settled on the Río de las Trampas in 1727. Evidence bearing on later decades in the eighteenth century, to be discussed below, also indicates that Jicarillas were living south of the Río de las Trampas (see J. Gunnerson 1969: 38), although their occupation probably shifted seasonally.

If the Cuartelejos, Carlanas, and Palomas were those "Jicarillas" who fled from the Jicarilla mission ca. 1733, and if they did return to El Cuartelejo, they may have abandoned that region again before 1739. Unfortunately, primary documents reveal nothing concerning their whereabouts for almost two decades, but it is probable that from about 1733 to 1750 they were living beyond the frontiers of New Mexico, unwilling to seek refuge among the settlements for fear that detention would be the price of Spanish protection.

In 1739 the party of French traders headed by the Mallet Brothers went through former Apache territory on the way to

Santa Fé without seeing any Apaches. However, these French-men found Comanches ("Laitanes") on the Arkansas River well out on the Plains and also in the "Spanish Mountains" (Folmer 1939: 166; Grinnell 1920: 253, 257; Margry 1875–1886 VI: 457–58). With the Comanches in this area, it is unlikely that the Apaches were maintaining semi-permanent villages in El Cuarte-lejo. It may be that other French sources will eventually yield some details on the final withdrawal of the Apaches from the Central Plains. Meanwhile, they have cast some light on events that preceded it.

As early as 1716 a Spanish friar, who was getting information from Caddoan Indians of eastern Texas and from the French, learned that some of the "Pannis" (Pawnees) who bordered on Apache territory were carrying on great wars with the latter and that the Pawnees were winning (Swanton 1942: 269–70). The conflicts he refers to were probably those between the Paloma Apaches and the Pawnees that caused the Palomas to abandon their lands and join the Cuartelejos, as Valverde re-ported in 1719 (G & G 1971).

But the French, who had at first helped the Caddoan tribes against the Apaches (whom the French called Padoucas), were much interested in establishing trade with the Spaniards in New Mexico. Knowing that the Padoucas already had trade relations with the Spaniards, the French planned not only to make a treaty with the Padoucas themselves but to establish peace be-tween the Padoucas and the tribes east of them. Grinnell (1920) claims (and he seems correct) that the Padoucas with whom Bourgmont succeeded in making an alliance in 1724 were not Comanches, as some scholars have believed, but Apaches, and specifically Cuartelejo Apaches. These Padoucas lived in Cuar-telejo territory, raised corn and pumpkins, and had well-estab-lished trade relations with the Spaniards. This description does not agree with what is known of the Comanches at this point in time.

Bourgmont had brought with him a large amount of merchan-dise, including guns and ammunition, two things which the Spaniards would not trade even to friendly tribes. All this he

presented to the Padoucas as gifts. Overwhelmed by such
generosity, the Padouca chief made derogatory remarks about
the Spaniards and agreed to receive French trading parties.
He even promised to conduct Frenchmen to New Mexico if they
desired to go (Folmer 1937; Margry 1875–1886 VI: 398–449).
Hence it was very probably true that there were Frenchmen
among the Cuartelejo Apaches in 1726 and 1727, as Jicarillas
reported to Governor Bustamante in Santa Fé. Bustamante was
astute in surmising that the French had won over most of the
Plains Indians. Other evidence that helps identify Bourgmont's
Padoucas as Apaches is that French traders *were* being guided
to New Mexico by *Apaches* by 1727. In other words, the French
had attained the end toward which the Padoucas were to be a
means—access to New Mexico. According to Pichardo, Bustamante told the viceroy on 30 April 1727: "They (the French)
come frequently to this kingdom and their access to it is by
means of the alliance and trade which they have with the said
Apaches, who conduct them to these places" (Hackett 1931–
1946 III: 244; see also Thomas 1935: 258).

The alliance between the French and the Cuartelejo Apaches
probably ceased to be effective before 1730 if the Cuartelejos
were driven from their lands by that year. Certainly it was not
with the help of Padoucas that the Mallet party reached Santa
Fé, and the Laitanes or Comanches that they met were not
particularly friendly. On their return, however, members of
the Mallet party reported to the French authorities that the
small amount of trade goods they had given to the Laitanes had
had a considerable effect and that the tribe could be entirely
won over if a trading post were to be established in their territory
(Folmer 1939: 167).

Eventually French officials followed up this lead and made peace
between the Comanches and the Jumanos sometime between 1746
and 1748. After this the French not only began to pass through
the Comanches to New Mexico (Thomas 1940: 17), but the
Comanches, having access to guns through both the French and
Jumanos, began to raid New Mexico settlements with more
deadly effect. The Spaniards interpreted French strategy ac-

curately. They realized that the French were making peace between tribes hostile to one another so that the way to New
Mexico would be safe, and the Spaniards arrested those French
traders who succeeded in reaching the province. But they could
not deal so easily with the Comanches, and the need for a military
post at La Jicarilla became even more pressing than in the past.
As the Comanche menace increased, the friendly Apaches once
again became important to the Spaniards—not now as buffers to
keep raiders away from the province entirely but as scouts and
as reinforcements for the garrisons at pueblos and Spanish towns.
As auxiliaries, these Apaches lived among, and at times in, the
settlements.

Our knowledge of the Jicarillas proper in the first half of the
decade 1740–1750 is limited to Menchero's statement in 1744
that they were still coming to seek the Franciscan Fathers at
their former mission. However, in the second half of the decade
the Utes and Comanches again became actively hostile, and it
may have been in their outbreaks of this period, if not before,
that they finally forced the Jicarillas to give up their adobe-
house villages east of the mountains.

On 4 February 1746, Governor Codallos y Rabal issued fourteen orders. The fifth of these states that the governor had
learned that the Taos had made a treaty with the Comanches and
were trading with them, and this he forbade (SANM 495). The
willingness of the Taos to trade with the Comanches, enemies of
their friends the Jicarillas and chancy associates for the Taos Indians themselves, emphasizes the importance of buffalo meat,
hides, salt, and other products of the Plains to the inhabitants of
New Mexico. With the Comanches more or less in control of
much of the Buffalo Plains, it had become economically necessary
to do business with this tribe in spite of the danger it entailed.

In June 1746, the Comanches raided Pecos, killing twelve inhabitants and committing depredations elsewhere in the vicinity.
After correspondence with the viceroy in Mexico City and
lengthy consideration, the governor of New Mexico finally
retaliated in October 1747. In a full-scale campaign that utilized
more than five hundred soldiers and allies, he defeated the

Comanches and Utes beyond Abiquiú (Bancroft 1889: 249). At about this same time the Utes were giving the Navajos so much trouble that the Franciscans were forced to give up plans to establish missions in the Navajo country (Bancroft 1889: 247–48).

On 20 January 1748, the priest resident at Pecos sent Governor Codallos the news that a large number of Comanches had gathered at "the place of the arrow tree," which the Indians who carried the letter said was about two and a half leagues from Pecos. At the same time the Comanches were said to have a hundred lodges on the "Jicarilla river," which was probably the present Rayado. Upon receipt of the message the governor went to Pecos where "some seventy young men gathered, including some Gentile Indians of the Jicarilla tribe, of those who live in peace in the shelter of the pueblo." The anticipated battle took place one week later, "the Christian Indians and Jicarillas shooting with their arrows, as arranged by the governor." One Jicarilla was killed in the engagement. The account of this fight is given by an eye witness, Fray Lorenzo Antonio Estremera, secretary of Fray Juan Miguel Menchero, then father commissary (Lummis 1898: 74–78).

One month later the parish priest of Taos informed Governor Codallos by letter that seven Comanches had entered Taos seeking tobacco. They had told the priest that a hundred lodges of their people were on the Jicarilla River, where they were tanning buffalo hides to bring in to barter as soon as the snow decreased in the mountains. Thirty-three Frenchmen had been among them trading muskets for mules and had left two of their number to come to Taos with the Comanches to barter. In relaying this news to the viceroy, Codallos said that the Comanches were camped "forty leagues distant, more or less (according to some settlers) [parentheses in original] from the Pueblo of San Geronimo de Taos." His statement suggests that he was not altogether sure of the distance. He also says that the Comanches regularly entered New Mexico by way of the Jicarilla River and that on two occasions the French had entered by the same route. Like his predecessors, Valverde and Bustamante, he urged the viceroy to establish a *presidio* at La Jicarilla.

> I deem it very fitting and necessary that your Excellency's greatness order the establishment of a garrison with the endowment of fifty mounted soldiers, including captain and subaltern officers at a point called the Jicarilla, distant from the said Pueblo of Taos twenty leagues. This location is very convenient, as to lands, water, pasturage and timber. Here were located, in times past, the Indians of the Jicarilla nation (a branch of the Apaches) [all parentheses appear in original], who were numerous and had houses, palisade huts and other shelters. Thence the Gentile Cumanches despoiled them, killing most of them; the few that remained of said Jicarillas have sheltered and maintained themselves in peace nearby the Pueblos of Taos and Pecos, with their families. Said site of the Jicarilla is the pass (or defile); literally "throat" (for shutting of the aforesaid populous nation of Cumanches—and the French, if they tried to make any entrance to this said Kingdom.) (Twitchell 1914 I: 148–50)

In spite of Codallos's misgivings about the Comanches he apparently gave a friendly reception to six hundred of them at Taos not long after the battle at Pecos—after they assured him that they had had nothing to do with the recent raids.

> Later in the year, by the viceroy's orders, a junta was held at Santa Fé to determine whether the Comanches should be permitted to attend the fairs at Taos for purposes of trade. All admitted the unreliable and treacherous character of the tribe; but a majority favored a continuance of trade because the skins, meats, and horses they brought for sale were much needed in the province; and moreover, their presence at the fairs would bring them within Christian influences, especially the captives they brought for sale, who might otherwise be killed. The governor decided accordingly, against the views of the padre custodio. (Bancroft 1889: 249–50)

Sometime between October 1747 and April 1749, an event occurred that was to make one band of the Utes an effective ally of the Jicarillas for more than a century to come—the Utes and Comanches not only ceased to be allies but became the bitterest of enemies. The reason is not known. It has been suggested that the essentially complete victory these tribes had gained over the Apaches in northeastern New Mexico and on the contiguous plains made them less valuable to one another (Thomas 1940: 29).

When Codallos defeated the Comanches beyond Abiquiú in October 1747 there were Utes with them, but sometime before Codallos's successor, Thomas Vélez Cachupín, took office in April 1749, the Utes came to New Mexico to seek aid against the Comanches. Unfortunately, Spanish soldiers, who were unaware of the Utes' purpose, attacked them. The Utes retaliated and put part of New Mexico in a state of "lamentable ruin" (in which Vélez says he found it). The governor was eventually able to establish peace with these former enemies (Thomas 1940: 29–30, 131). How soon the Utes became associated with the Jicarillas is not known, but the two tribes were confederated by 1754 (Thomas 1940: 136–37).

On 31 December 1749, proceedings were conducted at Taos to decide what to do about some Comanches who had been committing depredations in the area. In keeping with the long-time Spanish policy of ignoring minor infractions of the peace, it was decided to do nothing, especially since the Utes were still hostile, and the province did not have men enough to fight two wars at once (SANM 509).

Information on the Jicarillas and allied Apache tribes during the decade 1750–1759 comes largely from documents pertaining to the first term of Governor Thomas Vélez Cachupín (1749–1754). In general, throughout the history of New Mexico the activities of aggressive enemy tribes tended to dominate the records. Therefore, it is undoubtedly to Vélez's policy of establishing and maintaining friendship with all the Gentile tribes that we owe his informative if brief discussions of friendly Apaches. This governor stated that on his arrival in New Mexico (1749) he had found

> the Carlanas, with their other subordinate groups, Cuartelejos, Chilpaines, and the rest of those on the plains who live to the east of this province as far as the boundaries of Texas . . . with little communication with the province and with not a few indications of enmity. (Thomas 1940: 135)

By his own account, Vélez was able to win their friendship.

This statement, though brief, is significant. It suggests that the Carlanas, who were with the Cuartelejos on the Plains in 1726, were still allied with that group more than twenty years later. And since there is no evidence to the contrary, it is possible that the Carlanas, Cuartelejos, and Palomas had indeed remained largely aloof from New Mexico until Vélez Cachupín's administration. Moreover, the governor's statement that the Chilpaines, a band of Faraon Apaches, were a group subordinate to the Carlanas may indicate a union of these previously unassociated and even mutually hostile bands for defense against the Comanches.

Meanwhile, the Jicarillas proper were becoming ever more oriented toward the Río Grande Valley. The 1750 census of Taos Pueblo reveals that a number of Apaches, who could only be Jicarillas, were actually living inside (Adams 1953–1954: 215). However, such intimate relations between the Taos Indians and the Jicarillas did not prevent commercial relations between the Taos and the Comanches from increasing. In July 1751 a Comanche *ranchería* of forty tipis arrived in Taos to sell skins and Indian captives, including, according to the governor, some "grown women from the Carlanas, our friends" (Thomas 1940: 68).

Vélez allowed them to trade after warning them against making any raids, and the rest of the summer was quiet. However, on 27 November 1751, the governor reported a recent Comanche attack on Pecos for which he had punished the aggressors thoroughly (Thomas 1940: 68–76). By showing mercy to the survivors of the battle, however, he was able to lay the foundations for friendship with the Comanches during his term. One of the greatest obstacles to dealing effectively with this tribe was the fact that it consisted of several widely scattered divisions that acted independently under different chiefs. None of these chiefs followed the same policy in their relations with the New Mexico settlements. The independence of the bands made it necessary to determine after each attack which band was guilty and to make war on that group alone. Nevertheless, it was Vélez's opinion that Comanches should always be given free access to the fairs and liberal gifts when they made their appearance (Thomas 1940: 79–80).

In 1752 the Carlana Apaches were mentioned in association with the Jicarillas for the first time since 1723–1724. On 6 August 1752, two Frenchmen arrived at Pecos with merchandise to trade, an event that occasioned several official documents. First, the priest at Pecos Pueblo wrote immediately to the governor saying that the Frenchmen had arrived with an Indian woman whom they brought from the Canosso "and the rest of the Carlana Apaches" (Thomas 1940: 90). The same day, in an order for the removal of the Frenchmen to Santa Fé, Vélez said they had been guided by the *Jicarilla and Carlana* Apaches. Accordingly, Thomas (1940: 102) suggests that the term "Canosso" in the priest's letter referred to the Jicarillas, and this probability is strengthened by the fact that in reporting the incident to the viceroy the governor said that the Frenchmen had arrived at Pecos "in company with Carlana and Jicarilla Apaches whom they met on the Rio de Ganillas [Gallinas], fifteen leagues distant from that pueblo" (Thomas 1940: 108). It would appear from these references that some of the Jicarillas proper were camping with the Carlanas and hence that the friendship of these two groups had been maintained. Another possibility is that Jicarilla and Carlana were being used as alternative names for the same band which, judging from location, would in this case have been Carlanas. By 28 August 1752, the Utes had had a battle with the Comanches. This was apparently not their only fight since their estrangement because it was referred to as "the last battle they had to the northeast" (Thomas 1940: 114–15).

In a letter to the viceroy dated 29 September 1752, Vélez told how five Comanches on foot had crossed the Sierra Blanca to steal horses from settlers at La Soledad on the upper Río Grande. While these Comanches were stealing horses at La Soledad, others were discussing peace not far away at the Pueblo of Taos. When they departed, the *alcalde mayor* "provided them with an escort from Taos to the valley of La Jicarilla so that the Apaches would not attack them, a gesture they esteemed highly" (Thomas 1940: 121). The Apaches referred to here could only have been Jicarillas, and the statement suggests that while the Comanches occupied the valley of La Jicarilla when they pleased, the Jicarillas had merely retreated to less accessible places in the mountains between their former home and Taos.

By this time, too, apparently with Vélez's active encouragement, the Carlanas, Cuartelejos, and Palomas had developed the custom of living among the New Mexico settlements.

> Likewise, the Apaches, Carlanas, Palomas, and Cuartelejos will continue trustworthy. During the past winter, three hundred men of these tribes have been in the environs of the pueblo of Pecos with their families, living so sociably and neighborly as to indicate their general love for this province. Leaving their women and children in the pueblo of Pecos, they are accustomed to go to the plains to hunt buffalo for their support. I keep them in this limited area with whatever guile I can in expectation of an action on the part of the Comanches and to enlarge my troop with their support in case of necessity. I avail myself of them for use as spies. They are so active and astute that they have confidence in their ability to reconnoiter for one hundred leagues because of their extensive knowledge of the land. This activity is very rare and risky for the Indians of these pueblos. (Thomas 1940: 124)

Nothing in this passage suggests that these Apaches had been forced into New Mexico by the Comanches. By the governor's own statement he had found these bands to have little contact with New Mexico in 1749. Moreover, he says that he had to use guile to keep them among the settlements. The fact that they were not afraid to hunt on the Plains or to undertake extensive reconnaisance suggests that they were still able to deal with the Comanches. On the other hand, it was obviously an advantage for them to be able to leave their families in safety when they went on expeditions.

The only reference to Jicarillas in 1753 was that by an official in Mexico City. The royal auditor, a partisan of Governor Vélez, stated that the latter had established "peace and tranquility among all the ferocious, warlike, enemy tribes," and he included

the Jicarillas in a list of these (Thomas 1940: 127). Since the
Jicarillas proper were not warlike, the auditor may have been
referring to the Carlanas as Jicarillas, and the Carlanas may well
have been raiding Spanish settlements—not in New Mexico but
in Texas, as they appear to have done later under the names
Lipiyanes and Llaneros.

In spite of the efforts of his friends, Governor Vélez Cachupín
had to give up his office to Francisco Marín de Valle. His suggestions to his successor on how to win the confidence and
friendship of the Gentile Indians foreshadowed what was ultimately (and necessarily) to become official Spanish policy. When
Vélez left the province the Carlanas and their affiliated bands
were still living within the limits of settled New Mexico, but
their ties with the Plains were strong.

> A large part of this nation is at present in the neighborhood of
> Pecos with such confidence in us that they have lived among
> these dispersed settlements except during the times when it is
> necessary for them to hunt buffalo or when some groups go back
> and forth to the plains to see their relatives. It is also extremely
> important to the security of this province to conserve their
> friendship and hold it without force. Positive friendship should
> be maintained with the Natageses and Faraones, and care should
> be taken that the latter do not associate with the Carlanas, who
> should be urged to remain independent, as I have done. I have
> always tried to keep them under my eye. Because of the trade
> which the Natageses carry on with the Carlanas on the plains,
> the first seeking buffalo meat, which resembles elk, and buffalo
> skins, which the Carlanas make into tents to trade for horses and
> mules, it is impossible to prevent the trade based upon their
> respective needs. One wants horses, which they lack, and the
> other, skins for shelter. These horses of the Natageses are those
> which they steal in company with the Sumas and Faraones in La
> Vizcaya and Sonora. While their exchanges cannot be com-
> pletely prevented, at least let it not be frequent with the Nata-
> geses and let it be only trade, not union and alliance against this
> province and La Vizcaya. In such case, the Natageses, strength-
> ened by the support and cunning of the Plains Apaches, would
> develop among the Sumas the greatest boldness, which would
> result in the total ruin of the frontiers of La Vizcaya and the
> Real of Chihuahua. Thus, for these reasons, if a change should
> come over the Comanches, the Apaches' chief enemy, the great-
> est consideration becomes keeping the Carlanas and the rest of

the Plains Indians at peace, always sympathetic and linked to our interests.

> If by accident the three nations, Comanches, Utes, and Apaches, should come at the same time to Taos (as has happened in my time) [parentheses in original], your grace should prevent the two latter tribes from doing any injury to the Comanches, their chief enemy. Protect and ward off any annoyance which the two confederates might attempt toward the Comanches. I have always kept between them in this meeting as much harmony as if they were friends. They have exchanged their horses and arms without the least altercation in my presence and I have helped the Apaches ransom their relatives from the possession of the Comanches. (Thomas 1940: 135–37)

These statements by Vélez Cachupín underscore the new shift in attitude of the Spaniards toward friendly Apaches. During the war with France (1718–1720), Spanish officials had looked upon the Jicarillas and other peaceful Apache tribes as a possible buffer against the encroachment of Frenchmen from the northeast. But in 1723–1724, the Utes and Comanches proved that the semi-sedentary Apaches could not withstand a mobile enemy. Unfortunately, the Spaniards, who had not themselves experienced the full force of Comanche raids, chose the cheapest way of discharging their obligations to the Jicarillas, whom they had made vassals of the king. They tried to resettle them west of the Sangre de Cristos rather than to strengthen their position in La Jicarilla. Moreover the Spaniards, still not foreseeing the seriousness of the Comanche threat, came to look upon the Jicarillas as liabilities rather than as useful allies. By 1748 the Spaniards had cause to regret their failure to fortify La Jicarilla. The Comanches were raiding well into New Mexico, and the pass of La Jicarilla was their chief entrance. The Jicarilla Apaches were living in and near both Taos and Pecos (unless those at Pecos were actually Carlanas), paying for asylum by helping to fight the Comanches.

Meanwhile, probably after the failure of the Jicarilla mission in 1733, the Carlanas seem to have remained on the Plains, surviving the Comanche menace through alliance with not only the Palomas and Cuartelejos, old friends, but with some of the

Faraons, former enemies of at least the Jicarillas proper. The ability of the Carlanas and their allies to hold their own caused Governor Vélez to solicit their friendship early in his term. He was too wise to try to keep the Carlanas in New Mexico by force, or they might well have fled the province again. While the Carlanas had very probably maintained some contact with the Jicarillas proper over the years, their relationship may have been reintensified when the "Plains Apaches" came to live near Pecos. For some reason, the Spaniards considered the Carlanas more important than the Cuartelejos and Palomas, and in the records of Vélez's first term the latter tribes seem to have gradually lost their identity.

By Vélez Cachupín's time the Spaniards of New Mexico were well aware that they themselves needed help against the Comanches if the latter could not be kept peaceful, and friendship with the friendly Apaches and the Utes seemed the readiest solution. Vélez himself managed to keep the Comanches at peace; his successor not only failed in this respect but apparently allowed ties with the Carlana Apaches to weaken.

Early in his administration, on 26 November 1754, Marín de Valle issued a decree prohibiting the sale of horses, other animals, and firearms to the Indians. The "Apaches Carlanes" are mentioned as a tribe with whom the Spaniards were trading at the time (SANM 530). Such an edict was not likely to be popular with either the settlers or the Indians, and during the term of this official and the terms of the two ad interim governors who followed him, relations between the Spaniards and the Gentile tribes deteriorated, although there are few available details of events between the end of Vélez Cachupín's first term and the close of the decade.

Chapter Nine

In the Service of the King: The Jicarillas from 1760–1801

The decade of the 1760s was an important one in the affairs of the northern provinces of New Spain. In 1762 France ceded Louisiana to Spain, and although the transfer was not fully effected until 1769, in the interim the Spaniards were attempting to adjust to the new situation. The land cession left Spain's eastern military posts far behind the actual frontier, across which she now faced the English instead of the French. The Spaniards recognized a potential threat in their new neighbors, but their most pressing problem was the ever-increasing attacks of the Comanches and some of the Apache tribes whom the Comanches were forcing against the Spanish settlements. In addition, along with Louisiana, Spain had inherited the task of maintaining good relations with all the tribes of that vast territory who had formerly been loyal to the French. Faced with this problem, Spain had to revise its policy toward friendly Indians, and the Jicarillas ultimately benefited by the resulting innovations.

Tribes under the influence of the French in Louisiana had been accustomed to receiving not only guns and ammunition in trade but had been given substantial gifts periodically as a reward for continued loyalty. By contrast, Spanish policy had been to withhold weapons and horses from even friendly tribes and to spend as little of the king's money as possible on the frontier provinces. In Louisiana the Spaniards were forced to continue the much more liberal French customs or lose the allegiance of the Indians there, and eventually the practices followed in Louisiana were extended to New Mexico.

Moreover, new approaches to frontier defense called for Spanish military forces to take the initiative and make regular routine campaigns into enemy country, augmenting their strength with Indian allies. For the first time, substantial funds were allotted by the superior government for expenses connected with frontier defense, including gratification of friendly Indians. These changes put the services already being rendered by the Utes and Jicarillas on a regular and more profitable basis. Allied Indians who went on campaigns were fed and housed in Santa Fé and rewarded with trade goods. They were also allowed to share in the loot captured from vanquished enemies.

However, one feature of the new policy was not so agreeable to the Utes and Jicarillas. The Spaniards had always been alert to the desirability of accomplishing their own ends by using one tribe of Indians against another. Beset by both the Comanches and Southern Apaches, who were bitter enemies of one another, Spanish officials decided on an all-out effort to make peace with the Comanches and use them against hostile Apaches. Such a peace was finally concluded in 1786, and in the same year the Spaniards were able to sever a friendship between the Navajos and the Gila Apaches and add the Navajos to their roster of allies. Thus in 1786 the Jicarillas, Utes, Navajos, and Comanches, by virtue of their alliance with the Spaniards of New Mexico, became allies of one another. Well aware of the hatred that the first three tribes held for the Comanches, the Spaniards expected protests, and they came. The Utes argued long and passionately against a treaty with the Comanches, complaining with good reason that the Spaniards apparently preferred unfaithful rebels to obedient and faithful friends. The Jicarillas could justifiably have said the same, but there is no record of a protest from them. Either the Utes were speaking for them, or the Jicarillas were by then so tractable that the Spaniards were not concerned with their opinion.

The wishes of the Spaniards prevailed, and the Utes finally joined in the treaty with the Comanches. For many years the Spaniards were able to maintain the uneasy alliance without open rupture, and the governor of New Mexico could report to his superiors regularly, in a statement that became stereotyped, the continued good behavior of the "four allied tribes." But the ancient enmity of the Indians, kept under control in Spanish territory, continued to manifest itself beyond the confines of New Mexico.

This state of affairs apparently continued without significant change into and throughout the period of Mexican rule in New Mexico. In late Spanish colonial times there were indications that changing circumstances were beginning to make the roving life style of the Jicarillas impracticable and to build up tensions between them and the Mexican villagers. The advent of new tribes of Indians on the Buffalo Plains tended to confine the Jicarillas proper to the mountains, where game naturally grew more scarce as a result. Moreover, horticultural land became scarce as the Spanish inhabitants founded new villages and even granted land to aliens.

In the last half of the eighteenth century the Carlana Apaches, having absorbed the Cuartelejos and Palomas, were apparently drawn ever farther from New Mexico through their ties with the Natagés, a relationship which Governor Vélez had deplored in the early 1750s. In fact, it may well be that the peace Anza

contracted with the Comanches in 1786 finally alienated the
Carlanas, since they had become involved with the more southern
Apache tribes against whom the Comanches were used.

In any case, the Natagés had been known in both New Mexico
and Texas at least since Rivera's inspection of the frontiers in the
1720s (Thomas 1935: 213), and it is probably no coincidence
that at about the time the Carlana Apaches cease to be mentioned in documents originating in New Mexico, an Apache
group called Llaneros appears in Texas in connection with the
Natagés. In brief, it seems probable that in shifting their activities
to Texas for a time the Carlanas became known as Llaneros. The
long-time friendship between the Carlanas and the Jicarillas
proper supports this notion, for New Mexico documents of ca.
1800 make it finally and abundantly clear that the Llaneros were
part of the Jicarillas—that division which is today still known as
the Llanero Band.

In 1760 Pedro Tamarón, bishop of Durango, visited New
Mexico. At the Pueblo of Santo Domingo "the captain of the
peaceful Apache Indians" came to call on the bishop, who said
of him, "This man is esteemed in the kingdom because of his old
loyalty. He warns of the coming of Comanches, and in war he
and his men are a safe ally. But they have not been able to persuade him to become a Christian" (Adams 1953–1954: 203). This
Apache could have been either a Jicarilla or a Carlana, since both
groups were friends of the Spaniards in this decade, and both were
living near the settlements. He was probably a Carlana, however,
for the Jicarillas were apparently living north of Santa Cruz,
while the Carlanas are mentioned at Carnué, south of Albuquerque, or east of the Pecos River near its confluence with the
Río Gallinas. At Santa Fé, Tamarón "experienced another alarm
about the Comanches, the news of whose coming was given by
the peaceful heathen Apaches. The governor took precautions,
and the Comanches went in another direction" (Adams 1953–
1954: 212).

The bishop visited Picurís and from there took the road to
Taos, of which he says,

To reach this Indian pueblo, whose patron saint is San Geronimo, one traveled over pine covered mountains until making the
descent to the spacious and beautiful valley called Taos, in which
were encountered villages of peaceable heathen Apaches, who
are gathered under the protection of the Spaniards for defense
against the Comanches. Then a river was encountered which
they call Las Trampas, which has a good flow of water. Half a
day was spent in a large house of a rich Indian of Taos, very in-
telligent and well off. His house and lands are surrounded by
(*armas*) [parentheses in original] for defense. In the afternoon
the journey was continued through that valley. Three rivers
were crossed, of the same current and amount of water as the
first; all have plenty of water for irrigating, and are distant from
one another about a league and a half. After passing the last one,
the pueblo of Taos was entered, where a Franciscan missionary
curate resides. It is twelve leagues distant from Picuris to the
north. (Grant 1934: 282)

Tamarón's statement clearly indicates that these peaceful
Apaches, who could only have been Jicarillas, were living in
various small hamlets in Taos Valley along the established road or
trail between Picurís and Taos, specifically between the point
where the road left the mountains and the Trampas River. Since
it was summer, the Apaches may have been settled there only
until their crops were ready for harvest. However, their occupation of Taos Valley, seasonal or otherwise, may have dated back
to 1727 when the Jicarillas were first encouraged to settle in that
area.

The record of Tamarón's visitation indicates that the new
break between the Spanish and the Comanches, complete by the
time Vélez Cachupín returned to New Mexico in 1762, occurred
near the end of Marín de Valle's term (1754–1760). In 1760 the
Comanches were still attending the Taos fairs, as was the governor, a large part of the Santa Fé garrison, and people from all
over the province (Adams 1953–1954: 216). On 4 August of
that year, however, a large number of Comanches attacked Taos,
massacring the inhabitants of an outlying ranch. Marín de Valle,
using Apache auxiliaries, pursued them for nearly two hundred
leagues (Adams 1953–1954: 217).

While the Spaniards maintained friendship with some of the

Apaches in case of war with the Comanches, the Comanche threat, in turn, was regarded as an important inducement to the Apache allies to keep faith. Tamarón stated:

> Intelligent persons have told me that they (the Comanches) are useful in holding the rest of the Indians in check, because they all fear them and realize that the method of defending themselves against them is to resort to the Spaniards for aid. The Ute tribe is very numerous on the New Mexico border. Formerly they waged war, and now they are at peace because of their fear of the Comanches. The same applies to the Faraon Apaches. (Adams 1953–1954: 301–2)

The bishop's information that the Faraons were at peace in 1760 fits with Vélez's statements of the early 1750s and makes the friendship between the Carlanas and some bands of the Faraons more reasonable. It likewise helps explain the presence of the Carlanas in 1765 on the west side of the Sandía Mountains just south and east of Albuquerque—that is, in long-time Faraon territory.

In 1765, Governor Vélez investigated a complaint that the lieutenant *alcalde mayor* of Albuquerque had permitted settlers to trade illegally with Apaches in Carnué (blnmo). Testimony revealed that the Apaches in question were the Carlanas, referred to as "Apaches Amigos Carlanas," and that the trading had been carried on in the canyon of Carnué, near the settlement (*lugar, poblacion*) of San Miguel de Laredo. The Carlanas had bartered four mules for as many horses, some salt for maize and flour, and ten deerskins for two young calves. The official who permitted the trading was found guilty and sentenced to three days in the guard house in Santa Fé. It seems that his fault lay not in permitting the trade but in failing to notify the governor and obtain the appropriate permits.

The canyon of Carnué is shown on the Miera map of 1779 made for Governor Anza (Thomas 1932: opposite p. 87, 378 *n*48). Some Genízaros were living at Carnué in 1768 (sanm 636), and San Miguel de Laredo (see figure 7) may have been their village or church. The name Carnué later became Carnuel (A & C 1956: 254).

In 1766, in the jurisdiction of Santa Cruz de la Cañada, a

mestizo, by his own confession, killed a well-known Jicarilla Apache whom the Spaniards called El Chimayó. The subsequent investigation, which covered the period of April to October, reveals some interesting details concerning El Chimayó, his local group, and the relations of the Jicarillas with the Spanish in this decade (BLNMO).

Governor Vélez, urging the apprehension and prosecution of the murderer, spoke highly of El Chimayó. He said that although this Jicarilla was a heathen he was very loyal and had gone on expeditions in the royal service against enemy nations who were accustomed to invade and rob the province. El Chimayó had lived among the Spanish settlements with confidence in the friendship, good faith, and protection of the inhabitants. Vélez said that the murderer should be punished not only to satisfy justice but also to satisfy the Jicarilla Apache nation, which was a loyal friend and ally of the Pueblos of Christian Indians and the Spaniards.

During the legal proceedings, the testimony of several Spaniards was taken. Salvador García, a resident of the place of La Hoya and an officer of the militia company of the district of Our Lady of La Soledad stated that when El Chimayó disappeared, his people were living in a *ranchería* located about one league (approximately 2.65 miles) from García's house. It was their custom to live there at that time of year—i.e., in the spring. García said that he knew El Chimayó well and esteemed him for his good will and the frequency with which he used to come down to García's house.

According to García, the *mestizo* Juan Roybal, who had confessed the killing and taken refuge in the church at San Juan, was a servant in the house of Angela Martín (Roybal?). This woman lived opposite García's house on the other side of the river in the place of La Canoa. Juan Roybal had come to García's house, and had said that he was going where the Jicarilla Apaches were. Subsequently the Jicarilla El Chimayó had appeared at La Hoya looking for a missing horse, which he thought had been stolen. Interestingly enough, the Apache had gone to the *alcalde mayor* of the jurisdiction of Santa Cruz de la Cañada, who told him that he must make certain that someone had stolen the horse before anything could be done. The *alcalde*, Don Manuel García Parejas, lived at Nuestra Señora de la Soledad, two leagues from Salvador García's house at La Hoya.

According to another Spanish resident of La Hoya, Francisco Xavier Martín, the Apache El Chimayó trailed his horse to La Canoa and inquired about it at the house of the widow Angela Martín, where he spent the night. El Chimayó, who according to Francisco Martín was even better known as *barbitas*, had given the *mestizo* Juan Roybal his "*botas*" (boots?, saddlebags?) to help him look for his horse. The two had set out together, and the Apache was not seen again.

The information given by Spanish witnesses indicates that the Jicarillas near La Hoya were in some respects living according to Spanish pattern. El Chimayó, and certainly other Jicarillas, visited frequently with the settlers. He felt free to complain to the Spanish *alcalde* when his horse was stolen, and his tribesmen went to the Spanish governor when El Chimayó disappeared and could not be found. Some degree of social equality is suggested by the facts that El Chimayó spent the night before his murder inside the house of a Spanish settler and that he hired a *mestizo* servant of that settler to help him search for his horse.

Governor Vélez's statement that El Chimayó went on campaigns in the royal service validates other evidence that the use of Jicarillas as auxiliaries was already standard procedure by 1766, although it did not become part of formal Spanish policy until later. Moreover, the governor's remarks indicate that the entire Jicarilla tribe served the Spaniards as allies.

It has been assumed that the Jicarillas moved west of the Sangre de Cristos because they feared the Comanches, and the scarcity of references to the Jicarillas in Spanish documents after 1727 has led to the inference that the Jicarillas were so weakened by Comanche attacks as to be unimportant to the Spaniards. The Jicarillas did fear the Comanches, for as settled farmers in La Jicarilla they were hopelessly vulnerable to the attacks of a mobile foe. But it was probably not cowardice that caused them to move west of the mountains. The Jicarillas of the adobe houses and irrigated fields may have been so strongly oriented toward a sedentary existence that they chose to move into an area where they could continue this way of life after some fashion by means of a symbiotic alliance with the Spaniards and Pueblo Indians. For the Jicarillas did have a choice, as the history of the Carlanas shows. The Carlanas, like the Jicarillas, had once been sedentary foothills Apaches, apparently weaker than the Jicarillas since they had sought protection with the latter. Yet the Carlanas, by going to live on the Plains as allies of Plains Apaches and by becoming as mobile, perhaps, as the Comanches themselves, had managed not only to survive but to impress the Spaniards with their resourcefulness and courage in the 1750s. The Jicarillas might have done the same.

Actually, as has been pointed out earlier, the Jicarillas proper did not abandon the Sangre de Cristos. Documents of the 1760s suggest that they simply shifted their main bases of operation to the western slopes and canyons, and earlier and later documents suggest that they continued to exploit the higher valleys and eastern canyons whenever possible. In short, they showed that they were, as Opler (1936: 205) has deduced, basically a mountain people. As for the importance of the Jicarillas on the New Mexico scene, Vélez's remarks in 1766 show that they were indeed valued as friends and auxiliaries of the Spaniards, and it is not unreasonable to suppose that they were seldom mentioned in official documents because their loyalty was of such long-standing as to be taken for granted.

Since the documentary sources provide few details on the culture of the Jicarillas who lived near La Hoya, it is desirable to pinpoint the location of their village as closely as possible in the hope that it can be found and excavated by archeologists. First, however, it is necessary to locate the Spanish settlements mentioned which, with the exception of Santa Cruz, do not appear on modern maps. The problem is simplified to some extent by the fact that all the Spanish settlements mentioned in the document concerning the murder of El Chimayó were within the Sebastian Martín land grant, whose original boundaries are described by Twitchell as follows:

> The grant embraced the valley of the Rio Grande on both sides
> of the river from the boundary of the grant to the pueblo of
> San Juan on the south to the end of La Joya on the north and
> to the east as far as Las Trampas. The settlements of Plaza del
> Alcalde, Los Luceros, La Villita, and La Joya, are all within the
> original grant. The grant contained over 40,000 acres. (Twitch-
> ell 1914 I: 190)

The settlement referred to by Twitchell as La Joya is almost
certainly the La Hoya of the eighteenth century, and Twitchell's
spelling complicates an already complex problem. A settlement
named La Oya is shown on the Miera map of 1779 (Thomas
1932: opposite p. 87), north of Santa Cruz on the south bank of
the Truchas River near its confluence with the Río Grande.
Moreover, Father Morfi, in his account published in 1782, lists
a La Olla as one of the settlements of the *alcaldia* of Santa Cruz
de la Cañada (Thomas 1932: 94, 96). The locations given for
La Oya and La Olla, compared to the location of La Hoya in
1766, indicate that the names as given by Miera and Morfi were
variant spellings of La Hoya that arose because in the late
eighteenth century in New Mexico the "h" was not pronounced,
as is still the case in Castilian, and the "y" and "ll" were pronounced the same, a deviation from Castilian.

Harrington believes the name of the Ollero Band of the Jicarillas should have been written as Hoyero instead, and the
varying forms of the name of the Spanish settlement show that
confusion can indeed take place. According to Miller (1962:
291), the town now called Velarde was formerly called La Joya,
and Velarde is located approximately where La Oya is shown on
Miera's map. Harrington can probably be considered the final
authority on the place name in question. In speaking of the
present town of Velarde and its vicinity he points out that the
Spanish name La Hoya became in New Mexican Spanish La Joya
but still means the dell or the hollow.

> The Span. name is still in common use as a designation of the
> whole locality. It was formerly also used as the name of the
> settlement, which was recently changed from La Hoya to
> Velarde because of confusion with La Hoya on the Rio Grande
> below Albuquerque. In New Mexican Span. words beginning
> with a vowel or *h* are frequently pronounced with an initial *j*.

Hence the current misspelling "La Joya" for La Hoya. Hoya is a much applied geographical term in New Mexican Span. (Harrington 1916: 197–98)

In keeping with its former name, Velarde and its associated orchards (among the finest in New Mexico) are located in what is the largest of several *hoyas* or wide places that give opportunity for horticulture in a stretch of the Río Grande Canyon that is otherwise narrow and steep walled. The settlement of La Canoa still exists across the Río Grande from present Velarde.

As for Nuestra Señora de la Soledad, Twitchell (1914 II: 197–99), in his comments on the Martín family, says it was the name of Captain Sebastian Martín's private chapel. The Captain's daughter Angela, who married a Roybal in this chapel, was probably the widow Angela Martín of La Canoa, whose *mestizo* servant, Juan Roybal, killed El Chimayó. The name Nuestra Señora de la Soledad was apparently also applied to a village, for two legal documents, the will of Sebastian Martín's widow and a conveyance of lands, are dated at the "puesto [place] de Nuestra Señora de la Soledad del Rio Arriba" (Twitchell 1914 I: 74–75). This place may well have been the seat of the Martín family, for five brothers of Captain Sebastian lived with him on the grant, and it is probable that they lived close together for protection from hostile Indians. The extended family alone could have constituted a village. La Soledad, which in 1766 was the home of the *alcalde mayor* of the entire district of Santa Cruz, may be the town known in 1860 as Plaza del Alcalde, now shortened simply to Alcalde (Miller 1962: 291).

From the evidence, then, it appears that in 1766 and earlier some Jicarillas had a semi-permanent village to which they returned every spring, about one league from La Hoya (the oldest part of Velarde). It seems probable that the Jicarillas of this settlement were separate from and contemporaneous with those on the Trampas River to the north, for El Chimayó and his group had apparently been living seasonally near La Hoya for some time, and Bishop Tamarón had reported the villages near the Trampas River only six years before. Since El Chimayó came "down" to the Casa de la Hoya, he probably either lived a league upstream on the Río Grande, a league upstream on the Truchas, or on high land behind García's house.

During the very period when the death of this Jicarilla leader was being investigated, measures initiated by the King for the evaluation of New Spain's frontier defenses brought an important inspector, the Marqués de Rubí, to New Mexico. He was accompanied by the engineer Nicolas Lafora, who was assigned the duty of mapping and describing the regions visited, and by a cartographer, Ensign Joseph Urrutia (Kinnaird 1958: 2, 4). Since these two men traveled and worked together, it is interesting that on maps produced individually, Lafora (Kinnaird 1958: map) identified "Gentile" Indians living at the confluence of the Gallinas and Pecos Rivers as "Apaches Xicarillas," while on a map produced jointly by Lafora and Urrutia (Wheat 1957: 88, map 157), these Apaches are labeled as Carlanas. On yet another map bearing Lafora's name (Wheat 1957: map 155), the Indians shown at the confluence of the Pecos and Gallinas are labeled "Apaches Carlanes y Xicarillas" (figure 7). These map makers were probably getting their information from New Mexico officials whose tendency to use the name Jicarilla at times as an alternative for Carlana has already been mentioned.

Rubí's own comments, like the maps, are dated 1771 but presumably reflect conditions that existed in 1766, the year that he was in New Mexico.

> The Comanche in the northeast, he [Rubí] observed, were at peace and gave evidence of knowing how to keep their obligations. The Apaches who maintained a "perfidious peace," he described as extending from the Rio Grande north and northeast on both sides of the Pecos. They were known generically as the Natagées, but the various divisions of the tribe bore the names of Mescaleros, Carlanas, Salineros, Jicarillas, and other of their designated chiefs. With the groups on the plains, the Jicarillas, located near Pecos, had contact through the Sierra de Sandía. To the east they had been observed, it was thought, in San Sabá, while to the south and west they joined the Natagée and Gila to sweep through the unoccupied area just north of El Paso to raid that settlement, attack caravans on the camino real, and invade the jurisdiction of Albuquerque. (Thomas 1940: 36–37)

Among other measures, Rubí recommended that a military detachment be established north of El Paso at Robledo to block the communication of the Natagés, Jicarillas, and other eastern Apaches with the Gilas.

Earlier and later sources discredit Rubí's statement that all the Apaches he names were subdivisions of the Natagés. According to Curtis (1907–1930 I: 140), "na-ta" is a pan-Southern Athabascan term for mescal, but it would be inaccurate to equate the Natagés, or "Mescal People," with the modern Mescaleros. The scope of the term Natagé as a tribal designation seems to have changed through time. In 1796, for example, Cordero confined the term to a subdivision of the Llaneros (M & S 1957: 355), and it has not survived into recent times. More important, Rubí's statements concerning the Jicarillas located near Pecos seem incompatible with what New Mexico records reveal of the Jicarillas proper who were living on the upper Río Grande. His observations are consistent, however, with what Vélez Cachupín said of relations between the Carlanas, who *were* living in and near Pecos, and the Natagés in 1754. In that year, relinquishing office at the end of his first term, Vélez had warned his successor to watch the Carlanas.

> While their exchanges can not be completely prevented, at least let it not be frequent with the Natageses and let it be only trade, not union and alliance against this province and La Vizcaya. In such case, the Natageses, strengthened by the support and cunning of the Plains Apaches, would develop among the Sumas the greatest boldness, which would result in the total ruin of the frontiers of La Vizcaya and the Real of Chihuahua. (Thomas 1940: 136)

At the time of Rubí's inspection, the Carlanas were still maintaining more or less amicable relations in New Mexico itself, but some of Vélez's fears seem to have been realized because Jicarillas (Carlanas) had actually joined hostile Apaches in raids against settlements in Texas, northern Mexico, and even the Albuquerque district. It may well have been in this period that Spanish officials elsewhere in New Spain got the idea that the Jicarillas proper were closely related to more southern branches of the Apacheans (e.g., Cordero [M & S 1957: 353–54]).

It is interesting that Rubí's statements do not agree entirely with the following comments in Lafora's diary.

> The Apaches are a single nation, but are under the different names of Gileños, Carlanes, Chilpaines, Xicarillas, Pharaones, Mezcaleros, Natages, Lipanes, etc. These groups differ little in language. (Kinnaird 1958: 79)

Writing specifically of New Mexico he said:

> At the present time [1766] the nations of the Navajos, Moquinos, Yutas, Apaches, Carlanes and Chilpaines are at peace, and they are only troubled by the Apaches Gileños and Pharaones. (Kinnaird 1958: 93)

However, Governor Mendinueta, who succeeded Vélez Cachupín in 1767, wrote to the viceroy that on 24 May 1768

> about forty Apaches, Natagé and Sierra Blanca, arrived at the jurisdiction of Albuquerque, seeking, through their ambassadors, peace, which was granted them. They turned over two captives whom they had carried off in the past year from the same jurisdiction. They promised to keep the peace faithfully, which I doubt from experience with their unreliability. (Thomas 1940: 162)

Rubí may have had access to this information when he wrote in 1771.

Since the Carlana Apaches had been known as the Sierra Blancas at least as late as 1726 and since the Carlanas were friendly with the Natagés in the 1750s and 1760s, the Sierra Blancas mentioned here may have been Carlanas. If so, Mendinueta's statement suggests that the Carlanas were again drifting away from Spanish influence, as they had between 1726 and the beginning of Governor Vélez's first term (1749–1754).

When Mendinueta undertook a campaign against the Comanches in July 1768 there were Utes and Apaches, undoubtedly Jicarillas, with him as auxiliaries. However, when the Comanches were finally located, the Utes and Apaches warned them by rushing ahead before the order to attack was given (Thomas 1940: 165). In September of the same year Utes helped settlers of Ojo Caliente repulse an attack by twenty-four Comanches, killing or capturing all but two (Thomas 1940: 166). It was also reported that the Natagé and Sierra Blanca Apaches were maintaining faith with the Spaniards as they had promised in the spring. A captive who had escaped from the Apaches said they had asked for peace because the Comanches had raided the Natagé and because they knew that Spanish forces were coming against them from Nueva Vizcaya (Thomas 1940: 167–68).

The fact that the Carlana or Sierra Blanca Apaches were roaming in the 1760s in an area that included another mountain range called the Sierra Blancas, west of present Roswell, New Mexico, serves to complicate the picture. For in the end it was the Mescaleros who inhabited, and still inhabit, the Sierra Blancas of southeastern New Mexico.

Known documents pertaining to the decade 1770–1779 yield little specific information on either the Jicarillas proper or the Carlanas, but during this period Spanish officials were beginning to put into effect some of the new policies made necessary by changes on the international scene in the 1760s, and these, in turn, affected the Jicarillas in years to come (Bolton 1914; Worcester 1951; Kinnaird 1958; Thomas 1932; 1940). Several aspects of Spanish policy that were finally implemented throughout the Internal Provinces were suggested by Rubí as early as 1771. The friendship of the Comanches was to be cultivated on the assumption that these Indians, considered superior in some ways to the Apaches, would keep treaties. The Comanches were to be used against the Apaches, who as a result would be driven to take refuge at Spanish missions and *presidios* where they would not be granted peace unless they agreed to settle far within Mexico. There they would be dispersed into small groups that would lose their identity among other tribes. After the useless Spanish settlements and *presidios* of eastern Texas were abandoned, Indian agents were to be appointed to administer to the tribes of that area, after the French custom.

On the basis of these recommendations, both José de Gálvez, Minister of the Indies, and the viceroy of New Spain, suggested that the Northern Provinces be separated from the vice-royalty of Mexico and placed under a military government. Accordingly, by a *reglamento* (ordinance) in 1772, certain Texas *presidios* were relocated. Although steps may have been taken at this time to set aside the Northern Provinces, it was not until 1776 that the separation was formally accomplished by a royal order which also appointed Teodoro de Croix as commander general. Croix, who assumed his duties in 1777, made a tour of inspection and held three important councils of war in Monclova, San Antonio, and Chihuahua. While it was decided that the relocation of *presidios* according to Rubí's plan had been a mistake, his idea of an alliance with the Comanches was adopted as desirable policy, and officials also decided that vigorous aggressive war should be made on the Lipans, Natagés *or Lipiyanes* and Mescaleros.

Changes were made in the administrative organization of the Internal Provinces from time to time until 1793, but these did not seem to affect everyday affairs in New Mexico. In fact, none of the benefits of the new approach to Indian affairs were felt in that province until Don Juan Bautista de Anza, appointed governor in 1777, arrived to assume his duties late in 1778. When Anza arrived in Santa Fé it was with orders to open a new route between New Mexico and Sonora as soon as possible to facilitate expeditions against the southern Apaches. However, the condition in which he found the province put under his charge led him to make a campaign against the Comanches his first major objective. Even then it was not until 15 August 1779 that he began the march northward from Santa Fé that was to end with the decisive defeat of the Comanches and the death of their head chief, Cuerna Verde, or Green Horn.

On 20 August at the Río Conejos in present Colorado reinforcements presented themselves.

> At the end of the afternoon two hundred men of the Ute and Apache nation also joined me with one of their principal captains. Of the first were those who ever since my assumption of this government have asked me, and have reiterated incessantly with prayers that they be admitted into my company in confirmation of our friendship, provided I should go on a campaign against the Comanches. I agreed to grant this to them, as much to take advantage of this increase of people as to try in this way to civilize them so that they may at least be more useful to us against the enemy itself than they have been formerly.

> With this intent I indicated that they must be at my orders
> as to what of spoils belonged to them in case of encounters and
> defeats of the enemy. This, with the exception of personal cap-
> tures, they would have to agree to divide equally with all my
> men. To these proposals they consented, promising to observe
> them. (Thomas 1932: 125)

Anza found and defeated a large number of Comanches, capturing so much loot that it could not be loaded on a hundred
horses. This material was divided equally without any un-
pleasantness. After the horses belonging to the defeated Comanches had also been found and caught, "without giving any
notice, most of the Ute nation left for their country" (Thomas
1932: 132).

From some captured Comanches Anza learned that the chief
Cuerna Verde had gone to attack Taos, and accordingly the
general chose a homeward route that would be likely to inter-
cept the Comanches' return trail. After he met and defeated
Cuerna Verde, he went home as he had come, via the pass of
Sangre de Cristo. Between this stream and the Río de Culebra

> that part of the Ute nation which had remained, left for their
> country enriched and satisfied, and without farewells, for their
> barbarity and desire again to see their country did not admit
> this civility. (Thomas 1932: 137)

Presumably the Apache auxiliaries left with one or the other of
the Ute contingents.

At Taos, Anza found that the Comanches had indeed attacked
the Pueblo, but the *alcalde* had been warned six days before the
assault by "our Apache friends" and therefore had been able to
repel it. Nor had the last been heard from the "heathen" auxiliaries. When Anza arrived in Santa Fé on 10 September, word
awaited him from the first Utes to leave his forces that they had
surprised and killed a small group of Comanches on their own
(Thomas 1932: 139).

The Apaches mentioned in Anza's diary can only have been
Jicarillas, and they were identified as Jicarillas by Croix in 1781
(Thomas 1941: 109). Therefore, the diary is of considerable
significance for Jicarilla history. Sources of the previous decade
indicated that Jicarillas were living in at least two different

rancherías in the Upper Río Grande area. But, although Jicarillas and Utes were allies as early as 1754, Anza's diary is the
first document to actually locate Jicarilla Apaches as far north
and west as the Conejos River.

The value of the Jicarillas as scouts is well illustrated by
Cuerna Verde's defeat at Taos. On the other hand, the generous
policy of sharing spoils equally with Indian auxiliaries was undoubtedly a welcome source of goods for the Jicarillas, not to
speak of the satisfaction they must have experienced in helping
to inflict such a crushing defeat on their worst enemies.

Additional light was shed on the Jicarillas and Carlanas in the
late 1700s by Don Bernardo Miera y Pacheco, "engineer, retired
captain, and citizen of Santa Fe." Arriving in America in 1743,
this man became a soldier at El Paso, where he made maps of the
country as well as fought Indians. In 1754, he went to Santa Fé
with Governor Marín de Valle and settled there. As *alcalde* and
captain at Pecos and Galisteo he not only made campaigns
against the Comanches but mapped the country he traversed on
such expeditions. Between 1762 and 1767, Miera served as captain of militia in New Mexico under Vélez Cachupín, during
that governor's second term. His greatest recognition has come
from the fact that he accompanied Escalante and Dominguez as
engineer and mapped the territory they explored (Bolton 1950:
11–13).

Miera's knowledge of northeastern New Mexico is of most interest for this study, and if he campaigned against Comanches
he almost certainly had occasion to follow them north to the
Arkansas River or beyond. It has been pointed out earlier that
some Miera maps of 1778 show a lone peak representing the
"Cerro de la Xicarilla" rising from the plains well east of the
Sangre de Cristos. On the version of this map in the Archivo
General in Mexico City (figure 3) designated by Wheat (1957:
113) as "Type C, copy 2," the name of the peak is fully written
out. In addition, it is shown more or less straight east of the point
where the Canadian River (el Río Rojo) emerges from the
mountains. This version of the map reinforces the probability
that the Cerro de la Xicarilla was Capulin Mountain, and it is in-

teresting to note that the landmark still bore its original name in
1778 (see also Hackett 1931–1946 IV: 161). On this map, also,
Miera included the statement that the Comanches controlled all
the Buffalo Plains, having driven out the Apaches, formerly the
most wide-spread tribe known in America. He said that the
Apaches had "holed up" (*arrinconado*) on the frontiers of New
Spain.

Not only did Miera prepare a map after his return from the
journey led by Escalante and Dominguez, but on 26 October
1777, from Chihuahua, he wrote to the king of Spain suggesting
new measures for the defense of the frontiers. Among other innovations, he suggested that a "flying company" should operate
between the "Presido of Elceareo" [*sic*] and San Juan Bautista
on the lower Río Grande "to ward off the incursions of the
Apaches of the plains, who are the Carlanes, Natajees, and
Lipanes" (Bolton 1950: 249). From this it would appear that the
Carlanas were ranging well south of New Mexico indeed and
that even New Mexicans were aware that they were raiding in
Mexico.

On the agenda of a council of war held at Monclova on 11
December 1777 a name not previously found in the Santa Fé
Archives appears in an item designed to elicit information on
various Apache tribes. The enumeration includes the "Natajes, or
Lipiyanes" (Bolton 1914 II: 147, 150). Everyone present at the
council agreed that "the Natages live regularly on the plains in
the vicinity of the pueblo of El Paso and New Mexico, and
sometimes with their relatives the Lipanes" (Bolton 1914 II:
153), and that the "Lipiyanes" made war on New Mexico (Bolton 1914 II: 154). The same agenda was discussed at two more
major councils of war, one at San Antonio (Bolton 1914 II: 163–
70) and one at Chihuahua (Thomas 1940: 193–213).

In none of these councils were the Carlanas mentioned, nor the
Llaneros, whose name was soon to appear frequently in documents. Later records, however, indicate that the Lipiyanes were
part of, or the same as, the Llaneros who eventually proved to be
the Llanero Band of the modern Jicarillas. It is probable, then,
that the Lipiyanes were the Carlanas appearing in Texas and

northern Mexico under an Athabascan name. In spite of their defections, however, the Carlanas continued to appear in New Mexico from time to time under their old name. In establishing contacts with Lipans, the Carlanas may have been reuniting with that half of their tribe who did not join the Jicarillas in 1718. It has been suggested elsewhere (G & G 1971) that the "Chief Flaco" to whom half of the Carlanas fled in 1718 was a Lipan because of the continuity of this chief name among the Lipans. Since the paper cited above was written, additional research reveals that the name occurs more often than previously indicated. In 1775, fifty-six years after the dispersion of the Carlanas, there was a chief called El Flaco among the Lipans (Moorhead 1968: 38), and in 1843 Sam Houston wrote a glowing eulogy to his friend General Flaco, head chief of the Lower Lipans, who had recently died. Most significant, in 1844, the year after Houston eulogized Chief Flaco of the Lipans, a "Flaco Chico" (Flaco the Younger) was summoned to a meeting held for purposes of making a treaty, and on 28 October 1851, a "Captain John Flaco" (Flaco Chico?) of the Lipans signed a treaty (Winfrey 1959–1966 I: 164–65; II: 67; III: 149; Sjoberg 1953: 79).

Since the Lipans are said to have had a kind of hereditary chieftainship (Sjoberg 1953: 94), it is very possible that the Chief Flaco to whom half the Carlanas fled in 1718 belonged to a line of chiefs of that name, especially in view of evidence from other Apache groups. Among the Chiricahuas, for example, sons apparently succeeded their fathers in command, even if they were very young (Moorhead 1968: 192). Mooney records one case in which a Kiowa Apache subchief had inherited his name from his grandfather (Mooney 1898*b*: 445, pl. LXXIV), and in another case (Moorhead 1968: 242) not only the status but the name of a Mescalero Chief, Patule El Viejo (Patule the Elder) passed to his brother, Patule El Chico (Patule the Younger). If the Lipans did absorb half the Carlanas in 1718, and the rest of the Carlanas eventually became part of the Llanero Band of the modern Jicarillas, such circumstances would do much to explain not only some of the marked similarities between Lipan and Jicarilla culture in recent times but would also have facilitated the alliance between the Carlanas and the Lipans noted by Miera in 1777.

Historical evidence indicates, too, that the Lipans, along with other Apache groups with whom they were allied, converged on the Spaniards at San Antonio from the north or northwest, beginning to make their presence felt not long after the Carlanas were driven from southeastern Colorado. But by coincidence the *presidio* of San Antonio de Béxar and the associated mission, San Antonio de Valero, were themselves founded in 1718 (Castañeda 1935 I: 190), and their presence may have been in part what drew Apaches southward. Father Morfi's statement of ca. 1779 that the "Ipandis," who have been accepted as Lipans, were among the Indians for whom the mission at San Antonio was originally founded (Castañeda 1935 I: 190) is tantalizing, but this idea has not yet been verified in a primary source.

Dunn (1911: 267–68) cites a Spanish statement that the "Ypandis alias Pelones" were the least daring of the Apaches, had lived farthest north from San Antonio on the "Caudachos (Red) River," and were the first whom the Comanches had compelled to give up their lands. All these statements fit the Carlanas if one remembers that the Canadian (called first by the Spaniards the Río Colorado and later, occasionally, the Río Rojo) was erroneously considered to be the upper part of the Red River of Texas until well into the 1800s. Also worth mentioning is the fact that in 1723, when the Spaniards at San Antonio were trying to find out all they could about the Apaches some twenty days' journey to the north, an Apache woman captive from that area gave a description of the political and military organization of her people that is almost identical with that described to Bourgmont in Kansas in 1724 by the chief who called himself the "Emperor of all the Padoucas" (Apaches) (Margry 1875–1886 VI: 442).

By the late 1770s the Lipans, long in need of allies, were in more desperate straits than ever. Dunn (1911), Bolton (1914), and Newcomb (Tunnel and Newcomb 1969) have outlined the story of how the Lipans were harassed by the Comanches and "Nations of the North" (including the Wichitas), how they were pressed southward where they preyed upon Spanish settlements in Texas and northern Mexico, and how the Spaniards (it must be said in their favor) tried to protect and civilize the Lipans, whose depredations in large measure stimulated Spanish officials to attempt for the first time a truly organized approach to solving the "Apache Problem." Their efforts must be called an attempt because the problem was by then too complex for a simple solution, and none was ever really achieved—there was still an "Apache Problem" when the United States took over Texas, New Mexico, and Arizona.

It was unfortunate for both the Apaches and the Spaniards that, beginning with the recommendations of the Marqués de Rubí in 1768, the governors and presidial officers and, later, the commander generals of the Internal Provinces themselves, had to deal with hostile Indian tribes under a series of official regulations that were mutually inconsistent (Moorhead 1968: 116). Not until Viceroy Gálvez's *Instrucción* of 1786 (Worcester 1951) was a synthesis of previous edicts accomplished. Because it was a synthesis, the *Instrucción* contained elements that were brutal, cynical, and insidious along with provisions for tempering the Spanish version of justice with mercy. Actually, it made the Spaniards almost as politically flexible as the Indians by permitting them to wage war against tribes that were hostile but grant peace whenever (although not wherever) it was requested. All the specific measures, of course, were intended to contribute toward the eventual dominance of the Spaniards. Enlightened self-interest even lay behind the practice, regularized and adequately supported for the first time, of giving gifts to Indians at peace and essentially paying Indian auxiliaries. It was hoped that by this means, during intervals of peace, hostile tribes would become so dependent on European foods and other goods that they would eventually stay at peace in order to get these things. The complexities of the trial-and-error process by means of which the Spaniards evolved a workable Indian policy in the late eighteenth century have been discussed at length by several historians, while the implications of that policy for the Apaches have been effectively oversimplified by Nelson (1940: 459):

The future of the Apaches had been fixed and their death warrant signed at that fateful series of conferences on problems and policy held by Croix and his subordinates the winter of 1777–1778. . . . Nothing was to be done to offend the Comanches, all things were to be endured from them. The Apaches, on the contrary, if they kept the peace with the Spaniards, were to be left to the not too tender mercy of their hereditary enemies. If they broke the peace the Spaniards would merely join in a war of extermination against them. They lost either way.

All this should not have affected the Jicarillas proper, so long friendly toward the Spaniards and the Pueblo peoples, and most of the strategy was admittedly aimed against southern Apache tribes. However, to the Spaniards, especially top administrators far from New Mexico who often misunderstood or misinterpreted the information fed in from provincial officials, one Gentile Indian was much like another. And as enemy tribes on the one hand and Spanish troops on the other began to effect a vast "drag net" or "surround," the southernmost Apache tribes, impounded like hunted animals, began to mill about desperately seeking a way out of the trap. They went from one *presidio* to another seeking protection under different names. They made agreements to settle down that both they and the Spaniards knew were unrealistic because of the difficulty of providing subsistence for large sedentary groups in a restricted area. Various tribes resorted to making raids disguised as other Apache tribes, and in any case, because they were so much alike in language, clothing, and habits, the Spaniards could not always tell one group from another. Officials began to express again the idea that all Apaches were one and the same people and that none of them could be trusted because they were likely to help each other.

Hard beset by external pressures the Apacheans did turn to one another increasingly for aid, and the Spaniards were ready with countermeasures. They forced various Apachean groups to fight one another with threats of trade boycotts or military retaliation if they refused. Thus when the Gilas turned to the Navajos, the latter were soon forced not only to reject these southern kinsmen but to actively attack them so that they would not be likely to seek an alliance again. Likewise the Lipans and Mescaleros were encouraged to betray one another.

It is understandable, then, that the friendship of the tribe that emerged in Texas rather suddenly as Lipiyanes-Llaneros was important to the Lipans, but even alliance could not save these tribes. First the Lipans and then the Lipiyanes-Llaneros appeared in New Mexico asking for asylum, which over-all Spanish policy denied them. It was then that the Lipiyanes-Llaneros, finally to be known simply as Llaneros, put the first serious strain on relations between the Spaniards and the faithful Jicarillas proper by persuading the Jicarillas to hide them. In the end it was apparently the complete inability of the Spaniards to distinguish Llaneros from Jicarillas proper, and the avowed kinship of the two, that made it possible for the Llaneros to move back to the comparative safety of New Mexico.

While the metamorphosis of the Carlanas into the Llaneros was taking place off the New Mexico stage, the Jicarillas proper continued to maintain and enhance their standing with the Spaniards. They had probably been the first Gentile tribe to serve the Spaniards as auxiliaries in New Mexico, even offering to fight against their congeners the Faraons as early as 1715. Under Governors Vélez Cachupín and Anza they had gained something approaching the status of the Christian Pueblo Indian auxiliaries and the Spanish settler-soldiers, or militia. They had apparently become semi-sedentary, returning every spring to plant crops in areas that were conceded to be theirs—after all, they were vassals of the king.

With the changes in Spanish policy promulgated in 1786, which emphasized the greater tactical advantage of using friendly "barbarian" tribes against hostile barbarians (Thomas 1941: 94), the Jicarillas and those Utes allied with them became, for all practical purposes, mercenary soldiers subject to call like the militia itself. Special quarters were used to feed and house them when they were in Santa Fé; they were issued rations while on campaigns and were granted a share of spoils taken from enemies.

From Chihuahua in July 1780, Teodoro de Croix, commander general of the Internal Provinces, acknowledged receipt of letters and documents from Anza. It appears that after the latter's decisive campaign of 1779 against the Comanches, that tribe had already attempted to make peace. Anza had probably expressed his concern that the Utes and Jicarillas would attempt to block such a move, for Croix pointed out that it was Anza's task to conserve the friendship of the Utes and Jicarillas and still prepare them to accept an alliance with the Comanches if this could be accomplished (SANM 799).

The day book of the *presidio* at Santa Fé for January 1781 (SANM 816a) yields important details on the Carlanas, the last found thus far in a primary document. These Apaches, who had formerly lived in a "Sierra Blanca" northeast of Taos, were again living in a "Sierra Blanca"—this time almost certainly the range still known by that name southeast of Santa Fé. They are referred to as "Apaches Carlanes de la Sierra blanca" and "Apaches en la Sierra blanca." Interestingly enough, Utes allied with the Jicarillas were visiting back and forth with these Carlanas, the first specific indication that the Utes were also friendly with this band of Apaches.

On 24 January an Apache chief called Pajarito (Little Bird), identified in later documents as a Jicarilla, came in with two Ute chiefs, Moara and Antonio, to give the news that they had killed twelve Comanches beyond the "Sierra de jumanas." At the same time the Ute chief Antonio had given up a Spanish boy named Moya who had been a captive among Indians for four years. It seems that originally he had been captured by Comanches but that the preceding summer all the Carlanas, accompanied by Lipans, had gone on a campaign against the Comanches, who had gone to the Jumanos (Wichitas), taking him to sell. The boy said the Jumanos had many captives that the Comanches had stolen from the New Mexico settlement of Tomé and sold to them. Also, among the Jumanos was a Frenchman who could read and write. The Spanish boy, who was from the Plaza de Las Lunas, had escaped from the Comanches and fallen in with the Carlana Apaches, among whom he had remained until found there by the Ute chief, Antonio.

From this source it becomes evident that in 1781 the Carlanas were in the Sierra Blancas of southeastern New Mexico where they were being visited by both Jicarillas and Utes. Other portions of the document indicate that while the New Mexico Spaniards were not at war against the Carlanas, they were keeping them under surveillance, probably because of their raids against Spanish settlements elsewhere and because of their alliance with the Lipans, with whom the Spaniards were only reluctantly at peace.

On 30 October 1781, Teodoro de Croix completed a General Report on the Internal Provinces addressed to José de Gálvez, minister of the Indies. In his account of the province of Texas he reported:

> Another band of sixteen Comanche, who were attacking the neighborhood of the Villa of San Fernando, had an encounter with a detachment of forty-eight men from the presidio of Bejar. Ten of the enemy and two of our men met death. The troops and settlers of New Mexico, with the aid of the Ute and Jicarilla Apache, have persecuted and punished them with rigor. Certainly it is not strange that the Comanche, insatiable (as are all Indians) in their vengeance, unable to resist the forces of New Mexico allied with the brave Ute and treacherous Jicarilla, and urged by the necessity of providing themselves with horses for their bison hunts, give vent to their cruelties and natural inclination to steal and commit murder in the province of Texas where they find less resistance, greater helplessness, and cowardice in some settlers who have become accustomed to living in the bosom of peace. (Thomas 1941: 75)

Again, the choice of the word "treacherous" to describe the Jicarillas is puzzling, since it does not fit what is known of the Jicarillas proper. Of New Mexico, Croix said:

> The Comanche and all the Apache, with the exception of the Navajo and Jicarilla now at peace, attack in this province . . . the numerous and valiant Ute nation remains friendly and aids us happily against the Comanche. (Thomas 1941: 105)

In 1786 Governor Anza of New Mexico began negotiations with the Comanches that were to relieve that province of its most serious Indian problem. In 1785 the Comanches had sought peace at Taos and were told they would be granted it, but only as an entire tribe. The Comanches themselves then undertook to unite all their bands for treaty purposes (Thomas 1932: 292–96). When the bands that could be brought together had selected a representative, emissaries asked permission for him to come to Santa Fé "by way of the route through the pueblo of Pecos, entreating that while he was doing so, Anza should warn the Jicarilla Apaches who live under our protection not to molest him with their thefts," and "with regard to his petition, the Jicarilla Apaches were warned not to interfere with him" (Thomas 1932: 296, 297).

The Utes were not to be dealt with so easily as the Jicarillas.

> The reports [of negotiations with the Comanches] tended to cause uneasiness among the Utes who were wintering on the northern extremity of that kingdom. These Indians, whose loyalty to the Spaniards is as well known as their hate of the Comanches is ancient, persuaded that their friendship and services would preponderate in our consideration against the peace which was going to be established with their enemies, resolved to prevent it. They despatched to the governor without loss of an instant two of their most authoritative chiefs called Moara and Pinto who arrived at Santa Fe on the 7th of the same January. They heatedly declared against the attempted peace, advancing the most vindictive and even insulting and barbarous arguments to destroy it, even stating to that chief, Anza, that he preferred frequent, unfaithful rebels to friends always obedient and faithful. They were so inflamed that for more than four hours while they repeated their arguments, they did not wish to smoke or accept any other present. (Thomas 1932: 297)

Anza finally succeeded in winning over the Utes and persuading them to make a peace with the Comanches also (Thomas 1932: 298 ff.). Nevertheless, in the course of visits connected with the negotiations, Anza saw fit at one point to provide a military escort for Comanche emissaries for one day's journey beyond Pecos to protect them from attacks by Utes and Apaches (SANM 928). And as part of the treaty agreements, the Spaniards promised to forbid the Jicarilla Apaches to steal from the Comanches, who were to report any such thefts immediately (Thomas 1932: 307). Thus did Anza acquire for the Spaniards their most powerful Indian ally, so that the Plains soon became safe for the *Comancheros*, or Spanish and Pueblo Indian traders to the Comanches. Eventually, too, some of the Comanches came to live among the settlements as the Apaches had done before them (Kenner 1969).

Meanwhile, in 1786 the new Comanche allies lost no time in proving their good faith. By 30 April they had forced Apaches to abandon the eastern part of the Sierra Blancas (Thomas 1932: 309). The identity of these Apaches is not specified, but in July of the next year it was Faraons that the Comanches routed in the Sierras Blancas (Moorhead 1968: 160). And according to Moorhead:

> Since November of 1786, members of the Lipán Apache tribe, who enjoyed peace with Coahuila and Texas to the south, were filtering into New Mexico and making overtures for a similar arrangement with that province. This disturbed the Comanches, who now begged Anza not to make such a concession. If he did, they declared, the Comanches would then have no enemies on whom to make war and would consequently become effeminate. After receiving a number of such reports, Ugarte ordered first Anza and then his successor to maintain peace in New Mexico only with the Comanches, Utes, Navahos and Jicarilla Apaches, and not even to listen to the propositions of the Lipanes, Lipiyanes, Natagees, Faraones, Mescaleros, Gileños, or Apaches under any other name. Since the granting of trade and protection to the Lipanes would endanger the permanence of the peace conceded to the Comanches, the governors were to dissuade them gracefully from seeking protection in New Mexico, even though they enjoyed it in Texas and Coahuila. Viceroy Flores not only approved Ugarte's position in this matter, but vigorously insisted upon it. (Moorhead 1968: 160–61)

However, Simmons (1970) has published translations of some of the documents bearing on the attempts of the supposed Lipan Apaches to re-establish trade with the people of New Mexico at Pecos Pueblo, and evidence contained in these documents indicates that the Apaches concerned were not Lipans, as Governors Anza and Concha thought, but Lipiyanes, or Llaneros, who became the Llanero Band of the Jicarillas. Taken in conjunction with documents cited later in the present work, Simmons's translations strengthen the thesis that the Lipiyanes, or Llaneros, had been previously known as Carlana, Cuartelejo, and Paloma Apaches.

For example, on 8 November 1786, the "Lipans" who presented themselves before Governor Anza requested permission to re-establish the commerce which 35 to 40 years ago they carried on at the Pueblo of Pecos in this province, and from which they withdrew, transferring themselves to that of Coahuila on account of the terror caused them by the coming of the Comanches to this (province). . . . The people of this province, influenced more by the profits which may be realized from such commerce with those who are seeking it than worries about possible treachery on the part of the (Lipans), hope and entreat that restoration of such trade may be brought about. (Simmons 1970: 37)

It has already been pointed out herein (and see G & G 1970) that the Apaches who had been living in and near Pecos thirty-five to forty years before 1786 were the Carlanas, then in the process of assimilating the Cuartelejos and Palomas. And Miera (Bolton 1950: 249) indicated in 1777 that the Carlanas had indeed moved south to the border of Coahuila.

Anza, unwilling to repudiate the Apaches he had mistakenly identified as Lipans entirely, told them they could return to New Mexico if they would bring a letter from the governor of Coahuila stating they were actually at peace in that province (Simmons 1970: 37). Accordingly on November fourth of the next year, "the head Lipillan chief, called Strong Arm Lipan," brought Concha, the new governor of New Mexico, a passport from Juan de Ugalde, the governor of Coahuila (Simmons 1970: 38) with whom the chief had engaged in preliminary peace negotiations the preceding July (Moorhead 1968: 222, 248–49; Nelson 1940: 442–44). Thus Concha, too, mistook Lipiyanes (who were actually Llaneros) for Lipans, a matter on which his superiors eventually corrected him (see below).

In November 1787, the Lipiyanes (Llaneros) had apparently come to New Mexico rather specifically to see the Jicarillas, whose camps they visited with Concha's permission. It is interesting that when they left, some Utes went with them to go buffalo hunting. The efforts of the Lipiyanes-Llaneros under "Strong Arm" (also called "Brazo de Fierro" and "El Calvo") to re-establish themselves in New Mexico failed, for Concha's superior, Commander Ugarte, absolutely forbade him to negotiate with these Apaches (Simmons 1970: 38, 40). The eagerness of the New Mexico settlers themselves to reopen trade with the Lipiyanes should be kept in mind, however, for it seems that in following years New Mexico officials observed the prohibitions of distant administrators in this matter only reluctantly.

Bernardo de Gálvez, viceroy of New Spain, signed his famous *Instrucción* to Don Jacobo Ugarte y Loyola (Worcester 1951) on 26 August 1786. In it he included Jicarillas among tribes who lived at peace in one area and raided in others.

> Some hostilities are usually experienced in the province, presidio, or town where peace has been established, and the Indians never desist from committing outrages in other territories. All these arise from the same causes: the unsatisfied necessity which obliges them to rob in order to eat and greediness to acquire the things that they desire—liberty, idleness, and the same poverty that engenders and foments their perverse inclinations. If their hunger is great, they do not relieve it by committing robberies where they have been offered friendship. If it is not great, they preserve the peace with good faith, and truly they do not break it, for they commit their hostilities in other places. More than once they have made this candid confession, persuading themselves that they do not offend their friends by the harm which they impute to other subjects of the king who live in territories where actually no peace has been made. This happened with all the Apaches in the town of El Paso and the presidio of Janos, with the Mescaleros in Nueva Vizcaya, with the Jicarillas, Navajos, Utes, and Comanches in New Mexico, with the Lipans in Coahuila, and with the Nations of the North in Texas, and the practice continues. (Worcester 1951: 41–42)

Here, again, it may be that the "Jicarillas" he refers to were the Plains Band (Carlanas-Lipiyanes-Llaneros). In any case, he specified that peace should be maintained with the Jicarillas and Utes, and that "the Comanches never should be denied whatever they request in Taos." To Gálvez's insistence that he (and consequently his successors) be kept informed of all that went on in the Internal Provinces, especially in the way of warfare, we undoubtedly owe in part the greater number of documents relevant to Indians (Worcester 1951: 30, 72) that appear in the years following.

Although Ugarte did not receive Gálvez's formal directions until 14 November 1786 (Moorhead 1968: 66), his own judgment had already led him to implement some of the viceroy's policies. In a letter dated 5 October 1786, Ugarte suggested that Governor Anza of New Mexico assign "interpreters" (who were essentially Indian agents) to the Comanches as well as to the Navajos (Thomas 1932: 335), and this practice was eventually extended to all the tribes with whom the Spaniards had dealings. Ugarte also promised Anza six thousand pesos yearly to be expended in gratifying friendly Indian tribes (Thomas 1932: 342).

From this time, reports on the conduct of "the four allied tribes"—Comanches, Utes, Navajos, and Jicarillas—appear regularly in reports from the Santa Fé garrison, along with statements as to the amount expended in feeding Indians in Santa Fé before and after campaigns. The records reveal, also, the kinds of gifts presented to the Indians.

Meanwhile, in Texas, Spanish forces campaigning under Juan de Ugalde were becoming aware that the Apaches already referred to infrequently in the records as Lipiyanes were also called Llaneros (Nelson 1940). By June 1787, Ugalde had already heard persistent rumors of a warlike group of Apaches living on the Plains about eighty leagues north of present Pecos, Texas. Their lands contained numerous bison, and to defend their territory they had successfully fought many battles with the formidable Comanches. In fact, they boasted that since their country contained all that they needed, including an abundance of wild mustangs that they could catch and break, they had had no need either to seek shelter in Spanish *presidios* or to raid them. Their chief, whose Apachean name, Picax-ande Ins-tinsle, meant Strong-arm, was called El Calvo, the Bald One, by the Spaniards. This man, judged by Ugalde to be about fifty years old, was such an outstanding leader that even Indians from other Apachean tribes chose to follow him. His group was apparently especially intimate with the Lipans.

When Ugalde entered the country of these Lipiyan-Llaneros, his observations confirmed its richness in natural resources, and he found the Llanero leader, El Calvo, as remarkable as he had been represented. At their first meeting in July 1787, El Calvo and Ugalde, after a certain amount of verbal sparring, agreed to make a treaty in the future. Ugalde even requested the viceroy to give El Calvo a formal commission as head chief of the "Lipiyán, Lipan, Mescalero, Sendé, Nit-ajende and Cachu-ende Apaches" over whom he was apparently already exerting great influence because of his personal character. After months of delay (during which he had tried vainly to establish his people in New Mexico), El Calvo finally met Ugalde again in early March 1788 at the *presidio* of Santa Rosa in Coahuila. In conference El Calvo pointed out that if the Comanches stopped pressing southward on the Apaches the latter would not be forced to raid in Spanish territory. He promised to exterminate the Comanches if the Spaniards would aid him. Ugalde, of course, could not grant this request because of general Spanish policy and because the Spaniards had already made a treaty with the Comanches. Failing in this bid for help, El Calvo requested that the Comanches at least not be given arms, ammunition, and supplies at Santa Fé and San Antonio. To this Ugalde agreed, although he could not change the situation at Santa Fé, which was not in his jurisdiction.

El Calvo left the conference with a new Spanish name, "Manuel [for Viceroy Flores] de Ugalde," and an official cane or staff as a symbol of his authority. If the Carlanas, including the Cuartelejos and Palomas, had become the Lipiyan-Llaneros, then those bands whose aid had been so important to Governor Vélez Cachupín of New Mexico in the 1750s had produced the most outstanding Apache leader of the late eighteenth century and the last to cope effectively with the Comanches (Nelson 1940: 438–64). Unfortunately, the Spaniards were never able to make order out of the chaos of Apachean and Spanish names of tribes, bands, and sub-bands (Moorhead 1968: 248–49; Simmons 1970: 36), and thus far the historians have failed to improve significantly on their efforts.

Joseph Rengel, commander inspector of the Internal Provinces of New Spain, acknowledged a report on 30 December 1787 from Governor Concha of New Mexico. Concha had apparently informed his superior that the Comanches, Utes, Navajos, Jicarillas, and even the Lipans were peaceful and that peace negotiations between the Utes and Comanches had been brought to a successful conclusion (SANM 978). On 23 January 1788, Commander General Ugarte wrote to Concha expressing his satisfaction with Indian affairs in New Mexico. He refers to some undescribed but meritorious action of the Jicarilla chief Pajarito, whose name appears often in documents concerning Indian allies.[1] Again in this letter Ugarte admonished Concha not to negotiate with the Lipans in New Mexico—that they should be granted peace and asylum only in Coahuila (SANM 997).

A statement of expenses incurred in providing gifts and supplies for the allied tribes—Comanches, Utes, Jicarillas, and Navajos—in 1787–1788 has several entries indicating the kinds of goods being distributed to the Jicarillas. There is frequent mention of *piloncillo,* raw sugar molded in the form of little pylons or truncated cones, *cigarros* and *boletas* (cigarette papers?).

The Jicarillas accompanied Spanish troops on military campaigns several times during this period, once specifically to the Sierra Obscura (SANM 1025) in southeastern New Mexico where they may have been moving against Faraons, Natagés, or even their own friends the Carlanas-Llaneros.

Concha reported again to Ugarte on 18 November 1789 that the behavior and attitude of the four friendly tribes (the Comanches, Utes, Navajos, and Jicarillas) remained unchanged. They were maintaining excellent relations and peaceful trade with the Spanish settlers and Pueblo Indians of New Mexico. However, the Utes and Comanches had fought repeatedly between themselves because, in spite of Concha's remonstrances, the Utes had attacked Comanche horse herds (SANM 1064).

Two days later, Concha reported to Ugarte that Comanches had made attacks on the "Apaches Llaneros" and on those of the Sierra Blancas. In addition, the Jicarillas had informed the Spaniards that the Comanches had attacked other Apache *rancherías* in the Sierra del Carrizo, three days' travel from Comanche country (SANM 1066). It is probable that the benefits of alliance with the Spaniards had given new impetus to the Comanche thrust, so

---

1 Unfortunately, in this case, as in so many others, only one side of the correspondence between a governor of New Mexico and his superiors is available in the Santa Fé Archives.

that even the Llaneros could hold out no longer on the Plains
without some place of refuge. On 15 December 1789, Concha
wrote to the viceroy, Revilla Gigedo, confirming the excellent
state of relations with the four allied tribes (SANM 1071).

In Coahuila, Commander Ugalde had attempted to use the followers of the Llanero chief El Calvo against rebel Mescaleros and
other hostile Apaches only to discover that the great chief had
encouraged a Mescalero revolt, was harboring some of the fugitives in his camp, and had received goods stolen in their raids.
Also, it turned out that El Calvo had close ties with the Mescaleros through marriage, since he and a Mescalero chief had each
married a sister of the other. Disillusioned, Ugalde declared war
on his Llanero protégé but never managed to encounter him in
battle. El Calvo had taken his people northward to the Sierra
Obscura in New Mexico, and the Upper Lipans also retreated to
the area between the Sacramento range and the Sierra Blancas,
not far from the Llaneros. By December 1790, both Natagés and
the Llaneros were said to be on the slopes of the Sacramentos
(Moorhead 1967: 252–69), poised between Spanish officialdom
in Santa Fé and the *presidios* of Texas and northern Mexico.

By July 1790, western as well as eastern Apaches began to
cluster in mountains midway between Santa Fé and the *presidios*
of northern Mexico. Some of these Apaches were Gilas. Although they had solicited peace with the Spaniards of New
Mexico, Governor Concha had not committed himself absolutely.
He thought it might be possible to make a treaty with the Gilas
eventually because they had been behaving well on their visits
and trading expeditions among the Spaniards and Pueblo Indians.
Concha had presented the Gilas with the conditions under which
he would grant peace. They must patrol their area, keeping a
lookout for Natagés or other hostile tribes. They must not commit any depredations either in New Mexico or Spanish provinces
to the south. They must settle down and raise crops like the Jicarillas and Navajos, who were just as much Apaches as they were.
Concha was explicit in his hope that the example of the Jicarillas
and Navajos would influence other Apache tribes toward a more
sedentary life among the New Mexico villages (SANM 1086).

The Natagés had been singled out as a special target because since the preceding November, when they had moved northward, they had raided in New Mexico twice. In July, a hundred and fifty men set out from Santa Fé to comb the ranges called "Sierras de Jumanes, Carrizo, Blanca, y Obscura" in search of this enemy (SANM 1087). Since the Llanero Apaches under El Calvo had presumably wintered with the Natagés (Moorhead 1968: 267–68), they, too, were probably considered hostiles, although not mentioned as such in this document.

In 1790, also, the Comanches, who had long dominated the Plains, acknowledged the threat posed by other tribes crowding them on the north. Apparently the Jupe and Yamparica Comanches were afraid of the Pawnees, for in June of that year Concha yielded to the persistent pleas of their chief and gave them a military escort so they could not only go on a buffalo hunt without fear but search out and attack the Pawnees at the same time. No encounter with the Pawnees resulted, but Concha was reprimanded for undertaking to aid one tribe against another and, in this particular case, possibly drawing the wrath of new, far-away tribes on the Spaniards (SANM 1137).

For purposes of this study the most interesting document connected with this incident is the diary of the sergeant in charge of the escort, Juan de Dios Peña, who left Santa Fé on 12 June 1790, went north to Taos and thence across the Sangre de Cristos by way of the Taos-Rayado trail used earlier in the century by Ulibarri, Valverde, and probably Bustamante. It is noteworthy that, whereas in Bustamante's time an Apache chief named Churlique had lived in the Rayado area (Thomas 1935: 198–99), in 1790 Peña camped on a river called the Río Churlique. Between that river and the Río Colorado (the Canadian) he was joined by a Jicarilla Apache who said he was coming along to serve as a hunter for the expedition (SANM 1089). Thus in 1790 a river near the east end of the Taos-Rayado trail bore the same name as an Apache chief who had lived in the area in the 1720s, and there were still Jicarillas in the region that had been known as "La Jicarilla."

In September 1790 Concha reported to Commander General

Ugarte that the good behavior of the Utes, Comanches, Navajos, and Jicarillas had not varied (SANM 1090). He apparently repeated this statement in November in a message acknowledged by Ugarte's successor, Pedro de Nava, who expressed satisfaction not only with the way in which these allied tribes were employed but with the trust and good faith they manifested (SANM 1113).

Concha's list of "extraordinary expenses" for 1790 (SANM 1110) showed payments made on behalf of Jicarillas and other tribes. Forty-five pesos had been paid for the maintenance of fifteen Jicarillas who went on a campaign, apparently in mid-March. One of their chiefs named "El Mexico" and nine of his companions had been given gifts twice during that month, and another entry showed that twenty pesos had been paid for maize for "Apaches Xicarillas." On 2 September 1790, goods were given to Jicarillas who went on a campaign as scouts, and they were rewarded again when they returned.

With the tighter organization and more efficient administration on the frontiers under the *Comandancia General*, communication between the far-flung *presidios* had improved and continued to improve as time went on. From El Paso under date of 20 February 1791, Lieutenant Governor Francisco Uranga informed Concha that according to some Indians the "Capitancillo" Calvo wanted to go to ask for peace in New Mexico and establish himself with his people in the Sierra Blanca (SANM 1115). The use of a diminutive form of the title of the great Llanero chief, previously designated as the "Gran Capitan," seems inappropriate, unless it reflects efforts of the Spaniards to disparage him.

Concha again confirmed (20 April) that the four allied tribes were continuing with the same good conduct, harmony and good faith (SANM 1118, listed in Twitchell 1914 II as 1119–*1*), and he repeated the same statement on 12 July to both Commander General Pedro de Nava (SANM 1131) and Viceroy Revilla Gigedo (SANM 1132).

On 25 July, Nava acknowledged Concha's April report on the allied tribes, the most interesting aspect of the document being his spelling of the name as "Gicarillas" (SANM 1136). The viceroy, Revilla Gigedo, used the same spelling when he acknowledged Concha's July report (SANM 1152–2). In the same group of communiqués he said that he was waiting to hear the results of the campaign that was to have been undertaken by nearly a thousand "Cumanches, y Jumanes ó Tahuayases" (Wichitas) against "los Apaches Mescaleros, Lipanes Lipiyanes, y Llaneros" (SANM 1151–3). Seemingly Concha had informed Nava on 2 July 1791 that about a thousand Comanches had assembled in the vicinity of the Taovayases (Wichitas) to go on a campaign against the Lipan Apaches, the Mescaleros, and the Lipiyanes (Llaneros). Nava, too, asked to be informed of what happened to these "common enemies" of the Spaniards and Comanches (SANM 1135). The massive campaign of the Comanches apparently failed, and to an explicit request by Nava that Concha cooperate as fully as possible with officials of the eastern provinces by sending Comanche allies against the eastern Apaches ("la Apacheria Oriental"), the governor of New Mexico replied with a letter that might have been written by a frustrated officer of the United States cavalry operating in the same area more than a half century later.

While the Comanches, with the advantage obtained by getting horses and guns first, had been able to harass peaceful foothills Apaches and drive some Plains Apaches into the mountains, their advantage ended in the arid basins and ranges of southern New Mexico and Arizona where the Apaches were unequaled as fighters. Concha enumerated to his superior the difficulties and obstacles that prevented the Comanches from operating successfully against the "Lipanes, Lipiyanes y Llaneros." These Apaches were living at a great distance from Santa Fé in immense "llanos" (deserts?) where waterholes were scarce. They used hiding places of which even the local people who knew the country best were totally ignorant. What is more, the Apaches knew how to live in and off of, waterless, inhospitable terrain, giving their horses drinks from "jícaras" (pitch-covered basketry water bottles?). The Comanches, lacking such skill and experience, were reluctant to enter the country for fear of losing their horse herds. They had therefore directed their campaigns along the

banks of the Pecos, Canadian, and Arkansas Rivers, totally without results. But Concha promised, in spite of the difficulties involved, to continue to do the best he could against the Apaches
(SANM 1164–2).

In another letter written at the same time, Concha indicates
that the status of the Comanches was also changing on the Plains.
As mentioned earlier, he had been reprimanded by Nava for
sending a military escort to protect and aid Comanches against
Pawnees. Nava thought that Concha had thereby run the risk of
inciting the distant and little-known Pawnees to approach Spanish settlements in search of the Comanches (SANM 1137). Concha's reply (SANM 1164–1; see also Nasatir 1952: 146–48) was
stiff and defensive. He pointed out that the Pawnees should not
be considered unknown, since they lived only 160 leagues from
Santa Fé. It is obvious that Concha was aware of many other
tribes that lay beyond the Comanches, including the Sioux, and
that he had already come to view the Comanches as a barrier or
buffer between New Mexico and this potential threat. Thus, in
terms of Spanish strategy, the role of the Comanches was already
subtly changing. Like the Jicarillas before them, they were ceas-
ing to be primarily a powerful ally; they were beginning to need
Spanish protection rather than to obviate the need for Spanish
action. Moreover, just as Codallos had realized in 1748 that it had
been a mistake not to fortify La Jicarilla against the Comanches
(Twitchell 1914 I: 148–50), Concha pointed out that the Spaniards would not be having so much trouble with the eastern
Apaches had they not "regarded with indifference the Comanches' throwing the Lipans, Lipiyanes and Llaneros from
their lands, which I urged guarding against, since I consider
these [latter] also of some importance" (SANM 1164–1). Here
Concha reveals some sympathy for the eastern Apaches, and he
was probably not the only New Mexican to feel this way. After
all, New Mexico had not suffered greatly from hostilities of the
Lipans and Llaneros. It may be for these reasons that in spite of
continued orders from the commander general and the viceroy
the Llaneros were eventually accepted again in New Mexico. On
14 April 1792, Concha made a routine report on the "good be-

havior, harmony, and close friendship" that prevailed between the citizens of New Mexico and the Comanches, Utes, Navajos, and Jicarillas (SANM 1191–2).

In late April and early May of 1792, Domingo Díaz, at Presidio del Norte, reported to Pedro de Nava that the Apache chief El Calvo and also El Natagé had been in his *presidio*. There had been two Utes with them, and according to Díaz the Utes maintained a close friendship with the people of these two chiefs and also with the Lipans, visiting them often. In conferences the Indians insinuated that large numbers of Lipans, Llaneros, Natagés, and Utes were going to unite and attack the Comanches in retaliation for a defeat the Comanches had inflicted on the Lipans the year before. Díaz commented that the Utes and Comanches remained at peace with one another in New Mexico, but elsewhere ("en el Campo") they were mortal enemies. Nava transmitted this information from Díaz to Governor Concha of New Mexico in June (SANM 1196).

Meanwhile, Nava also corresponded with Viceroy Revilla Gigedo on the matter. The officials were afraid that if the Utes participated in an attack on the Comanches it would disrupt relations between the four allied tribes in New Mexico. It was urged that any alliance between the Utes and the Lipans be stopped and good relations promoted between the Utes and Comanches (SANM 1197).

In New Mexico, meanwhile, Concha, still ignorant of Díaz's observations at Presidio del Norte, reported to Nava on 20 July 1792 that the Comanches had recently begun a campaign against the Lipans, Lipiyanes, and Llaneros aided by Spanish equipment (SANM 1200). Two days later, Concha also reported the continuing good conduct of the friendly Comanches, Utes, Navajos, and Jicarillas (SANM 1203–2), as he did again on 8 November 1792 (SANM 1215–4). On the latter date he also discounted Díaz's statements about Utes being among the "Apaches Oriental." Concha said that the Utes' maintaining contact with the Lipiyanes (Llaneros) was implausible because to do so they would have to cross Comanche territory. The long distance and their fear of the Comanches would prevent visits. He added that the only thing that might have happened was that a Ute named Sagape, married into and living among the Jicarillas, might have gone with some of them to visit Iron Arm (Brazo de Fierro, otherwise called El Calvo). Concha insisted that it was not credible that other Utes should have gone in large numbers (SANM 1217). This document is highly significant because it reveals that Concha was aware that Jicarillas proper went to visit the Llaneros and did so in spite of the distance and danger involved. The old friendship between the Jicarillas and the Carlanas-turned-Llaneros persisted still. On 1 December 1792, before he could have received Concha's evaluation of the affair, Nava ordered that precautions be taken to prevent alliance between the Utes and the Lipans (SANM 1219).

On 15 March 1793, Concha submitted a statement of expenses incurred in maintaining good relations with Indians in 1792 (SANM 1228). During that year Jicarillas had been entertained and given gifts on several occasions. On 28 February, Chief "Sul" and six warriors of his *rancheria* were rewarded. Chief Pajarito and ten of his men had come into Santa Fé on 12 March. On 26 July the Spaniards had entertained the Jicarilla chief called "El Mexico" and ten of his people. All three chiefs—Pajarito, El Mexico, and Sul (also spelled Zul)—had been in Santa Fé with thirty-two of their men on 20 September. Sul and Mexico had come in again in October with seven warriors, and on 20 November, Pajarito and eighteen companions appeared. Since every Jicarilla chief could probably be expected to appear in Santa Fé in any one year, this document suggests that in 1792 the Jicarillas proper had three principal leaders: Pajarito, El Mexico, and El Zul. Eight times during the year one or more of these had been entertained in the capital.

Writing to the viceroy on 6 May 1793, Concha reported trouble among the "four allied tribes" (SANM 1234). The Comanches, Utes, Navajos, and Jicarillas all continued to keep the peace with the citizens of New Mexico, but among themselves they had fought several battles stemming from the hatred that the three latter tribes had for the Comanches. Specifically, some Utes and Navajos had banded together and gone to attack the

Comanches. They had found a *ranchería* whose men were hunting, had killed and captured the women and children, and had stolen the horse herd. The Comanches had retaliated by destroying a Ute village. Concha was afraid that the Comanches could not be calmed in their just anger against the Navajos. But if they sought the Navajos out in their *torreons* (defensive towers), it would totally disrupt the calm prevailing in the province. Thus he attempted to get the captive Comanches back from the Navajos. It is noteworthy that in spite of their close relations with both the Navajos and the Utes, the Jicarillas had not joined in this infraction of the peace.

Later in the year, the Gila Apaches attacked the Navajos, who were behaving well at the time. Concha sent some Keres Indians to help the Navajos retaliate, and some Utes accompanied the expedition (SANM 1266). In an account of the Franciscan missions in New Mexico dated 30 October 1795,[2] but dealing with their condition and progress in the years 1793 and 1794, there occurs an item concerning relations with the Indians. The description states that while all the missions were exposed, some more than others, to the hostilities of the Apaches, Utes, and Comanches, the most vulnerable were Picurís and Pecos. A new mission had been founded in the place called Mora ("lo de Mora"), and a new settlement had been started at a place called "el vado del Río de Pecos." The inhabitants of the village of Truchas ("puesto de las Truchas") were exposed to the attacks and thefts of the Faraon Apaches, although most of the missions suffered from these attacks most years, in some years more than in others. The Jicarilla Apaches were said to be settled in the vicinity of the missions most of the time, and it was believed that the Jicarillas attracted the others [Faraons?], "for all are one tribe." It was hoped that eventually, with time and effort, it would be possible to domesticate and convert the Jicarillas and thus avoid some of the harm being done to the missions.

This document echoes the opinion, apparently held by many, that all Apaches were alike. Implicitly, also, it suggests a close re-

2 Bruce T. Ellis, Associate in charge of History and Publications, Museum of New Mexico, kindly showed me this document in 1959.

lationship between the Jicarillas and the Faraons. At the same time, however, it indicates that the Jicarillas were settled most of the year and that they gave indications of becoming more so. The missionaries were not accusing the Jicarillas themselves of raids, but other Apaches whom they attracted to the region.

Whatever disruptions there may have been during 1794, Nava, on 31 December, expressed his satisfaction with the behavior of the four allied tribes and with the measures that Concha had taken to maintain the peace that existed in New Mexico (SANM 1303*A–1*).

The statement of expenses incurred in the maintenance of friendly relations with the Indian allies for 1794 (SANM 1320) has only two entries for Jicarillas, one in May and one in September. However, some of the entries use only the term "Apache," or give only the names of chiefs, so Jicarillas may have been entertained more often than it appears. The only recognizable name of a Jicarilla chief is that of Pajarito. On 26 June 1795, Nava again expressed his satisfaction with the behavior of the four allied tribes (SANM 1330).

Concha's successor as governor of New Mexico, Lieutenant Colonel don Fernando Chacón, had to report on 19 May 1796 that the Navajos had rebelled, joined the Gila Apaches, and broken the peace. Nava replied on 8 July suggesting that the Navajos be given more gifts, and if that measure was not effective, they should be punished,

> without ignoring the preservation of the friendship of the Cumanches, Jicarillas, and Utes, which so greatly interests us and which I recommend that your excellency cultivate and sustain most scrupulously. (SANM 1366)

Nava also suggested that both the Indian allies and the settlers would be more motivated to take part in expeditions if they were given the same share of spoils allotted to the regular troops.

In 1796 Lieutenant Colonel Antonio Cordero, under orders from Nava, prepared a report on the "Apache Nation" at El Paso (M & S 1957). This account, which contains much general information on the Apacheans of interest to anthropologists, is inaccurate in its one reference to the Jicarillas: Cordero stated that the Jicarillas were a branch of the Faraons (M & S 1957: 353–54), an error that undoubtedly reflected his lack of firsthand knowledge of New Mexico and the Jicarillas proper. Concerning the Llaneros, with whom he may have had personal contact, he says:

> These Indians occupy the plains and sandy places situated between the Pecos River, which they call Tjunchi, and the Colorado which they call Tjulchide. It is a group of some strength, and is divided into three parts, that is to say: Natajes, Lipiyanes and Llaneros. They check the Comanches in the continual fights and bloody actions which frequently occur, especially in the season of the buffalo hunts. They attack, although infrequently, the Spanish establishments, uniting themselves for this purpose with the Mescalero and Faraon Apaches, with whom they have a close friendship and alliance. They border to the north on the Comanches; and on the west with the Mescaleros; and on the east with the Lipanes, on the south with the line of the Spanish presidios. (M & S 1957: 354–55)

In another place Cordero indicated that the Apachean equivalent of Llaneros was "Cuelcajen-ne" (M & S 1957: 336).

Since the Natagés were a separate group by at least 1726, long before the Llaneros appear as such, they were allies of the Llaneros in Cordero's time rather than part of them. Moreover, the bulk of the evidence suggests that "Lipiyan" and "Llanero" are simply two names for the same group—the former an Athabascan name, the latter, of course, Spanish. In brief, what Cordero was listing as three divisions of the Llaneros were in reality two originally separate but later allied tribes, the Natagés and Llaneros, who maintained their own identities in the late 1700s under their respective leaders El Natagé and El Calvo.

It is possible, of course, that the Llaneros absorbed the Natagés, for the Llaneros are still identifiable and the Natagés are not. After all, the Llaneros themselves probably represented an amalgamation of Carlanas, Cuartelejos, and Palomas. Moreover, the southward drift of these latter tribes that carried them beyond the ken of New Mexico Spaniards in the mid-1700s came about partly as a result of their trade and association with the Natagés who were already south of the Organ Mountains in the vicinity of El Paso (Thomas 1935: 213). Cordero's statement is in part, then, the end product of change or confusion in the thinking of important Spanish officials after 1750. Rubí, it will be remembered, said that all the Apaches were known generically as Natagés (Thomas 1940: 37), whereas at the council of war held in Chihuahua in 1777 the name Natagé was apparently considered a synonym for Lipiyan (Thomas 1940: 198).

In 1797 the long-range strategy of the Spaniards was still operating smoothly in New Mexico. Late in the previous year the Navajos had reinstated themselves in the good graces of the officials (SANM 1375a). On 2 February 1797, Governor Chacón informed the commander general that five campaigns against hostile Indians had been mounted since November 1796. During the first four expeditions there had been no incidents, except that one company had captured the inhabitants of a small enemy *ranchería*—two adults and one child. These were in the possession of the Jicarilla Apaches, who had participated in the campaign (SANM 1375c). They were probably the Jicarillas' share of the spoils of war.

On 26 April 1797, Nava wrote to Chacón asking for complete sets of arms and clothing of the Comanches, Utes, Jicarillas, and Navajos and requesting that each article should be specified by name (SANM 1380). In due time (on 18 November 1797) Chacón announced that the items requested were being transmitted by cordón, along with an accompanying description (SANM 1404). One wonders whether the request reflects something like an ethnographer's interest in the four allied tribes and whether any of the items survive today.

On 19 October 1797, Nava ordered Chacón to induce some of the Comanches to campaign against the Mescaleros, now hostile, since the forces of Coahuila and El Paso had accomplished nothing. The Mescaleros were presumably allied with the "Lipiyanes" and Faraones, therefore the Comanches were to make war on all these groups (SANM 1399). This order initiated an exchange of correspondence that showed Chacón's confusion concerning the eastern Apaches and also revealed Nava's more exact information.

Chacón replied on the nineteenth of November that he had

communicated to the "general" and five principal "captains" of the Comanches Nava's order that they campaign against the Mescaleros and *Lipanes*. The Comanches had made excuses, saying they couldn't do it because their horse herd was in poor condition but would be willing to go out the next summer. These leaders had suggested that if the Spaniards wanted to punish the *Lipans*, it would be more appropriate to use the eastern Comanches ("Cumanches Orientales"), who were strategically located for such a purpose (SANM 1405).

To this Nava's reply, dated 3 January 1798, was direct: the Comanches were to campaign in spite of the obstacles they had mentioned. He pointed out that operations were to be conducted to punish

> los Mescaleros, Faraones, Lipiyanes o Llaneros: but you mistake this third group for La Lipana, who live at peace on the frontiers of Coahuila and Texas, and have not taken part in the hostilities that the said Mescaleros have engaged in. Though they [the Lipans] are bound up with them [the Mescaleros] through kinship, they are nevertheless cooperating to make war on them in union with our forces.

> The captain Braso de fierro alias el Calbo that you told me had presented himself on the 24th of September in the new settlement of el vado de Pecos asking to establish peace in that province is the head chief of the Apache tribe Lipiyana, or Llanera, though you thought it [the tribe] Lipan. His band has always been at war with us and the Comanches, and in one word, the Lipiyanes and the Lipans are different tribes though both are Apaches. . . .

> You did well not to yield to the petition of El Calbo or Braso de Fierro: and if he returns to present himself there renewing his requests to establish peace, whether for himself and his tribe [or] the Mescaleros and Faraones, your excellency should always reject them, doing the same with respect to the Lipans in case they should also at some time advance a similar solicitation. (SANM 1412)

The Indian expense account for New Mexico covering the period January through October 1797 was transmitted on 31 October. Only a few Jicarilla visitors are specified as such, although the tribal affiliation of the Apaches who came in is not always given. One entry is a charge for the rebuilding and arranging of the houses or *cuartels* of the allied nations. Two Apache couriers, or mail carriers, were also rewarded. It seems the Spaniards were finally utilizing the ability of the Apaches to move rapidly through the country instead of merely suffering from it (SANM 1400).

On 2 January 1798, after reviewing this expense account and suggesting economies, Nava commented that he was convinced the only (Gentile) Indians living in peace in New Mexico (i.e., settled in the province) were the Jicarillas and Navajos, and they did not have really permanent settlements near the pueblos (SANM 1410). On 19 April of the same year, Nava reiterated his instructions to Chacón concerning the eastern Apaches.

> Although both my predecessors and myself have admonished the governors of that province time and time again not to admit the Apaches Lipanes, Lipiyanes or Llaneros, or the Mescaleros into it [the province] in peace, I repeat to you now the same warning because it is very important to the service of His Majesty that one complies exactly with the orders sent that deal with this matter.
>
> You know that the Indians of these tribes from time to time have approached [us] pretending peace talks and that the chief of the Lipiyanes or Llaneros known on this frontier as El Calbo and there as Braso de fierro renewed them [overtures for peace] in September of last year [1797]. And finally the Lipanes and even the Mescaleros have tried to be admitted into that province on various occasions with the purpose of using this protection as a shield against the invasions of the Comanches and our [forces] when they find themselves in a declared war just as we have now with the aforementioned Mescaleros and Lipiyanes.
>
> One of the lesser chiefs of the Lipan tribe named Moreno presented himself last February to Lt. Colonel Don Antonio Cordero in the Presidio of Rio Grande [wearing] a manta like the kind embroidered in the Pueblos of Zuñi, Acoma and Laguna of that province. In the course of the conversation he confessed that it had been given to him by Captain Concha in the Pueblo of San Ildefonso and that his nation, that is the Lipan Apaches, was admitted there in the years [17]89 and [17]90 when they [the Lipan Apaches] were making bloody war with us under the name of Faraones and Llaneros and that his system has been to have safe asylum in one province by taking the name of a different tribe in order to make war in another [province] under a different guise as they have done when it seemed fit to do so.

Although this may not be true in all cases it demands more care and precaution on our part in order to defend ourselves from being deceived by the Indians. The Lipanes have been at peace since the first part of the year 1791. The Mescaleros and Lipiyanes are at open war with us and it being very difficult to distinguish the individuals of the three groups you should never listen to the overtures for peace that they present and you should send them away immediately when they approach to advance them [peace overtures]. (SANM 1416)

Two months later, Nava wrote Chacón again, repeating his warning about granting asylum to the Llaneros because these Apaches had suffered serious reverses in warfare, such that El Calvo had solicited peace in the south with urgency, and Nava had assigned him and his tribe lands on the frontier of Coahuila (SANM 1421).

Chacón answered the two preceding letters of Nava on 18 November 1798 as follows:

A few days after I received your lordship's two communiques of April 19 and June 13 in which you order scrupulous observance by this government of the order not to admit in peace any Mescaleros, Lipillanes or Llaneros, four braves who appeared to be Llaneros arrived accompanied by two Jicarillas. *They claimed to be individuals of this same nation and for that reason they were coming to live with them* [italics mine]. To reproach them we asked them why after having lived until this time on the plains they now wanted to join the Jicarillas who were living near the borders of this province. They responded that five years ago they left them [the Jicarillas] to look for a woman who had escaped to the Lipanes. When the [Lipanes] went in peace into Coahuila which is their land it was resolved to return to this land which is their own. They were anxious to see it and equally anxious to ransom a boy who was being held captive by the Comanches. This whole story seemed suspicious to me, and in respect to your decree, I ordered, after giving each a piece of cotton print and a sarape because they dressed completely in leather, that a patrol should lead them far from this province. They were warned that if they returned they would be harshly treated. At the same time I advised all the officers of the law in places where this band of heathen might enter to bring them to this capital as soon as they show up in order to carry out the aforementioned procedure. *But as these Apaches cannot be distinguished from the Jicarillas either in language, dress, weapons or anything else, it is not possible to preclude the possibility that on some other occasion they* [the Llaneros] *might be found among them [the Jicarillas] without one recognizing them* [italics mine]. Therefore, that which Moreno confessed to Don Antonio Cordero can very easily be true. What is certain is that the lesser chief of the Jicarillas known as Concha has died or has been taken prisoner in an attack that the aforementioned official [Cordero] recently carried out on the plains where *the members of this faction [the Jicarillas] gather without permission and often trade with the Lipillanes and Faraones* [italics mine], as a result of which one could explain the acquisition of the blanket by Moreno. (SANM 1430)

Chacón wrote to Nava in 1801 enclosing a diary of events (SANM 1548) that contains further details on relations between the Jicarillas proper and the Llaneros (still also being called Lipiyanes). In the diary the Llaneros are referred to twice as "Jicarillas who [have] lived on the plains." The death of the great Llanero chief El Calvo, killed by Comanches, is also mentioned. This occurrence must have been a catastrophic loss to the tribe and probably explains in part the behavior of the Llaneros. Without the leadership of El Calvo, who had been highly respected—almost revered—by his people (Nelson 1940), the Llaneros may have been temporarily unnerved. The Jicarillas themselves had evidently long traded and visited with the Llaneros on the Plains with the knowledge and tacit tolerance of the Spanish officials in New Mexico. But in 1801 they were suddenly faced with the problem of having their closest kinsmen beg to be hidden in New Mexico itself. It seemed that the Jicarillas would have to choose between having war with the Spaniards and rejecting their Llanero relatives. The Utes, by then long-time allies of the Jicarillas, did not hesitate to reject the latter to save their own status. Relevant portions of Chacón's letter and the accompanying diary follow.

I am sending to you three field reports and the report of events from April 1 to June 12. The incidents during the last expedition have shown clearly that the Jicarilla Apaches have demonstrated the bad faith and the mutual communication with the Lipiyanes and Llaneros that they are surmised to have had for a long time, helping those two groups in their robberies and murders and showing them the *Parages* [pastures] and *aguas* [waterholes] by way of which they should go in order to sack the greater part of the province under the certainty of not being recognized. Not content with this it seems that they plan to introduce them to the Nations of the North according to what was said by the Llaneros themselves, who came to unite with or to meet their relatives the Abajoses who last year showed up with the Cayguas [Kiowas], Aas, and Pananas [Pawnees] and whose plan provides that [word unreadable] have formed an alliance arranged by the Gicarillas and that it was they [the Jicarillas] the last time who had guided the nations of the north to our frontiers.

Consequent to this suspicion the interpreter Josef Mirabal reported that the Gicarillas have advanced to a certain place and arranged in it a signal of peace with various bundles of Punche [wild tobacco] which they have returned to check upon on two or three occasions.

The Utes, who have contracted a close friendship with the Jicarillas and defend them, constituting their protectors, are maintaining campsites near them [the Jicarillas] as has been noticed lately in the district of Taos to whose boundaries they [the Utes] approach under the pretext of trading even though this is not the place where they are accustomed to do this and they are doing it in a suspicious manner. It also should be noted that Captain Mano Mocha [of the Utes] promised to go and observe the aforementioned Nations of the North and to report what he discovered taking a month and a half to do so. He has returned without reporting [anything] or behaving in the customary manner; conduct which causes me concern.

In light of the facts, I have made the threat through the Jueces de Partido to the cited Utes and Gicarillas that if they continue in their treason I will declare war. Your lordship, notified of what has happened, can decide the manner in which one ought to deal with these two allied nations so that they do not likewise influence the Navajos.

In the meantime I have suspended for a time the monthly campaigns because after assigning detachments for Sevilleta, the horseherds and the escort of prisoners, there remain only 40 men in the area that can be called in case of an invasion or any other emergency.

The 13 Apaches [Lipiyanes, i.e., Llaneros] that were prisoners in Vado and Taos have been escorted to San Elseario by 70 men among which are soldiers, militia and Indians under the command of Sergeant Miguel Portillo. One exception is an old Lipan [Lipiyan] Indian woman, who, because she is old, blind and unable to travel has been placed among the Pueblo Indians who will care for her until she dies.

The sergeant has orders to bring back July's mail in order to save the troops at Tiburcios from this task.

I will let the commander of the region know the composition and location of the Apaches of Sacramento in the Sierra Capitana, Blanca and Carriso, whose numbers may be more than 400 and I will tell him, if he is disposed to search out and punish these gentiles, to announce an expedition to the Sierra de las Cumbres sending sealed orders to the commander of that region with orders not to open it until he reaches a specified place since the Apaches have spies in the Presidio and Jurisdiction of El Paso.

As to the 26 horses recaptured in the last campaign 15 are unbranded and of the rest, only two have been returned to their rightful owner as I have decided to add them to the royal stable which constantly suffers losses because of the work and rigorous temperatures of summer. In the meantime approve of this action unless you have a more convenient solution. (SANM 1548)

Following are relevant parts of the diary transmitted with the preceding letter:

Extract of the events that occurred in the Province of New Mexico from April 1 to June 12, 1801.

April

On the first a company of foot soldiers composed of 160 men including soldiers, militia, Genisaros and Indians departed under the command of one of the soldiers called Juan Lucero with orders to reconnoiter Carriso, Capitana, Punta de la Blanca and Malpayses. . . .

On April 19 a Ute chief and a brave arrived with the news that Chief Mano Mocha with 40 of his braves had gone to see if the nations of the North had worked their way into these lands as was witnessed last year estimating the time of 40 days for this expedition. . . .

May

Under date of [May] 1st, the agent at Bado informed the Lieutenant of Pecos, who at the time was in the Capitol, that there had arrived at that place an Apache Gicarilla who always had lived on the plains [*que siempre se mantenia en los Llanos*] known as Capatito, with the news that he had come with 16 Lipan *ranchos* who desired peace and trade relations. Feeling that the Indian could be a spy I ordered the aforementioned Lieutenant to depart immediately with the interpreter and go to Bado advising him to take Capatito prisoner and all those accompanying him. But upon his arrival, which was at two in the morning, he saw that the agent without awaiting an answer, had advised the Apache, trusting his word that they were Lipanes who accompanied him, that a patrol would leave for that country soon. He advised him at the same time to withdraw and with his people to move out of danger. And for that purpose he gave him 4 Genisaros so that they could lead them to a rancheria that was situated in Caballo Parado [that is,] Cañon Blanco. In view of such a strange decision on the part of the agent they [the soldiers] took him to the Villa to answer for the consequences.

Fortunately on May 5 the four Genisaros that were supposed dead or captive returned saying that the Apaches were four ranchos of Gicarillas *of those who lived on the plains* [italics mine] and the rest were Lipanes who received them well and who did not plan to move from where they were until the patrol passed. The patrol left at dawn on May 6 under the command of Josef Manrrique with 250 men with some of (your lordship's) [parentheses in original] troops. Considering that the opportune moment was lost in which to attack enemies that I soon realized were Lipiyanes or Llaneros rather than Lipanes, and that to chase them away or to attempt something against them could lead to their alerting the whole Eastern Cordillera with smoke signals, and that because no evil was done to the Genisaros they were to be commended for not killing them in cold blood, and not being able to change the direction of the patrol, I again advised Lieutenant Manrrique to try and find some advantage in this bad situation by sending the 4 Genisaros back with the order to suggest to the Apaches that two or three of the leaders meet with him to see if he could request scouts from them in order to reconnoiter from the Sierra Capitana onward, and that once the expedition was concluded he would notify them assuming that they would not move from the predetermined place, and that in no way could he accept them in peace without an order from the Commander General, and that they should move away from the frontier so that the rest of the patrols that would leave from there would not treat them like enemies. But when the Genisaros arrived at Cañon Blanco they did not find the Apaches there because as soon as they saw the company pass they [the Apaches] headed for Bado where they found the lieutenant who notified Manrrique, sending to him two lesser chiefs to confer with him, but from them he was not able at that time to obtain the scouts that were asked for and sending them away he notified me and although afterwards I found out through the lieutenant of Pecos that the Apaches had consented to give the scouts, I ordered the commander of the company to retreat with one squad and to send the Apaches ahead whether they wanted to or not to a place where he could direct them to their land, all the while taking advantage of their knowledge of the plain.

When this order reached Bado the Apaches had already gone 4 or 6 leagues into the interior and placed themselves in very rugged terrain in company with eight more ranchos of Gicarillas that seemed to have agreed to be waiting for them. Nevertheless Manrrique called for the same two lesser chiefs that then came, not without some misgivings, and giving the excuse that they had chosen the place in which they were found out of fear of the Comanches. After being notified of the order to return to their land they replied that they had come to join their relatives and friends the Gicarillas, Utes and Abajoses in order to take vengeance on the Comanches, but that nevertheless they would do what he ordered them to do and taking them at their word Lieutenant Manrrique sent them away with some Genisaros who returned saying that when they arrived at the place where the [two] lesser chiefs departed all the Apaches had already gone and had broken up into small groups of which I was given notice. Seeing my misgivings about the bad faith of the aforementioned Indians confirmed and so that in no way would the Gicarilla and the Llanero bands form a union with the Abajoses, I ordered Lieutenant Manrrique to regroup the company and pursue and punish the cited Indians even though they might be found with or sheltered by allied nations, at the same time advising the Alcaldes of Rio Arriba and Taos to make a wide search of the area and to notify the commander of the expedition of any reports that they might receive as to their [the Indians'] route.

On May 28 the lieutenant of Pecos reported that the new agent at Bado notified him that three Apache women had come to that post saying that in the Sierra de Pecuries Lieutenant Manrrique had overtaken the Apaches he had been following and had attacked them with the loss of some horses and part of their supplies and among those that were dispersed were those [the three Apache women]. Seeing that the Apaches rebuked them and wanted to abandon them, perhaps because they were old, they hid themselves with the intention of taking refuge at Bado. They also said that the Apaches headed for the Sierra Tecolote where they were followed by the Spanish.

On May 23 Lieutenant Manrrique notified me from Vado he had overtaken the Apaches in the Sierra de Pecuries and although his scouts were uneasy he attacked and dispersed them [the Indians], taking part of their equipment and making them continue in various groups. He again overtook them in the Sierra del Tecolote where he took all their horse herd which consisted of 31 animals and, in addition, tents and some skins. He observed that the Llaneros and Gicarillas that had come to Bado returned to the plains in two distinct groups, learning later from the Apaches they had agreed to meet in four days in the Piedra de Amolar (or Pintada) [parentheses in original]. The rest he states in his report.

In view of the facts and having found the horses skinny and with sore hooves I ordered Lieutenant Manrrique to release his people and return to the Capitol where he arrived on the 26th with no more incidents save that 5 of the captured horses had died from exhaustion.

In the confession which he took afterwards from the three Apache women one of them said that her people had divided into two troops beyond the valley of the Sierra de Pecuries with agreement to meet four days later at Piedra de Amolar and from there to head for Sierra de Tisón to join the Apaches that are found there. It is not easy for them to return to their [own] land because there are only a few of them left and the Comanches were attacking them almost every day: that the Apaches that are found in the aforementioned range of Carriso and Blanca are named Chief Estrella, Chiquito, Boca de Cavallo, Botas, Gusano, Bota de fierra, faca Ancha, Muchachito and those from the plains Chief Capote and Picado: that as soon as the Genisaros went away the last two [Indians mentioned] from Cavallo Parado or Canon Blanco sent 4 braves to notify those in the Sierra del Tizon that the company was going along the river: that the ones that call themselves Gicarillas are one with them and they were robbing horses from here northward and they were going to trade them for unbranded horses or for horses whose brands were not known: that the Gicarillas themselves joined with those of the plains and they showed the water holes in every direction. Since she thought that she would never return to her land she did not want to hide anything adding that her son together with Capote and various other Lipiyanes had been the ones that killed the son of the lieutenant at Pecos. They were also the ones who had stolen the cattle that were missing recently from Vado and that the Apaches that are occupying la Sierra Capitana, Blanca and Carriso number 400 warriors: that they have much stored meat and plenty of horses, and that they are there because the troops from Viscaya which pursue them a great deal, seldom go that far.

On May 29 the Alcalde of Taos reported that 5 Apaches with four women and a child came to that Pueblo expecting they would find in it Gicarillas or Utes with whom they planned to mix and lose themselves. When the Indians of the pueblo realized this they gave a war cry and they went to capture them without giving them a chance to reach their weapons. Nevertheless they put up strong resistance. A Ute in the pueblo found all this out and he notified the Ute chief called Mano Mocha who three days before had come to those parts under the pretext of trade. He, with one of his troops, arrived on horseback intimating to the Alcalde and to the Indians that they should free the Apaches and let them come to their tents to talk. He [the alcalde] did not consent to this and he sent them away in the best way possible [but] not daring to send them [the prisoners] to this capital for fear that cited Utes with the Apaches that are near by might commit the affront of overpowering the convoy of 20 men.

June

On June 2 a party of 20 men left under orders to take charge of the aforementioned prisoners and lead them to this Villa with the aid of the militia and Indians of the cited Pueblo.

On June 3 the Alcalde Mayor of Rio Abajo reported that 5 Apaches had stolen 13 animals and had killed a cow from which only the loins were taken and whose absence was not detected until three days later. For this reason he [the Alcalde] did not pursue the aggressors.

On June 9 the party that went to Taos returned leading 12 Apache prisoners both old and young among whom were counted two of the most important chiefs, known as Delgadito and Picado of the Lipanes [Lipiyanes], after Calbo alias Braso de Fierro was killed a short time ago by the Comanches. The prisoners concurred with everything that was stated before by the Apaches adding only that they had spent the entire summer with the Apaches of Sacramento whose principal chief is Botas de Fierro.

On June 11 the Ute chief Mano Mocha with 10 braves and 4 women came to this capital and having been reproached for the bad faith which he had shown the Spanish a little while before, he confessed to be true all the misgivings about them. Not only did he offer to make amends but also to separate completely from the Gicarillas and to join the Spanish in case the Nations of the North should fall upon the province as they had last year and to that end he proposed to scout the land for the Cerro of San Antonio to the source of the Rio del Norte and to promptly report all that he observed.

On June 12 a group of Lipanes [Lipiyanes] in chains escorted by a troop of militia and Indians will leave from this capital with orders to admit into its company the people from El Paso and other individuals who want to join the group as long as they do not carry heavy loads if they serve to hinder [the expedition]. (SANM 1548)

Obviously, Chacón, like his predecessors, had a hard time keeping the Lipans and the Lipiyanes straight.

The year 1801 was doubly important in the history of the Southern Athabascans because in the month of August one of the "interpreters" that the Spaniards had placed among the Navajos reported that among the new group of "Nations of the North" approaching the northern border of New Mexico was a tribe that spoke the same language as the Navajos and Jicarillas. If this interpretation of the badly written document (SANM 1563–2) is correct, this group of "Norteños" had preserved a tradition that they had been separated from the Navajos and Jicarillas when the Comanches overran the land they still occupied. In any case, the newcomers wished to become friends of the Navajos and Jicarillas. This Athabascan-speaking group from the north could only have been the Kiowa Apaches, apparently referred to in a document now missing but listed by Twitchell (1914 II: 531–32; SANM 2185) as "Apaches del Norte." Also, among these Nations of the North were the Kiowas, with whom the Kiowa Apaches were closely associated (G & G 1971).

Governor Chacón's letter conveying this information and a relevant excerpt from the accompanying diary of events, follows.

> I am sending to your lordship the report of events of this month through which I am informing you that the Apaches do not stop causing trouble in this province. I was planning to send out a company but I consider it more urgent to watch for the Nations of the North that I expect any day according to the reports they themselves have given. And although they claim to come in peace, the information given by the Ute woman which is cited in the report, assures [us] that they come with intent to make war. This agrees with what the Navajo interpreter has just reported. He was informed [by the Navajos] of the arrival of the *Indians from the north* ["Norteños"] and *that they came to make friends with them and with the Jicarillas because they consider themselves to be of the same people and speakers of the same language* [italics mine], preserving among themselves the tradition that when the Comanches overran the lands that they occupy they had come between [them and?] the Navajos and Jicarillas and had divided them.
>
> No matter for what reason the heathen may come I predict evil based on the knowledge that I have of the allied nations with

the exception of the Comanche Nation. They take advantage of these occasions to steal up and down the River and then place the blame on someone else whom they have lured to their side [?] for the purpose of putting their strategy into practice.

In addition to the aforestated, if the Navajos let these new Nations come in and introduce them to their neighbors the Mescaleros as the Jicarillas recently tried to do with the Llaneros and Lipiyanes the Apache Nation would become considerably larger. In the meantime I am treating this matter with the greatest care and according to any change in the circumstances I will try to give your lordship an immediate report. (SANM 1563–2)

Extract of the events which occurred in the Province of New Mexico from the 6th of this month to the present date [August 6–31, 1801].

In his letter of August 21 [1801] the alcalde mayor of Taos reported that 17 savages of those that had been seen last year arrived at the rancheria of Pajarito, a Jicarilla chief, with the news that there were in the Sierra del Almagre nine new nations of which they only recognized the names of three of them and who had come to ask peace with the Spanish. They demonstrated this desire by sending three crosses adding that with this same intent they were nearing little by little. For this reason I warned the alcalde to go out and observe them and to receive them with the six men who before had explored the area with the interpreter Mirabal and that at the same time to warn all the people in his jurisdiction and to send the same warning to the alcalde mayor of Rio Arriba. (SANM 1565)

Thus in the years 1798 and 1801 the Llanero Apaches arrived in New Mexico (see figure 8) insisting that they were actually part of the Jicarillas, and if this interpretation of events is valid, they were Carlanas, Cuartelejos, and Palomas returning to more or less the same areas in which they had lived ca. 1750, during the administration of Governor Vélez Cachupín. In spite of the strenuous objections of the Spanish officials, the Llaneros continued to live most of the time in eastern New Mexico until they were put on the present Jicarilla Reservation in 1887. Moreover, before that time they often camped and hunted with the Jicarillas proper who, in spite of increasing thefts due to their increasing poverty, continue to be referred to as allies and friends of the Spaniards in the New Mexico Archives through the Spanish colonial and Mexican Periods. In 1800 and 1801, also, there ap-

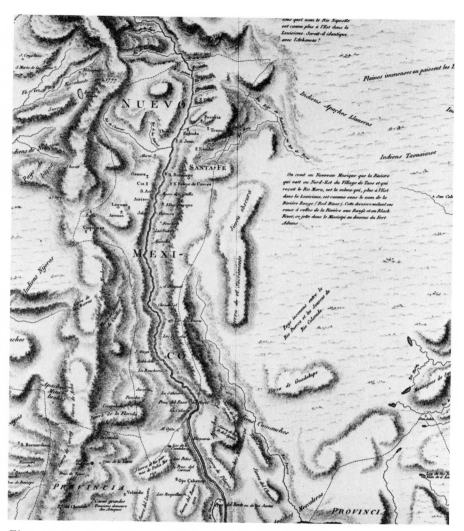

Figure 8. Section of Humboldt's map of New Spain drawn in 1803, showing the Llanero Apaches on the Plains east of settled New Mexico and mountain ranges that sheltered various Apache tribes ca. 1800. Reproduced from an original map in the Newberry Library, by permission of the trustees.

peared on the northern border of New Mexico an Athabascan-speaking group that could only have been the Kiowa Apaches. The last of the Apachean tribes had finally arrived on the New Mexico frontier.

The Jicarilla Apaches survived the impact of enemy tribes and alien cultures because of their flexibility in dealing with other peoples. For example, their amicable relations with the Spaniards and Pueblo Indians, especially those of the upper Río Grande, made it possible for them to seek shelter west of the Sangre de Cristos in the 1720s and live side by side with the inhabitants of Taos Valley.

In subsequent years the Jicarillas raised crops in *hoyas* or valleys not yet occupied by Spanish settlers (e.g., Cortez 1855). Through horticulture and hunting they were apparently largely self-supporting. There seems to be no clue in the Spanish documents as to when they began the active trade in pots and baskets for which they were already noted when the Anglo-Americans took New Mexico. As the Comanche menace to the entire province grew in the mid-1700s, the services of the Jicarillas as scouts and auxiliaries on military campaigns increased in importance. They apparently interacted more freely with the Spaniards than any other "Gentile" tribe. Their loyalty and friendship were unquestioned in New Mexico, and the suspicion with which officials elsewhere occasionally looked upon them may have resulted from the fact that the confederated Carlanas, Cuartelejos, and Palomas, later the Llanero Band of the Jicarillas, were committing depredations in other provinces. The adaptability of the Jicarillas is also shown by their acceptance of the Utes after the latter had broken with the Comanches. Again, the Jicarilla-Ute friendship, like that between the Jicarillas and the Taos Indians, has persisted into recent times.

Although I have not yet found archival materials that explicitly document a gradual reacceptance of the Llaneros by the Spaniards after 1801, that band did remain in the province. In records, however, the name Llanero was soon dropped in favor of the name Jicarilla. Although Spanish-American village people today still know the names Ollero and Llanero, this distinction does not exist in official documents. Early ethnologists seem to have introduced it to the literature.

Gradually, the lands on which the Jicarillas had farmed were pre-empted by Europeans. At the same time, new Indian tribes from the north such as the Kiowas, Pawnees, and Cheyennes made the Buffalo Plains more dangerous, and game grew more scarce in the mountains to which the Jicarillas clung. Still they tried to earn their own way, helping villagers harvest, working as shepherds, selling pots and baskets, perhaps more intensively than before. Often they resorted to appropriating livestock for food, and although the new government realized that under the circumstances this was their only alternative, for some reason this petty thievery seemed to annoy the officials more than the toll of human lives taken by the southern Apaches. The atypical instance in which a group of renegade Jicarillas attacked a wagon train, killing a white woman (Mrs. White) and kidnapping her daughter (Abel 1915: 269–74), seems to have aroused more public indignation than all the combined depredations of Gerónimo and Cochise. The Jicarillas were "at war" with the United States for only a year and a half and spent nearly all of that period eluding the troops rather than fighting. It is noteworthy that Kit Carson thought the Jicarillas had been forced into hostilities by the actions of officers and troops around Taos (Moody 1953; Goddard 1911: 242–43).

Moreover, the very knowledge of the Anglo-American authorities that the Spanish-American villagers had great sympathy for the Jicarillas and did not begrudge them the food that they appropriated made the Anglo-Americans uneasy; they did not trust the ex-Mexican nationals in their newly acquired territories nor did they trust the Taos Indians, those long-time friends of the Jicarillas who rebelled against the Anglos within months after Kearney marched into Santa Fé in 1846 (Gardner 1953).

No one has yet published a detailed and balanced account of the Jicarillas under United States rule. When it appears, hopefully it will be free of judgments reflecting the materialism and militarism rampant in the territorial period and not lacking in our culture today. On the other hand, one can hope that it will not descend to the sentimentality of a "Lo!-the-poor-Indian" approach, for the Jicarillas survived too long without this dubious benefit to be diminished by it now.

My own research suggests that the Jicarillas would have transferred their allegiance to the Americans and served them as faithfully as they had served the Spaniards if the Anglos had been willing to accept them as "friends" and allies. But the new conquerors of the Southwest had to go through all the trial-and-error groping toward a workable Indian policy that had characterized the Spanish regime. And where the Spaniards had felt a certain amount of responsibility for all the Indians living in their territories at peace, the Anglos, in general, tried to reject and exploit the Jicarillas at the same time. Like their Spanish predecessors who feared French and Comanche encroachment, some Anglo administrators recognized, especially in the Civil War years, that to control the basically peaceful Jicarillas was to hold "a balance of power" against more warlike tribes and against the Confederates (Seymour 1941: 189–91). As it was, the Jicarillas went on an expedition against Texans with Lucien Maxwell (Goddard 1911: 250–51) after he had moved to the Bosque Redondo. Seventy-two Jicarillas and Utes went with their former agent, Kit Carson, to Adobe Walls on the Canadian River in the Texas Panhandle where they helped fight a large group of Kiowas and Comanches (Pettis 1908; Goddard 1911: 250; Keleher 1964: 51–52).

The anthropologist who has studied the Jicarillas most extensively and intensively is Morris Opler. Although his information was collected at a time (1934–1935) when by all accounts the tribe was just emerging from a period of great stress, Opler generalized: "The keynote of the Jicarilla world conception is a tremendous enthusiasm for life; a conception of a personified universe with which man may identify himself" (Opler 1936: 205). And the Jicarilla myths and tales published by Opler (1938) suggest a vigorous people with a positive outlook—imaginative, even whimsical; dignified, but with a sense of humor. Opler found that Jicarilla culture was accurately reflected in Jicarilla mythology, and I have wondered whether his comments on Jicarilla myths and the way these myths are handled by those who tell them do not provide a key to understanding the Jicarilla capacity for survival. According to Opler, Jicarilla mythology has developed "a rare degree of vitality and flexibility." It "admits of continuous change to accommodate or explain phases of the white man's culture as it impinges on the Jicarilla." There are "themal associations, fundamental to Jicarilla thought and culture" that are "unifying threads which run through all the myths." Moreover, "the close correspondence between the myth and the reality acts ever as a brake to hold each tale to a consistent and intelligible part of the mythological whole." Yet there are "generous concessions to individual taste, artistry, and imagination permitted in the treatment of Jicarilla mythology," and these variations are agreeable rather than disruptive because both the narrator and his hearers believe in the basic themes (Opler 1938: xvi–xvii).

I suggest that in these respects Jicarilla culture has reflected Jicarilla mythology—the members of a band could disperse in order to hunt or evade an enemy and reunite days, months, or years later with their common bonds of culture intact. The Jicarillas could live among other, even proselytizing, peoples and make outward adjustments in peripheral details of existence without altering basic attitudes. The survival of the Jicarillas may be due, in brief, to a fortunate combination of external flexibility and core consistency.

Today, in their mountains in north-central New Mexico, the Jicarillas are a remote people, rarely seen in Santa Fé. But their agency town, Dulce, yearly grows larger as the people are encouraged to move in from the mountain valleys and canyons so they will be more effectively exposed to civilization. Only the future will reveal how well their resources from the past have served them in dealing with the present.

Abel, Annie H., ed.
> 1915. *The official correspondence of James S. Calhoun.* Washington: U.S. Government Printing Office.

Adams, E. B.
> 1953. Notes and documents concerning Bishop Crespo's visitation, 1730. *New Mexico Historical Review* 28: 222–33.
> 1953–1954. Bishop Tamarón's visitation of New Mexico, 1760. *New Mexico Historical Review* 28: 81–114, 192–221, 291–315; 29: 41–47.

Adams, E. B., and Fray Angélico Chávez.
> 1956. *The missions of New Mexico, 1776. A description by Fray Francisco Atanasio Dominguez, with other contemporary documents.* Albuquerque: University of New Mexico Press.

AGN Pro. Inter.
> *Archivo General Y Público de la Nación, Provincias Internas.* Housed in Palacio Nacional, Mexico, D.F. [For a guide see Bolton (1913).]

Ayer, Mrs. Edward E., trans.

1916. *The memorial of Fray Alonso de Benavides, 1630.* Chicago: privately printed.

Bailey, Jessie B.

1940. *Diego de Vargas and the reconquest of New Mexico.* Albuquerque: University of New Mexico Press.

Bancroft, Hubert H.

1883. *History of Mexico, 1521–1600.* Vol. II. San Francisco: A. L. Bancroft and Co.

1884. *History of the North Mexican states.* Vol. I. San Franciso: A. L. Bancroft and Co.

1889. *History of Arizona and New Mexico, 1530–1888.* San Francisco: The History Co.

Bandelier, A. F.

1890. *Contributions to the history of the southwestern portion of the United States.* Archaeological Institute of America, American Series Paper 5.

1890–1892. *Final report of investigations among the Indians of the southwestern United States, carried on mainly in the years from 1880 to 1885.* [Part I 1890; Part II 1892]. Archaeological Institute of America, American Series Paper 3.

1892. An outline of the documentary history of the Zuñi tribe. *A Journal of American Ethnology and Archaeology* 3: 1–115.

1910. *Documentary history of the Río Grande Pueblos of New Mexico. I, bibliographic introduction.* Archaeological Institute of America, School of American Archaeology Paper 13.

Birket-Smith, Kaj.

1930. *Contributions to Chipewyan ethnology.* Translated by W. E. Calvert. Copenhagen: Gyldendal.

BLNMO.

Bancroft Library New Mexico Originals. [Listed in Chávez (1950).]

Bloom, Lansing B.

1933. Fray Estévan de Perea's relación. *New Mexico Historical Review* 8: 211–35.

1933–1938. Bourke on the Southwest. *New Mexico Historical Review* 8: 1–30; 9: 33–77, 159–83, 274–89, 375–435; 10: 1–35, 275–322; 11: 77–122, 183–207, 217–82; 12: 41–77, 337–79; 13: 192–238.

Bolton, Herbert E.

1913. *Guide to materials for the history of the United States in the principal archives of Mexico.* Carnegie Institution of Washington Publication 163.

1914. *Athanase de Mézières and the Louisiana-Texas frontier 1768–1770.* 2 vols. Cleveland: The Arthur H. Clark Co.

1916. (ed.) *Spanish explorations in the Southwest, 1542–1706.* New York: Charles Scribner's Sons.

1917. French intrusions into New Mexico. In *The Pacific Ocean in history,* edited by H. M. Stephens and H. E. Bolton. pp. 389–407. New York: The Macmillan Company.

1950. *Pageant in the wilderness, the story of the Escalante expedition to the interior basin, 1776.* Salt Lake City: Utah State Historical Society.

Bourne, Edward Gaylord, ed.

1904. *Narratives of the career of Hernando De Soto.* 2 vols. New York: A. S. Barnes and Company.

Butler, Ruth Lapham.

1937. *A check list of manuscripts in the Edward E. Ayer collection.* Chicago: Newberry Library.

Carrol, H. B., and J. V. Haggard.

1942. *Three New Mexico chronicles.* Quivira Society Publication 11.

Castañeda, Carlos E., trans.

1935. *History of Texas 1673–1779 by Fray Juan Agustín Morfi.* 2 parts. Quivira Society Publication 6.

Champe, John L.

1949. White Cat Village. *American Antiquity* 14: 285–92.

Chávez, Fray Angélico.

1950. Some original New Mexico documents in California libraries. *New Mexico Historcial Review* 25: 244–53.

1954. *Origins of New Mexico families.* Santa Fe: Historical Society of New Mexico.

Cornell, Lois A.

1929. The Jicarilla Apaches: their history, customs, and present status. Unpublished thesis, University of Colorado.

Cortez, Don José.

1855. Territories occupied by the Apache and other tribes, to the northward of the province of New Mexico [dated 1799]. In *Pacific railroad report,* by A. T. Whipple, T. T. Eubank, and W. W. Turner. United States 33rd Congress, Second Session, House of Representatives Executive Document 91; Vol. 3, part 3; 118–27.

Cremony, John C.

1868a. *Life among the Apaches.* San Francisco: A. Roman.

1868b. The Apache race. *The Overland Monthly* 1: 201–9.

Curtis, Edward S.
> 1907–1930. *The North American Indian.* 20 vols. Cambridge: The University Press.

Domenech, Emmanuel H. D.
> 1860. *Seven years' residence in the great deserts of North America.* 2 vols. London: Longman, Green, Longman, and Roberts.

Dorsey, George A.
> 1905. *Traditions of the Caddo.* Carnegie Institution of Washington Publication 41.

Dort, Wakefield, Jr., and J. Knox Jones, Jr.
> 1970. *Pleistocene and recent environments of the Central Great Plains.* Department of Geology, University of Kansas Special Publication 3. Lawrence, Manhattan, Wichita: The University Press of Kansas.

Dunn, W. E.
> 1911. Apache relations in Texas, 1718–1750. *Southwestern Historical Quarterly* 14: 198–274.

[Escalante, Fray Silvestre Vélez de].
> 1962. Sesto Cuaderno. In *Documentos para servir a la historia del Nuevo Mexico 1538–1778.* Coleccion Chimalistac 13: 393–414. Madrid: Ediciones Jose Porrua Turanzas. [For identification of this work as Escalante's, see J. Espinosa 1942: 380.]

Espinosa, Gilberto, trans.
> 1933. *History of New Mexico by Gaspar Pérez de Villagrá, Alcalá, 1610.* The Quivira Society Publication 4.

Espinosa, J. Manuel.
> 1936. Governor Vargas in Colorado. *New Mexico Historical Review* 11: 179–87.
> 1940. (trans.) *First expedition of Vargas into New Mexico, 1692.* Albuquerque: University of New Mexico Press.
> 1942. *Crusaders of the Río Grande.* Chicago: Institute of Jesuit History Publications.

Folmer, H.
> 1937. De Bourgmont's expedition to the Padoucas in 1724, the first French approach to Colorado. *The Colorado Magazine* 14: 121–28.
> 1939. The Mallet expedition of 1739 through Nebraska, Kansas and Colorado to Santa Fe. *The Colorado Magazine* 16: 161–73.
> 1941. Contraband trade between Louisiana and New Mexico in the eighteenth century. *New Mexico Historical Review* 16: 249–74.

Forbes, Jack D.
>   1960. *Apache, Navaho and Spaniard*. Norman: University of Oklahoma Press.

Forrestal, Peter P.
>   1954. *Benavides' memorial of 1630*. Washington: Academy of American Franciscan History.

Franciscan Fathers.
>   1910. *An ethnologic dictionary of the Navaho language*. Saint Michaels, Arizona: The Franciscan Fathers.

Garcilaso de la Vega, el Inca.
>   1605. *La Florida de Ynca*. Lisbona: Impresso por Pedro Crasbeeck.

Gardner, Hamilton.
>   1963. Philip St. George Cooke and the Apache, 1854. *New Mexico Historical Review* 28: 115–32.

Gifford, E. W.
>   1940. *Culture element distributions: XII, Apache–Pueblo*. University of California Anthropological Records 4, no. 1.

Goddard, Pliny E.
>   1911. *Jicarilla Apache texts*. American Museum of Natural History Anthropological Paper 8.
>   1913. *Indians of the Southwest*. American Museum of Natural History Handbook Series 2.

Goodwin, Grenville
>   1942. *The social organization of the Western Apache*. Chicago: University of Chicago Press.

Grant, Blanche C.
>   1934. *When old trails were new, the story of Taos*. New York: The Press of the Pioneers.

Grinnell, G. B.
>   1920. Who were the Padouca? *American Anthropologist*, n.s. 22: 248–60.

Gunnerson, Dolores A.
>   1956. The Southern Athabascans: their arrival in the Southwest. *El Palacio* 63: 346–65.
>   1960. Review of *Apache, Navaho and Spaniard*, by Jack D. Forbes. *New Mexico Quarterly* 30: 315–16.
>   1972. Man and bison on the Plains in the protohistoric period. *Plains Anthropologist* 17: 1–10.

Gunnerson, James H.
>   1959. Archaeological survey in northeastern New Mexico. *El Palacio* 66: 145–54.
>   1969. Apache archaeology in northeastern New Mexico. *American Antiquity* 34: 23–39.

Gunnerson, James H., and Dolores A. Gunnerson.
 1970. Evidence of Apaches at Pecos. *El Palacio* 76: 1–6.
 1971. Apachean culture: a study in unity and diversity. In *Apachean culture history and ethnology.* Tucson: University of Arizona Press.
Hackett, Charles W., ed. and trans.
 1923–1937. *Historical documents relating to New Mexico, Nueva Vizcaya and approaches thereto, to 1773.* 3 vols. Carnegie Institution of Washington Publication 330.
 1931–1946. (ed.) *Pichardo's treatise on the limits of Louisiana and Texas.* 4 vols. Austin: The University of Texas Press.
 1942. (ed.) *Revolt of the Pueblo Indians of New Mexico and Otermin's attempted reconquest.* 2 vols. Albuquerque: University of New Mexico Press.
Hakluyt, Richard.
 1598–[1600]. *The principal navigations, voiages, traffiqves and discoueries of the English nation, made by sea or ouer-land, to the remote and farthest distant quarters of the earth, at any time within the compasse of these 1500. yeeres: deuided into three seuerall volumes, according to the positions of the regions, whereunto they were directed.* Vol. 3–[1600]. London: George Bishop, Ralph Newberie and Robert Barker.
Hale, Kenneth.
 1962. Jemez and Kiowa correspondences in reference to Kiowa-Tanoan. *International Journal of American Linguistics* 28: 1–5.
Hallenbeck, Cleve.
 1940. *Álvar Núñez Cabeza de Vaca. The journey and route of the first European to cross the continent of North America 1534–1536.* Glendale, California: Arthur H. Clark and Co.
 1950. *Land of the conquistadores.* Caldwell, Idaho: The Claxton Press.
Hammond, George P., and Agapito Rey.
 1927. *The Gallegos relation to the Rodriguez expedition to New Mexico.* Historical Society of New Mexico Publications in History 4.
 1928. *Obregóns history of 16th century explorations in Western America.* Los Angeles: Wetzel Publishing Company, Inc.
 1940. *Narratives of the Coronado expedition 1540–1542.* Albuquerque: University of New Mexico Press.
 1953. *Don Juan de Oñate colonizer of New Mexico 1595–1628.* 2 vols. Albuquerque: University of New Mexico Press.

1966. *The rediscovery of New Mexico 1580–1594.* Albuquerque:
University of New Mexico Press.

Harrington, J. P.
1916. *The ethnogeography of the Tewa Indians.* Bureau of
American Ethnology Annual Report 29.
1940. *Southern peripheral Athapaskawan origins, divisions, and
migrations.* Smithsonian Miscellaneous Collections 100: 503–
32.

Hill, W. W.
1940. *Some Navaho culture changes during two centuries.* Smithsonian Miscellaneous Collections 100: 395–415.
1948. Navaho trading and trading ritual. *Southwestern Journal
of Anthropology* 4: 371–96.

Hodge, F. W.
1895. The early Navajo and Apache. *American Anthropologist*
8: 223–40.
1907–1910. (ed.) *Handbook of American Indians north of
Mexico.* 2 parts. Bureau of American Ethnology Bulletin 30.
1929. French intrusion toward New Mexico. *New Mexico Historical Review* 4: 74–76.

Hodge, F. W., G. P. Hammond, and A. Rey.
1945. *Fray Alonso de Benavides' revised memorial of 1634.* Albuquerque: University of New Mexico Press.

Hoijer, Harry.
1938. The Southern Athapascan languages. *American Anthropologist* 40: 75–87.
1956a. The chronology of the Athapaskan languages. *International Journal of American Linguistics* 22: 219–32.
1956b. Athapaskan kinship systems. *American Anthropologist*
58: 308–33.

Hornaday, William T.
1889. *The extermination of the American bison, with a sketch of
its discovery and life history.* Smithsonian Institution Annual Report for 1887, part 2: 367–548.

Hotz, Gottfried.
1960. *Indianische ledermalereien.* Berlin: Verlag Von Dietrich
Reimer.
1970. *Indian skin paintings from the American Southwest.* Norman: University of Oklahoma Press.

Keleher, William A.
1964. *Maxwell Land Grant.* New York: Argosy-Antiquarian
Ltd.

Kelley, J. Charles.
1952. Factors involved in the abandonment of certain peripheral

Southwestern settlements. *American Anthropologist* 54: 356–87.

Kenner, Charles L.
1969. *A history of New Mexican-Plains Indian relations.* Norman: University of Oklahoma Press.

Kidder, A. V.
1932. *The artifacts of Pecos.* Phillips Academy Southwestern Expedition Paper 6.
1958. *Pecos, New Mexico: archaeological notes.* Robert S. Peabody Foundation for Archaeology Paper 5.

Kiddle, Lawrence B.
1944. *The Spanish Word Jícara, a word history.* Tulane University, Middle American Research Institute, Philological and Documentary Studies 1: 115–54.

Kinnaird, Lawrence, ed.
1958. *The frontiers of New Spain: Nicolás de Lafora's description, 1766–1768.* Quivira Society Publications 13.

Kluckhohn, Clyde, and Dorothea C. Leighton.
1946. *The Navaho.* Cambridge: Harvard University Press.

Krieger, Alex D.
1946. *Culture complexes and chronology in northern Texas.* University of Texas Publication 4640.
1947. The eastward extension of Puebloan datings toward cultures of the Mississippi Valley. *American Antiquity* 12: 141–48.

Lewis, Theodore H., ed.
1907. The narrative of the expedition of Hernando de Soto by the Gentleman of Elvas. In *Spanish explorers in the southern United States 1528–1543.* New York: Charles Scribner's Sons.

Lummis, V. F.
1898. A New Mexico episode in 1748. *Land of Sunshine* 8: 74–78.

McClintock, Walter.
1910. *The old north trail.* London: Macmillan and Co.

Margry, Pierre.
1875–1886. *Découvertes et établissements des Francais dans l'ouest et dans le sud de l'Amérique septentrionale (1614–1754) mémoires et documents originaux.* 6 vols. Paris: Imprimerie Jouaust et Sigaux.

Matson, Daniel S., and A. H. Schroeder, eds.
1957. Cordero's description of the Apache—1796. *New Mexico Historical Review* 32: 335–56.

Mecham, J. Lloyd.
    1968. *Francisco de Ibarra and Nueva Vizcaya*. New York:
    Greenwood Press.
Milich, Alicia R., trans.
    1966. *Relaciones by Zárate Salmerón*. Albuquerque: Horn and
    Wallace.
Miller, Joseph.
    1962. *New Mexico, a guide to the colorful state*. 3rd rvd. ed.
    New York: Hastings House.
Moody, Marshall D.
    1953. Kit Carson, agent to the Indians in New Mexico 1853–
    1861. *New Mexico Historical Review* 28: 1–20.
Mooney, James.
    1896. The ghost dance religion. *Annual Report of the Bureau of
    American Ethnology* 14: 640–1136.
    1898a. The Jicarilla genesis. *American Anthropologist* 11: 197–
    209.
    1898b. *Calendar history of the Kiowa Indians*. Bureau of Ameri-
    can Ethnology, Annual Report 17, part 1: 129–445.
Moorhead, Max L.
    1968. *The Apache frontier 1769–1791*. Norman: University of
    Oklahoma Press.
Nasatir, A. P.
    1952. *Before Lewis and Clark, documents illustrating the history
    of the Missouri 1785–1804*. 2 vols. St. Louis: St. Louis His-
    torical Documents Foundation.
Nelson, Al B.
    1940. Juan de Ugalde and Picax-ande Ins-tinsle 1787–1788. *The
    Southwestern Historical Quarterly* 43: 438–64.
Opler, Morris E.
    1936. A summary of Jicarilla Apache culture. *American Anthro-
    pologist* 38: 202–23.
    1938. *Myths and tales of the Jicarilla Apache Indians*. American
    Folklore Society Memoir 31.
    1940. *Myths and legends of the Lipan Apache Indians*. Ameri-
    can Folklore Society Memoir 36.
    1946. *Childhood and youth in Jicarilla Apache society*. South-
    west Museum: Frederick Webb Hodge Anniversary Fund
    Publication 5.
Paso y Troncoso, Francisco del, comp.
    1939–1942. *Epistolario de Nueva Espana, 1505–1818*. Mexico:
    Antigua librería Robredo, de J. Porrúa e hijos.

Pettis, George H.
    1908. *Kit Carson's fight with the Comanche and Kiowa Indians.*
    Historical Society of New Mexico Publication 12.
Porras, Guillermo, ed.
    1945. *Diario y derrotero de lo caminado, visto, y observado en
    el discurso de la visita general de precidios, situados en las
    Provincias Ynternas de Nueva España . . . 1724–1728,* by
    Pedro de Rivera Y Villalon. México: Librería Porrúa her-
    manos y cía.
Powell, Philip W.
    1969. *Soldiers, Indians and silver.* Berkeley and Los Angeles:
    University of California Press.
Priestley, Herbert I.
    1928. *The Luna papers.* 2 vols. Florida State Historical Society
    Publication 8.
Roe, Frank G.
    1951. *The North American buffalo.* Toronto: University of
    Toronto Press.
Sabin, Edwin L.
    1935. *Kit Carson days.* 2 vols. New York: Pioneer Press.
SANM.
    Spanish Archives of New Mexico. On deposit in State of New
    Mexico Records Center, Santa Fe. [For a guide see Twitch-
    ell (1914).]
Santamaria, Francisco J.
    1942. *Diccionario general de Americanismos.* Méjico: Editorial
    Pedro Robredo.
Sauer, Carl.
    1932. *The road to Cíbola.* Ibero-Americana 3.
    1937. The discovery of New Mexico reconsidered. *New Mexico
    Historical Review* 12: 270–87.
Schoenwetter, James, and Alfred E. Dittert, Jr.
    1968. An ecological interpretation of Anasazi settlement patterns.
    In *Anthropological Archaeology in the Americas,* pp. 41–
    66. Washington: The Anthropological Society of Wash-
    ington.
Scholes, France V.
    1936–1937. Church and state in New Mexico 1610–1650. *New
    Mexico Historical Review* 11: 9–76, 145–78, 283–94, 297–
    349; 12: 78–106.
    1937–1941. Troublous times in New Mexico, 1659–1670. *New
    Mexico Historical Review* 12: 134–74, 380–452; 13: 63–84;
    15: 249–68, 369–417; 16: 15–40, 313–27.

1938. Notes on the Jemez missions in the seventeenth century. *El Palacio* 44: 61–70.

1944. Juan Martinez de Montoya, settler and conquistador of New Mexico. *New Mexico Historical Review* 19: 337–42.

Scholes, France V., and H. P. Mera.

1940. *Some aspects of the Jumano problem.* Carnegie Institution of Washington Publication 523.

Schroeder, Albert H.

1952. Documentary evidence pertaining to the early historic period of southern Arizona. *New Mexico Historical Review* 27: 137–67.

1955–1956. Fray Marcos de Niza, Coronado and the Yavapai. *New Mexico Historical Review* 30: 265–96; 31: 24–37.

1959. A study of the Apache Indians. Part II, the Jicarilla Apaches. Mimeographed. Santa Fe, New Mexico.

1962. A re-analysis of the routes of Coronado and Oñate into the plains in 1541 and 1601. *Plains Anthropologist* 7: 2–23.

Schroeder, Albert H., and Dan S. Matson.

1965. *A colony on the move, Gaspar Castaño de Sosa's journal 1590–1591.* Santa Fe: The School of American Research.

Schwatka, Frederick.

1887. Among the Apaches. *Century Magazine* 34: 41–53.

Seymour, Flora.

1941. *Indian agents of the old frontier.* New York and London: D. Appleton Century Co., Inc.

Simmons, Marc, trans. and ed.

1970. Governor Anza, the Lipan Apaches and Pecos Pueblo. *El Palacio* 77: 35–40.

Sjoberg, A. F.

1953. Lipan Apache culture in historical perspective. *Southwestern Journal of Anthropology* 9: 76–98.

Smith, Buckingham, trans.

1871. *Relation of Núñez Cabeza de Vaca.* New York: March of America Facsimile Series 9. [Ann Arbor: University Microfilms, Inc., 1966.]

Stirling, M. W., and K. Glemser.

1963. John Peabody Harrington. *American Anthropologist* 65: 370–81.

Stubbs, Stanley A.

1950. *Bird's-eye view of the Pueblos.* Norman: University of Oklahoma Press.

Swanton, John R.

1939. *Final Report, United States De Soto Expedition Com-*

mission. United States 76th Congress, First Session, House Document No. 71.

1942. *Source material on the history and ethnology of the Caddo Indians.* Bureau of American Ethnology Bulletin 132.

1946. *The Indians of the southeastern United States.* Bureau of American Ethnology Bulletin 137.

Thomas, Alfred B.

1929. An anonymous description of New Mexico 1818. *Southwestern Historical Quarterly* 33: 50–74.

1932. *Forgotten frontiers.* Norman: University of Oklahoma Press.

1935. *After Coronado: Spanish exploration northeast of New Mexico, 1696–1727.* Norman: University of Oklahoma Press.

1940. *The Plains Indians and New Mexico, 1751–1778.* Albuquerque: University of New Mexico Press.

1941. *Teodoro de Croix and the northern frontier of New Spain.* Norman: University of Oklahoma Press.

Tunnell, C. D., and W. W. Newcomb, Jr.

1969. *A Lipan Apache mission.* Texas Memorial Museum Bulletin 14.

Turner, William W.

1852. The Apaches. *Literary World* 10 (272): 281–82.

Twitchell, Ralph E.

1914. *The Spanish Archives of New Mexico.* 2 vols. Cedar Rapids: The Torch Press.

Tyler, S. Lyman, and H. Darrel Taylor.

1958. The report of Fray Alonso de Posada in relation to Quivira and Teguayo. *New Mexico Historical Review* 33: 285–314.

Undreiner, George J.

1947. Fray Marcos de Niza and his journey to Cibola. *The Americas* 3: 415–86.

Varner, John Grier, and Jeannette J. Varner.

1951. *The Florida of the Inca.* Austin: University of Texas Press.

Velazquez, Mariano.

1955. *A new pronouncing dictionary of the Spanish and English languages.* Chicago and New York: Wilcox and Follett Co.

Villaseñor y Sanchez, Joseph Antonio de.

1748. *Theatro Americano.* 2 vols. in 1. Mexico: J. B. de Hogal.

Wedel, Waldo R.

1940. *Culture sequences in the central Great Plains.* Smithsonian Miscellaneous Collections 100: 291–352.

1941. *Environment and native subsistence economies in the central Great Plains.* Smithsonian Miscellaneous Collections 101 (3).

1942. *Archeological remains in central Kansas and their possible bearing on the location of Quivira.* Smithsonian Miscellaneous Collections 101 (7).

1959. *An introduction to Kansas archeology.* Bureau of American Ethnology Bulletin 174.

1961. *Prehistoric man on the Great Plains.* Norman: University of Oklahoma Press.

1968. Some thoughts on Central Plains–Southern Plains archaeological relationships. *Great Plains Journal* 7: 1–10.

Wheat, Carl I.
1957. *Mapping the transmississippi west 1540–1861.* Vol. I. San Francisco: Grabhorn Press.

Wilson, H. Clyde.
1964. *Jicarilla Apache political and economic structure.* University of California Publications 48: 297–360.

Winfrey, Dorman H., ed.
1959–1966. *Texas Indian papers.* Austin: Texas State Library.

Winship, George P.
1896. *The Coronado expedition, 1540–1542.* Bureau of American Ethnology, Annual Report 14: 329–613.

Wissler, Clark.
1908. Ethnographical problems of the Missouri Saskatchewan Area. *American Anthropologist,* n.s. 10: 197–207.

1950. *The American Indian,* 3rd. ed. New York: Peter Smith.

1967. *Indians of the United States.* rvd. ed. Gardner City: Doubleday and Company, Inc.

Wood, W. Raymond.
1971. Pottery sites near Limon, Colorado. *Southwestern Lore* 37: 53–85.

Worcester, Donald E., trans. and ed.
1951. *Instructions for governing the interior provinces of New Spain, 1786, by Bernardo de Gálvez.* Quivira Society Publication 12.

Zárate-Salmerón, G. de.
1899–1900. Relating all the things that have been seen and known in New Mexico. *Land of Sunshine* 11: 337–56; 12: 39–48, 104–13, 180–87.

The text of this book is set in Janson on Warren's Olde Style Wove.

The thirteen pen and ink sketches were drawn especially for this work by the Jicarilla artist, Carl A. Vicenti.

Manuscript editor for the book was Leslie L. Wildrick. Composition was by American Book–Stratford Press, Inc., Brattleboro, Vermont. Printing and binding was performed by Vail-Ballou Press, Inc., Binghamton, New York.

Design was by William Nicoll, Edit, Inc. of Chicago.

THE LIBRARY
ST. MARY'S COLLEGE OF MARYLAND
ST. MARY'S CITY, MARYLAND 20686

76073

E
99
.J5
G86

76073

Gunnerson, D.A.
The Jicarilla Apaches: a
study in survival. 7 8

DATE DUE			